Prometheus: Up & Running

Infrastructure and Application Performance Monitoring

Brian Brazil

Beijing · Boston · Farnham · Sebastopol · Tokyo

Prometheus: Up & Running

by Brian Brazil

Published by O'Reilly Media, Inc., 1005 Gravenstein Highway North, Sebastopol, CA 95472.

O'Reilly books may be purchased for educational, business, or sales promotional use. Online editions are also available for most titles (*http://oreilly.com/safari*). For more information, contact our corporate/institutional sales department: 800-998-9938 or *corporate@oreilly.com*.

Editor: Virginia Wilson
Production Editor: Nicholas Adams
Copyeditor: Christina Edwards
Proofreader: Sonia Saruba
Tech Reviewers: Julius Volz, Carl Bergquist, Andrew McMillan, and Greg Stark

Indexer: Ellen Troutman-Zaig
Interior Designer: David Futato
Cover Designer: Karen Montgomery
Illustrator: Rebecca Demarest

July 2018:   First Edition

Revision History for the First Edition
2018-07-06:   First Release

See *http://oreilly.com/catalog/errata.csp?isbn=9781492034148* for release details.

978-1-492-03414-8

[LSI]

Table of Contents

Part II.   Application Monitoring

Part III.   Infrastructure Monitoring

Part IV.   PromQL

Part V.   Alerting

Part VI.   Deployment

Preface

This book describes in detail how to use the Prometheus monitoring system to monitor, graph, and alert on the performance of your applications and infrastructure. This book is intended for application developers, system administrators, and everyone in between.

Expanding the Known

When it comes to monitoring, knowing that the systems you care about are turned on is important, but that's not where the real value is. The big wins are in understanding the performance of your systems.

By performance I don't only mean the response time of and CPU used by each request, but the broader meaning of performance. How many requests to the database are required for each customer order that is processed? Is it time to purchase higher throughput networking equipment? How many machines are your cache misses costing? Are enough of your users interacting with a complex feature in order to justify its continued existence?

These are the sort of questions that a metrics-based monitoring system can help you answer, and beyond that help you dig into why the answer is what it is. I see monitoring as getting insight from throughout your system, from high-level overviews down to the nitty-gritty details that are useful for debugging. A full set of monitoring tools for debugging and analysis includes not only metrics, but also logs, traces, and profiling; but metrics should be your first port of call when you want to answer systems-level questions.

Prometheus encourages you to have instrumentation liberally spread across your systems, from applications all the way down to the bare metal. With instrumentation you can observe how all your subsystems and components are interacting, and convert unknowns into knowns.

Conventions Used in This Book

The following typographical conventions are used in this book:

Italic
> Indicates new terms, URLs, email addresses, filenames, and file extensions.

`Constant width`
> Used for program listings, as well as within paragraphs to refer to program elements such as variable or function names, databases, data types, environment variables, statements, and keywords.

`Constant width bold`
> Shows commands or other text that should be typed literally by the user.

`Constant width italic`
> Shows text that should be replaced with user-supplied values or by values determined by context.

> This element signifies a tip or suggestion.

> This element signifies a general note.

> This element indicates a warning or caution.

Using Code Examples

Supplemental material (code examples, configuration files, etc.) is available for download at *https://github.com/prometheus-up-and-running/examples*.

This book is here to help you get your job done. In general, if example code is offered with this book, you may use it in your programs and documentation. You do not need to contact us for permission unless you're reproducing a significant portion of the code. For example, writing a program that uses several chunks of code from this book does not require permission. Selling or distributing a CD-ROM of examples from O'Reilly books does require permission. Answering a question by citing this book and quoting example code does not require permission. Incorporating a significant amount of example code from this book into your product's documentation does require permission.

We appreciate, but do not require, attribution. An attribution usually includes the title, author, publisher, and ISBN. For example: "*Prometheus: Up & Running* by Brian Brazil (O'Reilly). Copyright 2018 Robust Perception Ltd., 978-1-492-03414-8."

If you feel your use of code examples falls outside fair use or the permission given above, feel free to contact us at *permissions@oreilly.com*.

O'Reilly Safari

 Safari (formerly Safari Books Online) is a membership-based training and reference platform for enterprise, government, educators, and individuals.

Members have access to thousands of books, training videos, Learning Paths, interactive tutorials, and curated playlists from over 250 publishers, including O'Reilly Media, Harvard Business Review, Prentice Hall Professional, Addison-Wesley Professional, Microsoft Press, Sams, Que, Peachpit Press, Adobe, Focal Press, Cisco Press, John Wiley & Sons, Syngress, Morgan Kaufmann, IBM Redbooks, Packt, Adobe Press, FT Press, Apress, Manning, New Riders, McGraw-Hill, Jones & Bartlett, and Course Technology, among others.

For more information, please visit *http://oreilly.com/safari*.

How to Contact Us

Please address comments and questions concerning this book to the publisher:

O'Reilly Media, Inc.
1005 Gravenstein Highway North
Sebastopol, CA 95472
800-998-9938 (in the United States or Canada)
707-829-0515 (international or local)
707-829-0104 (fax)

We have a web page for this book, where we list errata, examples, and any additional information. You can access this page at *http://bit.ly/prometheus-up-and-running*.

To comment or ask technical questions about this book, send email to *bookquestions@oreilly.com*.

For more information about our books, courses, conferences, and news, see our website at *http://www.oreilly.com*.

Find us on Facebook: *http://facebook.com/oreilly*

Follow us on Twitter: *http://twitter.com/oreillymedia*

Watch us on YouTube: *http://www.youtube.com/oreillymedia*

Acknowledgments

This book would not have been possible without all the work of the Prometheus team, and the hundreds of contibutors to Prometheus and its ecosystem. A special thanks to Julius Volz, Richard Hartmann, Carl Bergquist, Andrew McMillan, and Greg Stark for providing feedback on initial drafts of this book.

Introduction

This section will introduce you to monitoring in general, and Prometheus more specifically.

In Chapter 1 you will learn about the many different meanings of monitoring and approaches to it, the metrics approach that Prometheus takes, and the architecture of Prometheus.

In Chapter 2 you will get your hands dirty running a simple Prometheus setup that scrapes machine metrics, evaluates queries, and sends alert notifications.

CHAPTER 1
What Is Prometheus?

Prometheus is an open source, metrics-based monitoring system. Of course, Prometheus is far from the only one of those out there, so what makes it notable?

Prometheus does one thing and it does it well. It has a simple yet powerful data model and a query language that lets you analyse how your applications and infrastructure are performing. It does not try to solve problems outside of the metrics space, leaving those to other more appropriate tools.

Since its beginnings with no more than a handful of developers working in Sound-Cloud in 2012, a community and ecosystem has grown around Prometheus. Prometheus is primarily written in Go and licensed under the Apache 2.0 license. There are hundreds of people who have contributed to the project itself, which is not controlled by any one company. It is always hard to tell how many users an open source project has, but I estimate that as of 2018, tens of thousands of organisations are using Prometheus in production. In 2016 the Prometheus project became the second member[1] of the Cloud Native Computing Foundation (CNCF).

For instrumenting your own code, there are client libraries in all the popular languages and runtimes, including Go, Java/JVM, C#/.Net, Python, Ruby, Node.js, Haskell, Erlang, and Rust. Software like Kubernetes and Docker are already instrumented with Prometheus client libraries. For third-party software that exposes metrics in a non-Prometheus format, there are hundreds of integrations available. These are called exporters, and include HAProxy, MySQL, PostgreSQL, Redis, JMX, SNMP, Consul, and Kafka. A friend of mine even added support for monitoring Minecraft servers, as he cares a lot about his frames per second.

---

1 Kubernetes was the first member.

A simple text format makes it easy to expose metrics to Prometheus. Other monitoring systems, both open source and commercial, have added support for this format. This allows all of these monitoring systems to focus more on core features, rather than each having to spend time duplicating effort to support every single piece of software a user like you may wish to monitor.

The data model identifies each time series not just with a name, but also with an unordered set of key-value pairs called labels. The PromQL query language allows aggregation across any of these labels, so you can analyse not just per process but also per datacenter and per service or by any other labels that you have defined. These can be graphed in dashboard systems such as Grafana.

Alerts can be defined using the exact same PromQL query language that you use for graphing. If you can graph it, you can alert on it. Labels make maintaining alerts easier, as you can create a single alert covering all possible label values. In some other monitoring systems you would have to individually create an alert per machine/application. Relatedly, service discovery can automatically determine what applications and machines should be scraped from sources such as Kubernetes, Consul, Amazon Elastic Compute Cloud (EC2), Azure, Google Compute Engine (GCE), and OpenStack.

For all these features and benefits, Prometheus is performant and simple to run. A single Prometheus server can ingest millions of samples per second. It is a single statically linked binary with a configuration file. All components of Prometheus can be run in containers, and they avoid doing anything fancy that would get in the way of configuration management tools. It is designed to be integrated into the infrastructure you already have and built on top of, not to be a management platform itself.

Now that you have an overview of what Prometheus is, let's step back for a minute and look at what is meant by "monitoring" in order to provide some context. Following that I will look at what the main components of Prometheus are, and what Prometheus is not.

What Is Monitoring?

In secondary school one of my teachers told us that if you were to ask ten economists what economics means, you'd get eleven answers. Monitoring has a similar lack of consensus as to what exactly it means. When I tell others what I do, people think my job entails everything from keeping an eye on temperature in factories, to employee monitoring where I was the one to find out who was accessing Facebook during working hours, and even detecting intruders on networks.

Prometheus wasn't built to do any of those things.[2] It was built to aid software developers and administrators in the operation of production computer systems, such as the applications, tools, databases, and networks backing popular websites.

So what is monitoring in that context? I like to narrow this sort of operational monitoring of computer systems down to four things:

Alerting
> Knowing when things are going wrong is usually the most important thing that you want monitoring for. You want the monitoring system to call in a human to take a look.

Debugging
> Now that you have called in a human, they need to investigate to determine the root cause and ultimately resolve whatever the issue is.

Trending
> Alerting and debugging usually happen on time scales on the order of minutes to hours. While less urgent, the ability to see how your systems are being used and changing over time is also useful. Trending can feed into design decisions and processes such as capacity planning.

Plumbing
> When all you have is a hammer, everything starts to look like a nail. At the end of the day all monitoring systems are data processing pipelines. Sometimes it is more convenient to appropriate part of your monitoring system for another purpose, rather than building a bespoke solution. This is not strictly monitoring, but it is common in practice so I like to include it.

Depending on who you talk to and their background, they may consider only some of these to be monitoring. This leads to many discussions about monitoring going around in circles, leaving everyone frustrated. To help you understand where others are coming from, I'm going to look at a small bit of the history of monitoring.

A Brief and Incomplete History of Monitoring

While monitoring has seen a shift toward tools including Prometheus in the past few years, the dominant solution remains some combination of Nagios and Graphite or their variants.

When I say Nagios I am including any software within the same broad family, such as Icinga, Zmon, and Sensu. They work primarily by regularly executing scripts called

---

2 Temperature monitoring of machines and datacenters is actually not uncommon. There are even a few users using Prometheus to track the weather for fun.

checks. If a check fails by returning a nonzero exit code, an alert is generated. Nagios was initially started by Ethan Galstad in 1996, as an MS-DOS application used to perform pings. It was first released as NetSaint in 1999, and renamed Nagios in 2002.

To talk about the history of Graphite, I need to go back to 1994. Tobias Oetiker created a Perl script that became Multi Router Traffic Grapher, or MRTG 1.0, in 1995. As the name indicates, it was mainly used for network monitoring via the Simple Network Management Protocol (SNMP). It could also obtain metrics by executing scripts.[3] The year 1997 brought big changes with a move of some code to C, and the creation of the Round Robin Database (RRD) which was used to store metric data. This brought notable performance improvements, and RRD was the basis for other tools including Smokeping and Graphite.

Started in 2006, Graphite uses Whisper for metrics storage, which has a similar design to RRD. Graphite does not collect data itself, rather it is sent in by collection tools such as collectd and Statsd, which were created in 2005 and 2010, respectively.

The key takeway here is that graphing and alerting were once completely separate concerns performed by different tools. You could write a check script to evaluate a query in Graphite and generate alerts on that basis, but most checks tended to be on unexpected states such as a process not running.

Another holdover from this era is the relatively manual approach to administering computer services. Services were deployed on individual machines and lovingly cared for by systems administrators. Alerts that might potentially indicate a problem were jumped upon by devoted engineers. As cloud and cloud native technologies such as EC2, Docker, and Kubernetes have come to prominence, treating individual machines and services like pets with each getting individual attention does not scale. Rather, they should be looked at more as cattle and administered and monitored as a group. In the same way that the industry has moved from doing management by hand, to tools like Chef and Ansible, to now starting to use technologies like Kubernetes, monitoring also needs to make a similar transition from checks on individual processes on individual machines to monitoring based on service health as a whole.

You may have noticed that I didn't mention logging. Historically logs have been used as something that you use tail, grep, and awk on by hand. You might have had an analysis tool such as AWStats to produce reports once a hour or day. In more recent years they have also been used as a significant part of monitoring, such as with the Elasticsearch, Logstash, and Kibana (ELK) stack.

Now that we have looked a bit at graphing and alerting, let's look at how metrics and logs fit into things. Are there more categories of monitoring than those two?

---

3 I have fond memories of setting up MRTG in the early 2000s, writing scripts to report temperature and network usage on my home computers.

Categories of Monitoring

At the end of the day, most monitoring is about the same thing: events. Events can be almost anything, including:

- Receiving a HTTP request
- Sending a HTTP 400 response
- Entering a function
- Reaching the `else` of an `if` statement
- Leaving a function
- A user logging in
- Writing data to disk
- Reading data from the network
- Requesting more memory from the kernel

All events also have context. A HTTP request will have the IP address it is coming from and going to, the URL being requested, the cookies that are set, and the user who made the request. A HTTP response will have how long the response took, the HTTP status code, and the length of the response body. Events involving functions have the call stack of the functions above them, and whatever triggered this part of the stack such as a HTTP request.

Having all the context for all the events would be great for debugging and understanding how your systems are performing in both technical and business terms, but that amount of data is not practical to process and store. Thus there are what I would see as roughly four ways to approach reducing that volume of data to something workable, namely profiling, tracing, logging, and metrics.

Profiling

Profiling takes the approach that you can't have all the context for all of the events all of the time, but you can have some of the context for limited periods of time.

Tcpdump is one example of a profiling tool. It allows you to record network traffic based on a specified filter. It's an essential debugging tool, but you can't really turn it on all the time as you will run out of disk space.

Debug builds of binaries that track profiling data are another example. They provide a plethora of useful information, but the performance impact of gathering all that information, such as timings of every function call, means that it is not generally practical to run it in production on an ongoing basis.

In the Linux kernel, enhanced Berkeley Packet Filters (eBPF) allow detailed profiling of kernel events from filesystem operations to network oddities. These provide access to a level of insight that was not generally available previously, and I'd recommend reading Brendan Gregg's writings (*http://www.brendangregg.com/ebpf.html*) on the subject.

Profiling is largely for tactical debugging. If it is being used on a longer term basis, then the data volume must be cut down in order to fit into one of the other categories of monitoring.

Tracing

Tracing doesn't look at all events, rather it takes some proportion of events such as one in a hundred that pass through some functions of interest. Tracing will note the functions in the stack trace of the points of interest, and often also how long each of these functions took to execute. From this you can get an idea of where your program is spending time and which code paths are most contributing to latency.

Rather than doing snapshots of stack traces at points of interest, some tracing systems trace and record timings of every function call below the function of interest. For example, one in a hundred user HTTP requests might be sampled, and for those requests you could see how much time was spent talking to backends such as data-bases and caches. This allows you to see how timings differ based on factors like cache hits versus cache misses.

Distributed tracing takes this a step further. It makes tracing work across processes by attaching unique IDs to requests that are passed from one process to another in remote procedure calls (RPCs) in addition to whether this request is one that should be traced. The traces from different processes and machines can be stitched back together based on the request ID. This is a vital tool for debugging distributed micro-services architectures. Technologies in this space include OpenZipkin and Jaeger.

For tracing, it is the sampling that keeps the data volumes and instrumentation per-formance impact within reason.

Logging

Logging looks at a limited set of events and records some of the context for each of these events. For example, it may look at all incoming HTTP requests, or all outgoing database calls. To avoid consuming too much resources, as a rule of thumb you are limited to somewhere around a hundred fields per log entry. Beyond that, bandwidth and storage space tend to become a concern.

For example, for a server handling a thousand requests per second, a log entry with a hundred fields each taking ten bytes works out as a megabyte per second. That's a nontrivial proportion of a 100 Mbit network card, and 84 GB of storage per day just for logging.

A big benefit of logging is that there is (usually) no sampling of events, so even though there is a limit on the number of fields, it is practical to determine how slow requests are affecting one particular user talking to one particular API endpoint.

Just as monitoring means different things to different people, logging also means different things depending on who you ask, which can cause confusion. Different types of logging have different uses, durability, and retention requirements. As I see it, there are four general and somewhat overlapping categories:

Transaction logs
These are the critical business records that you must keep safe at all costs, likely forever. Anything touching on money or that is used for critical user-facing features tends to be in this category.

Request logs
If you are tracking every HTTP request, or every database call, that's a request log. They may be processed in order to implement user facing features, or just for internal optimisations. You don't generally want to lose them, but it's not the end of the world if some of them go missing.

Application logs
Not all logs are about requests; some are about the process itself. Startup messages, background maintenance tasks, and other process-level log lines are typical. These logs are often read directly by a human, so you should try to avoid having more than a few per minute in normal operations.

Debug logs
Debug logs tend to be very detailed and thus expensive to create and store. They are often only used in very narrow debugging situations, and are tending towards profiling due to their data volume. Reliability and retention requirements tend to be low, and debug logs may not even leave the machine they are generated on.

Treating the differing types of logs all in the same way can end you up in the worst of all worlds, where you have the data volume of debug logs combined with the extreme reliability requirements of transaction logs. Thus as your system grows you should plan on splitting out the debug logs so that they can be handled separately.

Examples of logging systems include the ELK stack and Graylog.

Metrics

Metrics largely ignore context, instead tracking aggregations over time of different types of events. To keep resource usage sane, the amount of different numbers being tracked needs to be limited: ten thousand per process is a reasonable upper bound for you to keep in mind.

Examples of the sort of metrics you might have would be the number of times you received HTTP requests, how much time was spent handling requests, and how many requests are currently in progress. By excluding any information about context, the data volumes and processing required are kept reasonable.

That is not to say, though, that context is always ignored. For a HTTP request you could decide to have a metric for each URL path. But the ten thousand metric guideline has to be kept in mind, as each distinct path now counts as a metric. Using context such as a user's email address would be unwise, as they have an unbounded cardinality.[4]

You can use metrics to track the latency and data volumes handled by each of the subsystems in your applications, making it easier to determine what exactly is causing a slowdown. Logs could not record that many fields, but once you know which subsystem is to blame, logs can help you figure out which exact user requests are involved.

This is where the tradeoff between logs and metrics becomes most apparent. Metrics allow you to collect information about events from all over your process, but with generally no more than one or two fields of context with bounded cardinality. Logs allow you to collect information about all of one type of event, but can only track a hundred fields of context with unbounded cardinality. This notion of cardinality and the limits it places on metrics is important to understand, and I will come back to it in later chapters.

As a metrics-based monitoring system, Prometheus is designed to track overall system health, behaviour, and performance rather than individual events. Put another way, Prometheus cares that there were 15 requests in the last minute that took 4 seconds to handle, resulted in 40 database calls, 17 cache hits, and 2 purchases by customers. The cost and code paths of the individual calls would be the concern of profiling or logging.

Now that you have an understanding of where Prometheus fits in the overall monitoring space, let's look at the various components of Prometheus.

Prometheus Architecture

Figure 1-1 shows the overall architecture of Prometheus. Prometheus discovers targets to scrape from service discovery. These can be your own instrumented applica-

---

4 Email addresses also tend to be personally identifiable information (PII), which bring with them compliance and privacy concerns that are best avoided in monitoring.

---

tions or third-party applications you can scrape via an exporter. The scraped data is stored, and you can use it in dashboards using PromQL or send alerts to the Alertmanager, which will convert them into pages, emails, and other notifications.

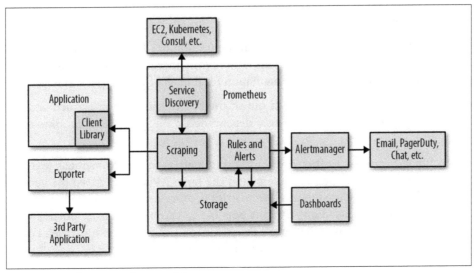

Figure 1-1. The Prometheus architecture

Client Libraries

Metrics do not typically magically spring forth from applications; someone has to add the instrumentation that produces them. This is where client libraries come in. With usually only two or three lines of code, you can both define a metric and add your desired instrumentation inline in code you control. This is referred to as direct instrumentation.

Client libraries are available for all the major languages and runtimes. The Prometheus project provides official client libraries in Go, Python, Java/JVM, and Ruby. There are also a variety of third-party client libraries, such as for C#/.Net, Node.js, Haskell, Erlang, and Rust.

Official Versus Unofficial

Don't be put off by integrations such as client libraries being unofficial or third party. With hundreds of applications and systems that you may wish to integrate with, it is not possible for the Prometheus project team to have the time and expertise to create and maintain them all. Thus the vast majority of integrations in the ecosystem are third party. In order to keep things reasonably consistent and working as you would expect, guidelines are available on how to write integrations.

Client libraries take care of all the nitty-gritty details such as thread-safety, bookkeeping, and producing the Prometheus text exposition format in response to HTTP requests. As metrics-based monitoring does not track individual events, client library memory usage does not increase the more events you have. Rather, memory is related to the number of metrics you have.

If one of the library dependencies of your application has Prometheus instrumentation, it will automatically be picked up. Thus by instrumenting a key library such as your RPC client, you can get instrumentation for it in all of your applications.

Some metrics are typically provided out of the box by client libraries such as CPU usage and garbage collection statistics, depending on the library and runtime environment.

Client libraries are not restricted to outputting metrics in the Prometheus text format. Prometheus is an open ecosystem, and the same APIs used to feed the generation text format can be used to produce metrics in other formats or to feed into other instrumentation systems. Similarly, it is possible to take metrics from other instrumentation systems and plumb it into a Prometheus client library, if you haven't quite converted everything to Prometheus instrumentation yet.

Exporters

Not all code you run is code that you can control or even have access to, and thus adding direct instrumentation isn't really an option. For example, it is unlikely that operating system kernels will start outputting Prometheus-formatted metrics over HTTP anytime soon.

Such software often has some interface through which you can access metrics. This might be an ad hoc format requiring custom parsing and handling, such as is required for many Linux metrics, or a well-established standard such as SNMP.

An exporter is a piece of software that you deploy right beside the application you want to obtain metrics from. It takes in requests from Prometheus, gathers the required data from the application, transforms them into the correct format, and finally returns them in a response to Prometheus. You can think of an exporter as a small one-to-one proxy, converting data between the metrics interface of an application and the Prometheus exposition format.

Unlike the direct instrumentation you would use for code you control, exporters use a different style of instrumentation known as *custom collectors* or *ConstMetrics*.[5]

---

5 The term ConstMetric is colloquial, and comes from the Go client library's `MustNewConstMetric` function used to produce metrics by exporters written in Go.

The good news is that given the size of the Prometheus community, the exporter you need probably already exists and can be used with little effort on your part. If the exporter is missing a metric you are interested in, you can always send a pull request to improve it, making it better for the next person to use it.

Service Discovery

Once you have all your applications instrumented and your exporters running, Prometheus needs to know where they are. This is so Prometheus will know what is meant to monitor, and be able to notice if something it is meant to be monitoring is not responding. With dynamic environments you cannot simply provide a list of applications and exporters once, as it will get out of date. This is where service discovery comes in.

You probably already have some database of your machines, applications, and what they do. It might be inside Chef's database, an inventory file for Ansible, based on tags on your EC2 instance, in labels and annotations in Kubernetes, or maybe just sitting in your documentation wiki.

Prometheus has integrations with many common service discovery mechanisms, such as Kubernetes, EC2, and Consul. There is also a generic integration for those whose setup is a little off the beaten path (see "File" on page 130).

This still leaves a problem though. Just because Prometheus has a list of machines and services doesn't mean we know how they fit into your architecture. For example, you might be using the EC2 Name tag[6] to indicate what application runs on a machine, whereas others might use a tag called app.

As every organisation does it slightly differently, Prometheus allows you to configure how metadata from service discovery is mapped to monitoring targets and their labels using *relabelling*.

Scraping

Service discovery and relabelling give us a list of targets to be monitored. Now Prometheus needs to fetch the metrics. Prometheus does this by sending a HTTP request called a *scrape*. The response to the scrape is parsed and ingested into storage. Several useful metrics are also added in, such as if the scrape succeeded and how long it took. Scrapes happen regularly; usually you would configure it to happen every 10 to 60 seconds for each target.

---

6 The EC2 Name tag is the display name of an EC2 instance in the EC2 web console.

Pull Versus Push

Prometheus is a pull-based system. It decides when and what to scrape, based on its configuration. There are also push-based systems, where the monitoring target decides if it is going to be monitored and how often.

There is vigorous debate online about the two designs, which often bears similarities to debates around Vim versus EMACS. Suffice to say both have pros and cons, and overall it doesn't matter much.

As a Prometheus user you should understand that pull is ingrained in the core of Prometheus, and attempting to make it do push instead is at best unwise.

Storage

Prometheus stores data locally in a custom database. Distributed systems are challenging to make reliable, so Prometheus does not attempt to do any form of clustering. In addition to reliability, this makes Prometheus easier to run.

Over the years, storage has gone through a number of redesigns, with the storage system in Prometheus 2.0 being the third iteration. The storage system can handle ingesting millions of samples per second, making it possible to monitor thousands of machines with a single Prometheus server. The compression algorithm used can achieve 1.3 bytes per sample on real-world data. An SSD is recommended, but not strictly required.

Dashboards

Prometheus has a number of HTTP APIs that allow you to both request raw data and evaluate PromQL queries. These can be used to produce graphs and dashboards. Out of the box, Prometheus provides the *expression browser*. It uses these APIs and is suitable for ad hoc querying and data exploration, but it is not a general dashboard system.

It is recommended that you use Grafana for dashboards. It has a wide variety of features, including official support for Prometheus as a data source. It can produce a wide variety of dashboards, such as the one in Figure 1-2. Grafana supports talking to multiple Prometheus servers, even within a single dashboard panel.

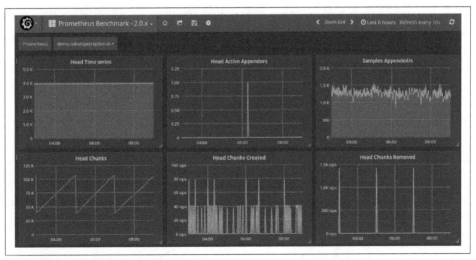

Figure 1-2. A Grafana dashboard

Recording Rules and Alerts

Although PromQL and the storage engine are powerful and efficient, aggregating metrics from thousands of machines on the fly every time you render a graph can get a little laggy. Recording rules allow PromQL expressions to be evaluated on a regular basis and their results ingested into the storage engine.

Alerting rules are another form of recording rules. They also evaluate PromQL expressions regularly, and any results from those expressions become alerts. Alerts are sent to the *Alertmanager*.

Alert Management

The Alertmanager receives alerts from Prometheus servers and turns them into notifications. Notifications can include email, chat applications such as Slack, and services such as PagerDuty.

The Alertmanager does more than blindly turn alerts into notifications on a one-to-one basis. Related alerts can be aggregated into one notification, throttled to reduce pager storms,[7] and different routing and notification outputs can be configured for each of your different teams. Alerts can also be silenced, perhaps to snooze an issue you are already aware of in advance when you know maintenance is scheduled.

---

7 A *page* is a notification to an oncall engineer which they are expected to prompty investigate or deal with. While you may receive a page via a traditional radio pager, these days it more likely comes to your mobile phone in the form of an SMS, notification, or phone call. A pager storm is when you receive a string of pages in rapid succession.

The Alertmanager's role stops at sending notifications; to manage human responses to incidents you should use services such as PagerDuty and ticketing systems.

 Alerts and their thresholds are configured in Prometheus, not in the Alertmanager.

Long-Term Storage

Since Prometheus stores data only on the local machine, you are limited by how much disk space you can fit on that machine.[8] While you usually care only about the most recent day or so worth of data, for long-term capacity planning a longer retention period is desirable.

Prometheus does not offer a clustered storage solution to store data across multiple machines, but there are remote read and write APIs that allow other systems to hook in and take on this role. These allow PromQL queries to be transparently run against both local and remote data.

What Prometheus Is Not

Now that you have an idea of where Prometheus fits in the broader monitoring landscape and what its major components are, let's look at some use cases for which Prometheus is not a particularly good choice.

As a metrics-based system, Prometheus is not suitable for storing event logs or individual events. Nor is it the best choice for high cardinality data, such as email addresses or usernames.

Prometheus is designed for operational monitoring, where small inaccuracies and race conditions due to factors like kernel scheduling and failed scrapes are a fact of life. Prometheus makes tradeoffs and prefers giving you data that is 99.9% correct over your monitoring breaking while waiting for perfect data. Thus in applications involving money or billing, Prometheus should be used with caution.

In the next chapter I will show you how to run Prometheus and do some basic monitoring.

---

8 However, modern machines can hold rather a lot of data locally, so a separate clustered storage system may not be necessary for you.

Getting Started with Prometheus

In this chapter you will set up and run Prometheus, the Node exporter, and the Alert-manager. This simple example will monitor a single machine and give you a small taste of what a full Prometheus deployment looks like. Later chapters will look at each aspect of this setup in detail.

This chapter requires a machine running any reasonable, modern version of Linux. Either bare metal or a virtual machine will do. You will use the command line and access services on the machine using a web browser. For simplicity I will assume that everything is running on localhost; if this is not the case, adjust the URLs as appropriate.

 A basic setup similar to the one used in this chapter is publicly available at *http://demo.robustperception.io/*.

Running Prometheus

Prebuilt versions of Prometheus and other components are available from the Prometheus website at *https://prometheus.io/download/*. Go to that page and download the latest version of Prometheus for the Linux OS with Arch amd64; the download page will look something like Figure 2-1.

Figure 2-1. Part of the Prometheus download page. The Linux/amd64 version is in the middle.

Here I am using Prometheus 2.2.1, so *prometheus-2.2.1.linux-amd64.tar.gz* is the file-name.

Stability Guarantees

Prometheus upgrades are intended to be safe between minor versions, such as from 2.0.0 to 2.0.1, 2.1.0, or 2.3.1. Even so, as with all software it is wise to read through the changelog.

Any 2.x.x version of Prometheus should suffice for this chapter.

Extract the tarball on the command line and change into its directory:[1]

```
hostname $ tar -xzf prometheus-*.linux-amd64.tar.gz
hostname $ cd prometheus-*.linux-amd64/
```

Now change the file called *prometheus.yml* to contain the following text:

```
global:
  scrape_interval: 10s
scrape_configs:
 - job_name: prometheus
   static_configs:
    - targets:
       - localhost:9090
```

---

1 This uses a glob for the version in case you are using a different version than I am. The star will match any text.

YAML

The Prometheus ecosystem uses Yet Another Markup Language (YAML) for its configuration files, as it is both approachable to humans and can be processed by tools. The format is sensitive to whitespace though, so make sure to copy examples exactly and use spaces rather than tabs.[2]

By default Prometheus runs on TCP port 9090, so this configuration instructs to scrape itself every 10 seconds. You can now run the Prometheus binary with **./prome theus**.

```
hostname $ ./prometheus
level=info ... msg="Starting Prometheus" version="(version=2.2.1, branch=HEAD,
    revision=bc6058c81272a8d938c05e75607371284236aadc)"
level=info ... build_context="(go=go1.10, user=root@149e5b3f0829,
    date=20180314-14:15:45)"
level=info ... host_details="(Linux 4.4.0-98-generic #121-Ubuntu..."
level=info ... fd_limits="(soft=1024, hard=1048576)"
level=info ... msg="Start listening for connections" address=0.0.0.0:9090
level=info ... msg="Starting TSDB ..."
level=info ... msg="TSDB started"
level=info ... msg="Loading configuration file" filename=prometheus.yml
level=info ... msg="Server is ready to receive web requests."
```

As you can see, Prometheus logs various useful information at startup, including its exact version and details of the machine it is running on. Now you can access the Prometheus UI in your browser at *http://localhost:9090/*, which will look like Figure 2-2.

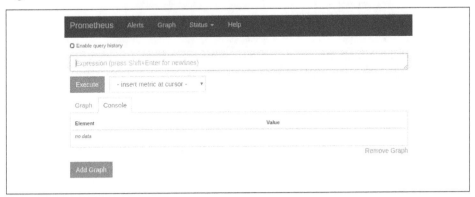

Figure 2-2. The Prometheus expression browser

---

2 You may wonder why Prometheus doesn't use JSON. JSON has its own issues such as being picky about commas, and unlike YAML does not support comments. As JSON is a subset of YAML, you can use JSON instead if you really want to.

This is the *expression browser* from which you can run PromQL queries. There are also several other pages in the UI to help you understand what Prometheus is doing, such as the Targets page under the Status tab, which looks like Figure 2-3.

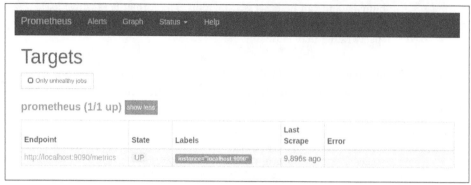

Figure 2-3. The target status page

On this page there is only a single Prometheus server in the UP state, meaning that the last scrape was successful. If there had been a problem with the last scrape, there would be a message in the Error field.

Another page you should look at is the */metrics* of Prometheus itself, as somewhat unsurprisingly Prometheus is itself instrumented with Prometheus metrics. These are metrics available on *http://localhost:9090/metrics* and are human readable as you can see in Figure 2-4.

```
# HELP go_gc_duration_seconds A summary of the GC invocation durations.
# TYPE go_gc_duration_seconds summary
go_gc_duration_seconds{quantile="0"} 2.8479e-05
go_gc_duration_seconds{quantile="0.25"} 6.2474e-05
go_gc_duration_seconds{quantile="0.5"} 9.5289e-05
go_gc_duration_seconds{quantile="0.75"} 0.000230219
go_gc_duration_seconds{quantile="1"} 0.000652444
go_gc_duration_seconds_sum 0.002677241
go_gc_duration_seconds_count 17
# HELP go_goroutines Number of goroutines that currently exist.
# TYPE go_goroutines gauge
go_goroutines 112
# HELP go_memstats_alloc_bytes Number of bytes allocated and still in use.
# TYPE go_memstats_alloc_bytes gauge
go_memstats_alloc_bytes 2.6763616e+07
# HELP go_memstats_alloc_bytes_total Total number of bytes allocated, even if freed.
# TYPE go_memstats_alloc_bytes_total counter
go_memstats_alloc_bytes_total 1.59820128e+08
# HELP go_memstats_buck_hash_sys_bytes Number of bytes used by the profiling bucket hash table.
# TYPE go_memstats_buck_hash_sys_bytes gauge
go_memstats_buck_hash_sys_bytes 1.475242e+06
# HELP go_memstats_frees_total Total number of frees.
# TYPE go_memstats_frees_total counter
go_memstats_frees_total 884863
```

Figure 2-4. The first part of Prometheus's /metrics

Note that there are not just metrics from the Prometheus code itself, but also about the Go runtime and the process.

Using the Expression Browser

The expression browser is useful for running ad hoc queries, developing PromQL expressions, and debugging both PromQL and the data inside Prometheus.

To start, make sure you are in the Console view, enter the expression **up**, and click Execute.

As Figure 2-5 shows, there is a single result with the value 1 and the name up{instance="localhost:9090",job="prometheus"}. up is a special metric added by Prometheus when it performs a scrape; 1 indicates that the scrape was successful. The instance is a label, indicating the target that was scraped. In this case it indicates it is the Prometheus itself.

Figure 2-5. The result of up in the expression browser

The job label here comes from the job_name in the *prometheus.yml*. Prometheus does not magically know that it is scraping a Prometheus and thus that it should use a job label with the value prometheus. Rather, this is a convention that requires configuration by the user. The job label indicates the type of application.

Next, you should evaluate **process_resident_memory_bytes** as shown in Figure 2-6.

Figure 2-6. The result of process_resident_memory_bytes in the expression browser

My Prometheus is using about 44 MB of memory. You may wonder why this metric is exposed using bytes rather than megabytes or gigabytes, which may be more readable. The answer is that what is more readable depends a lot on context, and even the same binary in different environments may have values differing by many orders of magnitude. An internal RPC may take microseconds, while polling a long-running process might take hours or even days. Thus the convention in Prometheus is to use base units such as bytes and seconds, and leave pretty printing it to frontend tools like Grafana.[3]

Knowing the current memory usage is great and all, but what would be really nice would be to see how it has changed over time. To do so, click Graph to switch to the graph view as shown in Figure 2-7.

---

3 This is the same logic behind why dates and times are generally best stored in UTC, and timezone transformations only applied just before they are shown to a human.

Figure 2-7. A graph of process_resident_memory_bytes in the expression browser

Metrics like process_resident_memory_bytes are called *gauges*. For a gauge, it is its current absolute value that is important to you. There is a second core type of metric called the *counter*. Counters track how many events have happened, or the total size of all the events. Let's look at a counter by graphing **prometheus_tsdb_head_samples_appended_total**, the number of samples Prometheus has ingested, which will look like Figure 2-8.

Figure 2-8. A graph of prometheus_tsdb_head_samples_appended_total in the expression browser

Counters are always increasing. This creates nice up and to the right graphs, but the values of counters are not much use on their own. What you really want to know is how fast the counter is increasing, which is where the `rate` function comes in. The `rate` function calculates how fast a counter is increasing per second. Adjust your expression to **`rate(prometheus_tsdb_head_samples_appended_total[1m])`**, which will calculate how many samples Prometheus is ingesting per second averaged over one minute and produce a result such as that shown in Figure 2-9.

Figure 2-9. A graph of rate(prometheus_tsdb_head_samples_appended_total[1m]) in the expression browser

You can see now that Prometheus is ingesting 68 or so samples per second on average. The `rate` function automatically handles counters resetting due to processes restarting and samples not being exactly aligned.[4]

---

4 This can lead to rates on integers returning noninteger results, but the results are correct on average. For more information, see "rate" on page 268.

Running the Node Exporter

The Node exporter exposes kernel- and machine-level metrics on Unix systems, such as Linux.[5] It provides all the standard metrics such as CPU, memory, disk space, disk I/O, and network bandwidth. In addition it provides a myriad of additional metrics exposed by the kernel, from load average to motherboard temperature.

What the Node exporter does not expose is metrics about individual processes, nor proxy metrics from other exporters or applications. In the Prometheus architecture you monitor applications and services directly, rather than entwining them into the machine metrics.

A prebuilt version of the Node exporter can be downloaded from *https://prome theus.io/download/*. Go to that page and download the latest version of Node exporter for the Linux OS with Arch amd64.

Again, the tarball will need to be extracted, but no configuration file is required so it can be run directly.

```
hostname $ tar -xzf node_exporter-*.linux-amd64.tar.gz
hostname $ cd node_exporter-*.linux-amd64/
hostname $ ./node_exporter
INFO[0000] Starting node_exporter (version=0.16.0, branch=HEAD,
    revision=d42bd70f4363dced6b77d8fc311ea57b63387e4f)
    source="node_exporter.go:82"
INFO[0000] Build context (go=go1.9.6, user=root@a67a9bc13a69,
    date=20180515-15:52:42)
    source="node_exporter.go:83"
INFO[0000] Enabled collectors:                      source="node_exporter.go:90"
INFO[0000]  - arp                                    source="node_exporter.go:97"
INFO[0000]  - bacahe                                 source="node_exporter.go:97"
...
various other collectors
...
INFO[0000] Listening on :9100                       source="node_exporter.go:111"
```

You can now access the Node exporter in your browser at *http://localhost:9100/* and visit its /metrics endpoint.

To get Prometheus to monitor the Node exporter, we need to update the *prome theus.yml* by adding an additional scrape config:

```
global:
  scrape_interval: 10s
scrape_configs:
 - job_name: prometheus
```

---

5 Windows users should use the wmi_exporter (*https://github.com/martinlindhe/wmi_exporter*) rather than the Node exporter.

```
    static_configs:
      - targets:
        - localhost:9090
  - job_name: node
    static_configs:
      - targets:
        - localhost:9100
```

Restart Prometheus to pick up the new configuration by using Ctrl-C to shut it down and then start it again.[6] If you look at the Targets page you should now see two targets, both in the UP state as shown in Figure 2-10.

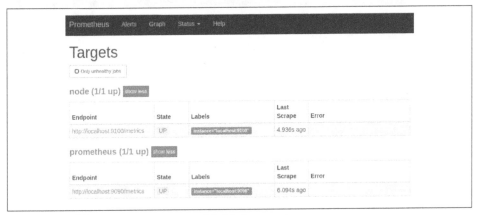

Figure 2-10. The target status page with Node exporter

If you now evaluate **up** in the Console view of the expression browser you will see two entries as shown in Figure 2-11.

Figure 2-11. There are now two results for up

---

6 It is possible to get Prometheus to reload the configuration file without restarting by using a `SIGHUP`.

As you add more jobs and scrape configs, it is rare that you will want to look at the same metric from different jobs at the same time. The memory usage of a Prometheus and a Node exporter are very different, for example, and extraneous data make debugging and investigation harder. You can graph the memory usage of just the Node exporters with **process_resident_memory_bytes{job="node"}**. The job="node" is called a *label matcher,* and it restricts the metrics that are returned, as you can see in Figure 2-12.

Figure 2-12. A graph of the resident memory of just the Node exporter

The process_resident_memory_bytes here is the memory used by the Node exporter process itself (as is hinted by the process prefix) and not the machine as a whole. Knowing the resource usage of the Node exporter is handy and all, but it is not why you run it.

As a final example evaluate **rate(node_network_receive_bytes_total[1m])** in Graph view to produce a graph like the one shown in Figure 2-13.

Figure 2-13. A graph of the network traffic received on several interfaces

node_network_receive_bytes_total is a counter for how many bytes have been received by network interfaces. The Node exporter automatically picked up all my network interfaces, and they can be worked with as a group in PromQL. This is useful for alerting, as labels avoid the need to exhaustively list every single thing you wish to alert on.

Alerting

There are two parts to alerting. First, adding alerting rules to Prometheus, defining the logic of what constitutes an alert. Second, the Alertmanager converts firing alerts into notifications, such as emails, pages, and chat messages.

Let's start off by creating a condition that you might want to alert on. Stop the Node exporter with Ctrl-C. After the next scrape, the Targets page will show the Node exporter in the DOWN state as shown in Figure 2-14, with the error *connection refused* as nothing is listening on the TCP port and the HTTP request is being rejected.[7]

Prometheus does not include failed scrapes in its application logs, as a failed scrape is an expected occurrence that does not indicate any problems in Prometheus itself. Aside from the Targets page, scrape errors are also available in the debug logs of Prometheus, which you can enable by passing the --log.level debug command-line flag.

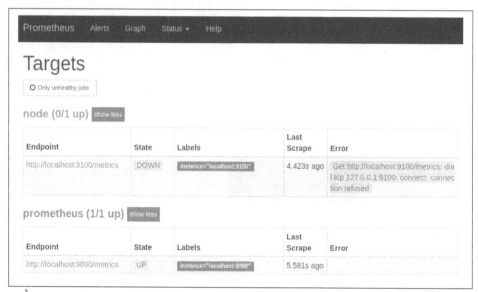

Figure 2-14. The target status page showing the Node exporter as down

Manually looking at the Targets page for down instances is not a good use of your time. Luckily, the up metric has your back, and when evaluating **up** in the Console

---

7 Another common error is *context deadline exceeded*. This indicates a timeout, usually due either to the other end being too slow or the network dropping packets.

view of the expression browser you will see that it now has a value of 0 for the Node exporter as shown in Figure 2-15.

Figure 2-15. *up is now 0 for the Node exporter*

For alerting rules you need a PromQL expression that returns only the results that you wish to alert on. In this case that is easy to do using the == operator. == will filter[8] away any time series whose values don't match. If you evaluate **up == 0** in the expression browser, only the down instance is returned, as Figure 2-16 shows.

Figure 2-16. *Only up metrics with the value 0 are returned*

---

8 There is also a bool mode that does not filter, covered in the section "bool modifier" on page 244.

Next, you need to add this expression in an alerting rule in Prometheus. I'm also going to jump ahead a little, and have you tell Prometheus which Alertmanager it will be talking to. You will need to expand your *prometheus.yml* to have the content from Example 2-1.

Example 2-1. prometheus.yml scraping two targets, loading a rule file, and talking to an Alertmanager

```
global:
  scrape_interval: 10s
  evaluation_interval: 10s
rule_files:
 - rules.yml
alerting:
  alertmanagers:
   - static_configs:
      - targets:
         - localhost:9093
scrape_configs:
 - job_name: prometheus
   static_configs:
    - targets:
       - localhost:9090
 - job_name: node
   static_configs:
    - targets:
       - localhost:9100
```

Next, create a new *rules.yml* file with the contents from Example 2-2, and then restart Prometheus.

Example 2-2. rules.yml with a single alerting rule

```
groups:
 - name: example
   rules:
   - alert: InstanceDown
     expr: up == 0
     for: 1m
```

The `InstanceDown` alert will be evaluated every 10 seconds in accordance with the `evaluation_interval`. If a series is continuously returned for at least a minute[9] (the `for`), then the alert will be considered to be firing. Until the required minute is up,

---

9 Usually a `for` of at least 5 minutes is recommended to reduce noise and mitigate various races inherent in monitoring. I am only using a minute here, so you don't have to wait too long when trying this out.

the alert will be in a *pending* state. On the Alerts page you can click this alert and see more detail, including its labels as seen in Figure 2-17.

Figure 2-17. A firing alert on the Alerts page

Now that you have a firing alert, you need an Alertmanager to do something with it. From *https://prometheus.io/download/*, download the latest version of the Alertmanager for the Linux OS with Arch amd64. Untar the Alertmanager and cd into its directory.

```
hostname $ tar -xzf alertmanager-*.linux-amd64.tar.gz
hostname $ cd alertmanager-*.linux-amd64/
```

You now need a configuration for the Alertmanager. There are a variety of ways that the Alertmanager can notify you, but most of the ones that work out of the box use commercial providers and have setup instructions that tend to change over time. Thus I am going to presume that you have an open SMTP smarthost available.[10] You should base your *alertmanager.yml* on Example 2-3, adjusting `smtp_smarthost`, `smtp_from`, and `to` to match your setup and email address.

Example 2-3. alertmanager.yml sending all alerts to email

```
global:
  smtp_smarthost: 'localhost:25'
  smtp_from: 'youraddress@example.org'
route:
  receiver: example-email
receivers:
```

---

10 Given how email security has evolved over the past decade this is not a good assumption, but your ISP will probably have one.

```
- name: example-email
  email_configs:
   - to: 'youraddress@example.org'
```

You can now start the Alertmanager with **./alertmanager**.

```
hostname $ ./alertmanager
level=info ... caller=main.go:174 msg="Starting Alertmanager"
    version="(version=0.15.0, branch=HEAD,
    revision=462c969d85cf1a473587754d55e4a3c4a2abc63c)"
level=info ... caller=main.go:175 build_context="(go=go1.10.3,
    user=root@bec9939eb862, date=20180622-11:58:41)"
level=info ... caller=cluster.go:155 component=cluster msg="setting advertise
    address explicitly" addr=192.168.1.13 port=9094
level=info ... caller=cluster.go:561 component=cluster msg="Waiting for
    gossip to settle..." interval=2s
level=info ... caller=main.go:311 msg="Loading configuration file"
    file=alertmanager.yml
level=info ... caller=main.go:387 msg=Listening address=:9093
level=info ... caller=cluster.go:586 component=cluster msg="gossip not settled"
    polls=0 before=0 now=1 elapsed=2.00011639s
level=info ... caller=cluster.go:578 component=cluster msg="gossip settled;
    proceeding" elapsed=10.000782554s
```

You can now access the Alertmanager in your browser at *http://localhost:9093/* where you will see your firing alert, which should look similar to Figure 2-18.

Figure 2-18. A InstanceDown alert in the Alertmanager

If everything is set up and working correctly, after a minute or two you should receive a notification from the Alertmanager in your email inbox that looks like Figure 2-19.

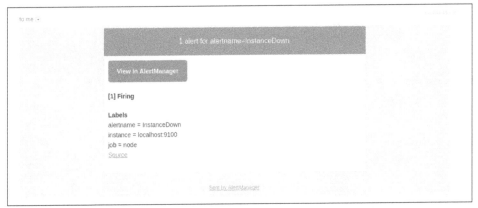

Figure 2-19. An email notification for an InstanceDown alert

This basic setup has given you a small taste of what Prometheus can do. You could add more targets to the *prometheus.yml* and your alert would automatically work for them too.

In the next chapter I am going to focus on one part of using Prometheus—adding instrumentation to your own applications.

Application Monitoring

You will realise the full benefits of Prometheus when you have easy access to the metrics you added to your own applications. This section covers adding and using this instrumentation.

In Chapter 3 you will learn how to add basic instrumentation, and what is benefical instrumentation to have.

In Chapter 4 I cover making the metrics from your application available to Prometheus.

In Chapter 5 you will learn about one of the most powerful features of Prometheus and how to use it in instrumentaton.

After you have your application metrics in Prometheus, Chapter 6 will show you how you can create dashboards that group related graphs together.

Instrumentation

The largest payoffs you will get from Prometheus are through instrumenting your own applications using *direct instrumentation* and a *client library*. Client libraries are available in a variety of languages, with official client libraries in Go, Python, Java, and Ruby.

I use Python 3 here as an example, but the same general principles apply to other languages and runtimes, although the syntax and utility methods will vary.

Most modern OSes come with Python 3. In the unlikely event that you don't already have it, download and install Python 3 from *https://www.python.org/downloads/*.

You will also need to install the latest Python client library. This can be done with `pip install prometheus_client`. The instrumentation examples can be found on GitHub (*https://github.com/prometheus-up-and-running/examples/tree/master/3*).

A Simple Program

To start things off, I have written a simple HTTP server shown in Example 3-1. If you run it with Python 3 and then visit *http://localhost:8001/* in your browser, you will get a Hello World response.

Example 3-1. A simple Hello World program that also exposes Prometheus metrics

```python
import http.server
from prometheus_client import start_http_server

class MyHandler(http.server.BaseHTTPRequestHandler):
    def do_GET(self):
        self.send_response(200)
        self.end_headers()
```

```
        self.wfile.write(b"Hello World")

if __name__ == "__main__":
    start_http_server(8000)
    server = http.server.HTTPServer(('localhost', 8001), MyHandler)
    server.serve_forever()
```

The start_http_server(8000) starts up a HTTP server on port 8000 to serve metrics to Prometheus. You can view these metrics at *http://localhost:8000/*, which will
look like Figure 3-1. Which metrics are returned out of the box varies based on the
platform, with Linux platforms tending to have the most metrics.

```
←  C  ⓘ localhost:8000/metrics

# HELP process_virtual_memory_bytes Virtual memory size in bytes.
# TYPE process_virtual_memory_bytes gauge
process_virtual_memory_bytes 371736576.0
# HELP process_resident_memory_bytes Resident memory size in bytes.
# TYPE process_resident_memory_bytes gauge
process_resident_memory_bytes 20480000.0
# HELP process_start_time_seconds Start time of the process since unix epoch in seconds.
# TYPE process_start_time_seconds gauge
process_start_time_seconds 1514904066.43
# HELP process_cpu_seconds_total Total user and system CPU time spent in seconds.
# TYPE process_cpu_seconds_total counter
process_cpu_seconds_total 0.13
# HELP process_open_fds Number of open file descriptors.
# TYPE process_open_fds gauge
process_open_fds 10.0
# HELP process_max_fds Maximum number of open file descriptors.
# TYPE process_max_fds gauge
process_max_fds 1024.0
# HELP python_info Python platform information
# TYPE python_info gauge
python_info{implementation="CPython",major="3",minor="5",patchlevel="2",version="3.5.2"} 1.0
```

Figure 3-1. The /metrics page when the simple program runs on Linux with CPython

While occasionally you will look at a /metrics page by hand, getting the metrics into
Prometheus is what you really want. Set up a Prometheus with the configuration in
Example 3-2 and get it running.

Example 3-2. prometheus.yml to scrape http://localhost:8000/metrics

```
global:
  scrape_interval: 10s
scrape_configs:
 - job_name: example
   static_configs:
    - targets:
      - localhost:8000
```

If you enter the PromQL expression **python_info** in the expression browser at *http://
localhost:9090/*, you should see something like Figure 3-2.

Figure 3-2. Evaluating the expression python_info produces one result

In the rest of this chapter I will presume that you have Prometheus running and scraping your example application. You will use the expression browser as you go along to work with the metrics you create.

The Counter

Counters are the type of metric you will probably use in instrumentation most often. Counters track either the number or size of events. They are mainly used to track how often a particular code path is executed.

Extend the above code as shown in Example 3-3 to add a new metric for how many times a Hello World was requested.

Example 3-3. REQUESTS tracks the number of Hello Worlds returned

```
from prometheus_client import Counter

REQUESTS = Counter('hello_worlds_total',
        'Hello Worlds requested.')

class MyHandler(http.server.BaseHTTPRequestHandler):
    def do_GET(self):
        REQUESTS.inc()
        self.send_response(200)
        self.end_headers()
        self.wfile.write(b"Hello World")
```

There are three parts here: the import, the metric definition, and the instrumentation.

Import

Python requires that you import functions and classes from other modules in order to use them. Accordingly, you must import the `Counter` class from the `prometheus_client` library at the top of the file.

Definition

Prometheus metrics must be defined before they are used. Here I define a counter called `hello_worlds_total`. It has a help string of `Hello Worlds requested.`, which will appear on the /metrics page to help you understand what the metric means.

Metrics are automatically registered with the client library in the *default registry*.[1] You do not need to pull the metric back to the `start_http_server` call; in fact, how the code is instrumented is completely decoupled from the exposition. If you have a transient dependency that includes Prometheus instrumentation, it will appear on your /metrics automatically.

Metrics must have unique names, and client libraries should report an error if you try to register the same metric twice. To avoid this, define your metrics at file level, not at class, function, or method level.

Instrumentation

Now that you have the metric object defined, you can use it. The `inc` method increments the counter's value by one.

Prometheus client libraries take care of all the nitty-gritty details like bookkeeping and thread-safety for you, so that is all there is to it.

When you run the program, the new metric will appear on the /metrics. It will start at zero and increase by one[2] every time you view the main URL of the application. You can view this in the expression browser and use the PromQL expression `rate(hello_worlds_total[1m])` to see how many Hello World requests are happening per second as Figure 3-3 shows.

---

1 Unfortunately not all client libraries can have this happen automatically for various technical reasons. In the Java library, for example, an extra function call is required, and depending on how you use the Go library you may also need to explicitly register metrics.

2 It may increase by two due to your browser also hitting the */favicon.ico* endpoint.

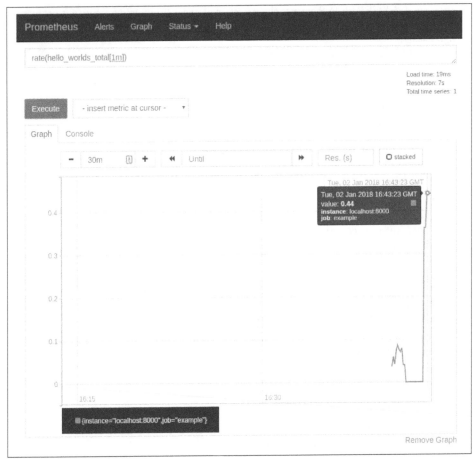

Figure 3-3. A graph of Hello Worlds per second

With just two lines of code you can add a counter to any library or application. These counters are useful to track how many times errors and unexpected situations occur. While you probably don't want to alert every single time there is an error, knowing how errors are trending over time is useful for debugging. But this is not restricted to errors. Knowing which are the most popular features and code paths of your application allows you to optimise how you allocate your development efforts.

Counting Exceptions

Client libraries provide not just core functionality, but also utilities and methods for common use cases. One of these in Python is the ability to count exceptions. You don't have to write your own instrumentation using a try...except; instead you can take advantage of the count_exceptions context manager and decorator as shown in Example 3-4.

Example 3-4. EXCEPTIONS counts the number of exceptions using a context manager

```
import random
from prometheus_client import Counter

REQUESTS = Counter('hello_worlds_total',
        'Hello Worlds requested.')
EXCEPTIONS = Counter('hello_world_exceptions_total',
        'Exceptions serving Hello World.')

class MyHandler(http.server.BaseHTTPRequestHandler):
    def do_GET(self):
        REQUESTS.inc()
        with EXCEPTIONS.count_exceptions():
          if random.random() < 0.2:
            raise Exception
        self.send_response(200)
        self.end_headers()
        self.wfile.write(b"Hello World")
```

count_exceptions will take care of passing the exception up by raising it, so it does not interfere with application logic. You can see the rate of exceptions with **rate(hello_world_exceptions_total[1m])**. The number of exceptions isn't that useful without knowing how many requests are going through. You can calculate the more useful ratio of exceptions with

```
  rate(hello_world_exceptions_total[1m])
/
  rate(hello_worlds_total[1m])
```

in the expression browser. This is how to generally expose ratios: expose two counters, then rate and divide them in PromQL.

> You may notice gaps in the exception ratio graph for periods when there are no requests. This is because you are dividing by zero, which in floating-point math results in a *NaN*, or Not a Number. Returning a zero would be incorrect as the exception ratio is not zero, it is undefined.

You can also use count_exceptions as a function decorator:

```
EXCEPTIONS = Counter('hello_world_exceptions_total',
        'Exceptions serving Hello World.')

class MyHandler(http.server.BaseHTTPRequestHandler):
    @EXCEPTIONS.count_exceptions()
    def do_GET(self):
        ...
```

Counting Size

Prometheus uses 64-bit floating-point numbers for values so you are not limited to incrementing counters by one. You can in fact increment counters by any non-negative number. This allows you to track the number of records processed, bytes served, or sales in Euros as shown in Example 3-5.

Example 3-5. SALES tracks sale value in Euros

```
import random
from prometheus_client import Counter

REQUESTS = Counter('hello_worlds_total',
        'Hello Worlds requested.')
SALES = Counter('hello_world_sales_euro_total',
        'Euros made serving Hello World.')

class MyHandler(http.server.BaseHTTPRequestHandler):
    def do_GET(self):
        REQUESTS.inc()
        euros = random.random()
        SALES.inc(euros)
        self.send_response(200)
        self.end_headers()
        self.wfile.write("Hello World for {} euros.".format(euros).encode())
```

You can see the rate of sales in Euros per second in the expression browser using the expression **rate(hello_world_sales_euro_total[1m])**, the same as for integer counters.

Attempting to increase a counter by a negative number is considered to be a programming error on your part, and will cause an exception to be raised.

It is important for PromQL that counters only ever increase, so that rate and friends don't misinterpret the decrease as counters resetting to zero when an application restarts. This also means there's no need to persist counter state across runs of an application, or reset counters on every scrape. This allows multiple Prometheus servers to scrape the same application without affecting each other.

The Gauge

Gauges are a snapshot of some current state. While for counters how fast it is increasing is what you care about, for gauges it is the actual value of the gauge. Accordingly, the values can go both up and down.

Examples of gauges include:

- the number of items in a queue
- memory usage of a cache
- number of active threads
- the last time a record was processed
- average requests per second in the last minute[3]

Using Gauges

Gauges have three main methods you can use: inc,[4] dec, and set. Similar to the methods on counters, inc and dec default to changing a gauge's value by one. You can pass an argument with a different value to change by if you want. Example 3-6 shows how gauges can be used to track the number of calls in progress and determine when the last one was completed.

Example 3-6. INPROGRESS and LAST track the number of calls in progress and when the last one was completed

```
import time
from prometheus_client import Gauge

INPROGRESS = Gauge('hello_worlds_inprogress',
        'Number of Hello Worlds in progress.')
LAST = Gauge('hello_world_last_time_seconds',
        'The last time a Hello World was served.')

class MyHandler(http.server.BaseHTTPRequestHandler):
    def do_GET(self):
        INPROGRESS.inc()
        self.send_response(200)
        self.end_headers()
        self.wfile.write(b"Hello World")
        LAST.set(time.time())
        INPROGRESS.dec()
```

These metrics can be used directly in the expression browser without any additional functions. For example, **hello_world_last_time_seconds** can be used to determine when the last Hello World was served. The main use case for such a metric is detect-

---

3 While this is a gauge, it is best exposed using a counter. You can convert a requests over time counter to a gauge in PromQL with the rate function.

4 Unlike counters, gauges can decrease, so it is fine to pass negative numbers to a gauge's inc method.

ing if it has been too long since a request was handled. The PromQL expression `time() - hello_world_last_time_seconds` will tell you how many seconds it is since the last request.

These are both very common use cases, so utility functions are also provided for them as you can see in Example 3-7. `track_inprogress` has the advantage of being both shorter and taking care of correctly handling exceptions for you. `set_to_current_time` is a little less useful in Python, as `time.time()` returns Unix time in seconds;[5] but in other languages' client libraries, the `set_to_current_time` equivalents make usage simpler and clearer.

Example 3-7. The same example as Example 3-6 but using the gauge utilities

```python
from prometheus_client import Gauge

INPROGRESS = Gauge('hello_worlds_inprogress',
        'Number of Hello Worlds in progress.')
LAST = Gauge('hello_world_last_time_seconds',
        'The last time a Hello World was served.')

class MyHandler(http.server.BaseHTTPRequestHandler):
    @INPROGRESS.track_inprogress()
    def do_GET(self):
        self.send_response(200)
        self.end_headers()
        self.wfile.write(b"Hello World")
        LAST.set_to_current_time()
```

Metric Suffixes

You may have noticed that the example counter metrics all ended with `_total`, while there is no such suffix on gauges. This is a convention within Prometheus that makes it easier to identify what type of metric you are working with.

In addition to `_total`, the `_count`, `_sum`, and `_bucket` suffixes also have other meanings and should not be used as suffixes in your metric names to avoid confusion.

It is also strongly recommended that you include the unit of your metric at the end of its name. For example, a counter for bytes processed might be `myapp_requests_processed_bytes_total`.

---

5 Seconds are the base unit for time, and thus preferred in Prometheus to other time units such as minutes, hours, days, milliseconds, microseconds, and nanoseconds.

Callbacks

To track the size or number of items in a cache, you should generally add `inc` and `dec` calls in each function where items are added or removed from the cache. With more complex logic this can get a bit tricky to get right and maintain as the code changes. The good news is that client libraries offer a shortcut to implement this, without having to use the interfaces that writing an exporter require.

In Python, gauges have a `set_function` method, which allows you to specify a function to be called at exposition time. Your function must return a floating point value for the metric when called, as demonstrated in Example 3-8. However, this strays a bit outside of direct instrumentation, so you will need to consider thread safety and may need to use mutexes.

Example 3-8. A trivial example of set_function to have a metric return the current time[6]

```
import time
from prometheus_client import Gauge

TIME = Gauge('time_seconds',
        'The current time.')
TIME.set_function(lambda: time.time())
```

The Summary

Knowing how long your application took to respond to a request or the latency of a backend are vital metrics when you are trying to understand the performance of your systems. Other instrumentation systems offer some form of Timer metric, but Prometheus views things more generically. Just as counters can be incremented by values other than one, you may wish to track things about events other than their latency. For example, in addition to backend latency you may also wish to track the size of the responses you get back.

The primary method of a summary is `observe`, to which you pass the size of the event. This must be a nonnegative value. Using `time.time()` you can track latency as shown in Example 3-9.

---

6 In practice, there is not much need for such a metric. The `timestamp` PromQL function will return the timestamp of a sample, and the `time` PromQL function the query evaluation time.

Example 3-9. LATENCY tracks how long the Hello World handler takes to run

```
import time
from prometheus_client import Summary

LATENCY = Summary('hello_world_latency_seconds',
        'Time for a request Hello World.')

class MyHandler(http.server.BaseHTTPRequestHandler):
    def do_GET(self):
        start = time.time()
        self.send_response(200)
        self.end_headers()
        self.wfile.write(b"Hello World")
        LATENCY.observe(time.time() - start)
```

If you look at the /metrics you will see that the hello_world_latency_seconds metric has two time series: hello_world_latency_seconds_count and hello_world_latency_seconds_sum.

hello_world_latency_seconds_count is the number of observe calls that have been made, so rate(hello_world_latency_seconds_count[1m]) in the expression browser would return the per-second rate of Hello World requests.

hello_world_latency_seconds_sum is the sum of the values passed to observe, so rate(hello_world_latency_seconds_sum[1m]) is the amount of time spent responding to requests per second.

If you divide these two expressions you get the average latency over the last minute. The full expression for average latency would be:

```
    rate(hello_world_latency_seconds_sum[1m])
  /
    rate(hello_world_latency_seconds_count[1m])
```

Let's take an example. Say in the last minute you had three requests that took 2, 4, and 9 seconds. The count would be 3 and the sum would be 15 seconds, so the average latency is 5 seconds. rate is per second rather than per minute, so you in principle need to divide both sides by 60, but that cancels out.

 Even though the hello_world_latency_seconds metric is using seconds as its unit in line with Prometheus conventions, this does not mean it only has second precision. Prometheus uses 64-bit floating-point values that can handle metrics ranging from days to nanoseconds. The preceding example takes about a quarter of a millisecond on my machine, for example.

As summarys are usually used to track latency, there is a `time` context manager and function decorator that makes this simpler, as you can see in Example 3-10. It also handles exceptions and time going backwards for you.[7]

Example 3-10. LATENCY tracking latency using the time function decorator

```python
from prometheus_client import Summary

LATENCY = Summary('hello_world_latency_seconds',
        'Time for a request Hello World.')

class MyHandler(http.server.BaseHTTPRequestHandler):
    @LATENCY.time()
    def do_GET(self):
        self.send_response(200)
        self.end_headers()
        self.wfile.write(b"Hello World")
```

Summary metrics may also include quantiles, although the Python client does not currently support these client-side quantiles. These should generally be avoided as you cannot do math such as averages on top of quantiles, preventing you from aggregating client-side quantiles from across the instances of your service. In addition, client-side quantiles are expensive compared to other instrumentation in terms of CPU usage (a factor of a hundred slower is not unusual). While the benefits of instrumentation generally greatly outweigh their resource costs, this may not be the case for quantiles.

The Histogram

A summary will provide the average latency, but what if you want a quantile? Quantiles tell you that a certain proportion of events had a size below a given value. For example, the 0.95 quantile being 300 ms means that 95% of requests took less than 300 ms.

Quantiles are useful when reasoning about actual end-user experience. If a user's browser makes 20 concurrent requests to your application, then it is the slowest of them that determines the user-visible latency. In this case the 95th percentile captures that latency.

---

7 System time can go backwards if the date is manually set in the kernel, or if a daemon is trying to keep things in sync with the Network Time Protocol (NTP).

Quantiles and Percentiles

The 95th percentile is the 0.95 quantile. As Prometheus prefers base units, it always uses quantiles, in the same way that ratios are preferred to percentages.

The instrumentation for histograms is the same as for summarys. The `observe` method allows you to do manual observations, and the `time` context manager and function decorator allow for easier timings as shown in Example 3-11.

Example 3-11. LATENCY histogram tracking latency using the time function decorator

```
from prometheus_client import Histogram

LATENCY = Histogram('hello_world_latency_seconds',
        'Time for a request Hello World.')

class MyHandler(http.server.BaseHTTPRequestHandler):
    @LATENCY.time()
    def do_GET(self):
        self.send_response(200)
        self.end_headers()
        self.wfile.write(b"Hello World")
```

This will produce a set of time series with the name `hello_world_latency_sec` `onds_bucket`, which are a set of counters. A histogram has a set of buckets, such as 1 ms, 10 ms, and 25 ms, that track the number of events that fall into each bucket. The `histogram_quantile` PromQL function can calculate a quantile from the buckets. For example, the 0.95 quantile (95th percentile) would be:

```
histogram_quantile(0.95, rate(hello_world_latency_seconds_bucket[1m]))
```

The `rate` is needed as the buckets' time series are counters.

Buckets

The default buckets cover a range of latencies from 1 ms to 10 s. This is intended to capture the typical range of latencies for a web application. But you can also override them and provide your own buckets when defining metrics. This might be done if the defaults are not suitable for your use case, or to add an explicit bucket for latency quantiles mentioned in your Service-Level Agreements (SLAs). In order to help you detect typos, the provided buckets must be sorted:

```
LATENCY = Histogram('hello_world_latency_seconds',
        'Time for a request Hello World.',
        buckets=[0.0001, 0.0002, 0.0005, 0.001, 0.01, 0.1])
```

If you want linear or exponential buckets, you can use Python list comprehensions. Client libraries for languages that do not have an equivalent to list comprehensions may include utility functions for these:

```
buckets=[0.1 * x for x in range(1, 10)]    # Linear
buckets=[0.1 * 2**x for x in range(1, 10)] # Exponential
```

Cumulative Histograms

If you have looked at a /metrics for a histogram, you probably noticed that the buckets aren't just a count of events that fall into them. The buckets also include a count of events in all the smaller buckets, all the way up to the +Inf, bucket which is the total number of events. This is known as a cumulative histogram, and why the bucket label is called le, standing for less than or equal to.

This is in addition to buckets being counters, so Prometheus histograms are cumulative in two different ways.

The reason they're cumulative is that if the number of buckets becomes a performance problem, some extraneous buckets[8] can be dropped using metric_relabel_configs (see "metric_relabel_configs" on page 148) in Prometheus while still allowing quantiles to be calculated. There is an example of this in Example 8-24.

You may be wondering how many buckets you should have for sufficient accuracy. I recommend sticking to somewhere around ten. This may seem like a small number, but buckets are not free, as each is an extra time series to be stored.[9] Fundamentally, a metrics-based system like Prometheus is not going to provide 100% accurate quantiles. For that you would need to calculate the quantiles from a log-based system. But what Prometheus provides is good enough for most practical alerting and debugging purposes.

The best way to think of buckets (and metrics generally) is that while they may not always be perfect, they generally give you sufficient information to determine the next step when you are debugging. So, for example, if Prometheus indicates that the 0.95 quantile jumped from 300 ms to 350 ms, but it was actually from 305 ms to 355 ms that doesn't matter that much. You still know that there was a big jump, and the next step in your investigation would be the same either way.

---

8 The +Inf bucket is required, and should never be dropped.

9 Particularly if the histogram has labels.

Latency SLAs will often be expressed as *95th percentile latency is at most 500 ms*. There is a nonobvious trap here, in that you may focus on the wrong number.

Calculating the 95th percentile accurately is tricky, requiring what may be significant computing resources if you want to get it perfect. Calculating how the proportion of requests that took more than 500 ms is easy though, you only need two counters. One for all requests and another for requests that took up to 500 ms.

By having a 500 ms bucket in your histogram you can accurately calculate the ratio of requests that take over 500 ms using

```
    my_latency_seconds_bucket{le="0.5"}
  / ignoring(le)
    my_latency_seconds_bucket{le="+Inf"}
```

to determine if you are meeting your SLA. The rest of the buckets will still give you a good estimate of the 95th percentile latency.

Quantiles are limited in that once you calculate them you cannot do any further math on them. It is not statistically correct to add, subtract, or average them, for example. This affects not just what you might attempt in PromQL, but also how you reason about a system while debugging it. A frontend may report a latency increase in the 0.95 quantile, yet the backend that caused it may show no such increase (or even a decrease!).

This can be very counterintuitive, especially when you have been woken up in the middle of the night to debug a problem. Averages, on the other hand, do not have this problem, they can be added and subtracted.[10] For example, if you see a 20 ms increase in latency in a frontend due to one of its backends, you will see a matching latency increase of around 20 ms in the backend. But there is no such guarantee with quantiles. So while quantiles are good for capturing end-user experience, they are tricky to debug with.

I recommend debugging latency issues primarily with averages rather than quantiles. Averages work the way you think they do, and once you have narrowed down the subsystem to blame for a latency increase using averages, you can switch back to quantiles if appropriate. To this end the histogram also includes _sum and _count time series. Just like with a summary, you can calculate average latency with:

---

10 However, it is not correct to average a set of averages. For example, if you had 3 events with an average of 5 and 4 events with an average of 6, the overall average would not be 5 + 6 / 2 = 5.5, but rather (3 * 5 + 4 * 6) / (3 + 4) = 5.57.

```
      rate(hello_world_latency_seconds_sum[1m])
  /
      rate(hello_world_latency_seconds_count[1m])
```

Unit Testing Instrumentation

Unit tests are a good way to avoid accidentally breaking your code as it changes over time. You should approach unit testing instrumentation the same way you approach unit tests for logs. Just as you would probably not test a debug-level log statement, neither should you test the majority of metrics that you sprinkle across your code base.

You would usually only unit test log statements for transaction logs and sometimes request logs.[11] Similarly it usually makes sense to unit test metrics where the metric is a key part of your application or library. For example, if you are writing an RPC library, it would make sense to have at least some basic tests to make sure the key requests, latency, and error metrics are working.

Without tests, some of the noncritical metrics you might use for degugging may not work, in my experience this will be the case for around 5% of debug metrics. Requiring all metrics to be unit tested would add friction to instrumentation, so rather than ending up with 20 metrics of which 19 are usable, you might instead end up with only 5 tested metrics. It would no longer be a case of adding two lines of code to add a metric. When it comes to using metrics for debugging and deep perfomance analysis, a wider breadth of metrics is always useful.

The Python client offers a `get_sample_value` function that will effectively scrape the registry and look for a time series. You can use `get_sample_value` as shown in Example 3-12 to test counter instrumentation. It is the increase of a counter that you care about, so you should compare the value of the counter before and after, rather than the absolute value. This will work even if other tests have also caused the counter to be incremented.

Example 3-12. Unit testing a counter in Python

```
import unittest
from prometheus_client import Counter, REGISTRY

FOOS = Counter('foos_total', 'The number of foo calls.')

def foo():
    FOOS.inc()
```

---

11 Categories of logs were mentioned in "Logging" on page 8.

```
class TestFoo(unittest.TestCase):
    def test_counter_inc(self):
        before = REGISTRY.get_sample_value('foos_total')
        foo()
        after = REGISTRY.get_sample_value('foos_total')
        self.assertEqual(1, after - before)
```

Approaching Instrumentation

Now that you know how to use instrumentation, it is important to know where and how much you should apply it.

What Should I Instrument?

When instrumenting, you will usually be looking to either instrument services or libraries.

Service instrumentation

Broadly speaking, there are three types of services, each with their own key metrics: online-serving systems, offline-serving systems, and batch jobs.

Online-serving systems are those where either a human or another service is waiting on a response. These include web servers and databases. The key metrics to include in service instrumentation are the request rate, latency, and error rate. Having request rate, latency, and error rate metrics is sometimes called the RED method, for Requests, Errors, and Duration. These metrics are not just useful to you from the server side, but also the client side. If you notice that the client is seeing more latency than the server, you might have network issues or an overloaded client.

> When instrumenting duration, don't be tempted to exclude failures. If you were to include only successes, then you might not notice high latency caused by many slow but failing requests.

Offline-serving systems do not have someone waiting on them. They usually batch up work and have multiple stages in a pipeline with queues between them. A log processing system is an example of an offline-serving system. For each stage you should have metrics for the amount of queued work, how much work is in progress, how fast you are processing items, and errors that occur. These metrics are also known as the USE method for Utilisation, Saturation, and Errors. Utilisation is how full your service is, saturation is the amount of queued work, and errors is self-explanatory. If you are using batches, then it is useful to have metrics both for the batches, and the individual items.

Batch jobs are the third type of service, and they are similar to offline-serving systems. However, batch jobs run on a regular schedule, whereas offline-serving systems run continuously. As batch jobs are not always running, scraping them doesn't work too well, so techniques such as the Pushgateway (discussed in "Pushgateway" on page 71) are used. At the end of a batch job you should record how long it took to run, how long each stage of the job took, and the time at which the job last succeeded. You can add alerts if the job hasn't succeeded recently enough, allowing you to tolerate individual batch job run failures.

Idempotency for Batch Jobs

Idempotency is the property that if you do something more than once, it has the same result as if it were only done once. This is a useful property for batch jobs as it means handling a failed job is simply a matter of retrying, so you don't have to worry as much about individual failures.

To achieve this you should avoid passing which items of work (such as the previous day's data) a batch job should work on. Instead you should have the batch job infer that and continue on from where it left off.

This has the additional benefit that you can have your batch jobs retry themselves. For example, you might have a daily batch job run instead a few times per day, so that even if there is a transient failure the next run will take care of it. Alert thresholds can be increased accordingly, as you will need to manually intervene less often.

Library instrumentation

Services are what you care about at a high level. Within each of your services there are libraries that you can think of as mini services. The majority will be online-serving subsystems, which is to say synchronous function calls, and benefit from the same metrics of requests, latency, and errors. For a cache you would want these metrics both for the cache overall and the cache misses that then need to calculate the result or request it from a backend.

Total and Failures, Not Success and Failures

With metrics for failures and total it is easy to calculate the failure ratio by division. With success and failures this is trickier,[12] as you first need to calculate the total.

Similarly for caches it is best to have either hits and total requests, or failures and total requests. All of total, hits, and misses works fine too.

It is beneficial to add metrics for any errors that occur and anywhere that you have logging. You might only keep your debug logs for a few days due to their volume, but with a metric you can still have a good of idea of the frequency of that log line over time.

Thread and worker pools should be instrumented similarly to offline-serving systems. You will want to have metrics for the queue size, active threads, any limit on the number of threads, and errors encountered.

Background maintenance tasks that run no more than a few times an hour are effectively batch jobs, and you should have similar metrics for these tasks.

How Much Should I Instrument?

While Prometheus is extremely efficient, there are limits to how many metrics it can handle. At some point the operational and resource costs outweigh the benefits for certain instrumentation strategies.

The good news is that most of the time you don't need to worry about this. Let's say that you had a Prometheus that could handle ten million metrics[13] and a thousand application instances. A single new metric on each of these instances would use 0.01% of your resources, making it effectively free. This means you are free to add individual metrics by hand where it is useful.

Where you need to be careful is when things get industrial. If you automatically add a metric for the duration of every function, that can add up fast (it is classic profiling after all). If you have metrics broken out by request type and HTTP URL,[14] all the potential combinations can easily take up a significant chunk of your resources. Histogram buckets expand that again. A metric with a cardinality of a hundred on each instance would take up 1% of your Prometheus server's resources, which is a less clear win and certainly not free. I discuss this further in "Cardinality" on page 93.

---

12 You should not try dividing the failures by the successes.

13 This was roughly the performance limit of Prometheus 1.x.

14 Chapter 5 looks at labels, which are a powerful feature of Prometheus that make this possible.

It is common for the ten biggest metrics in a Prometheus to constitute over half of its resource usage. If you are trying to manage the resource usage of your Prometheus, you will get a better return for your efforts by focusing on the ten biggest metrics.

As a rule of thumb, a simple service like a cache might have a hundred metrics in total, while a complex and well-instrumented service might have a thousand.

What Should I Name My Metrics?

The naming of metrics is more of an art than a science. There are some simple rules you can follow to avoid the more obvious pitfalls, and also general guidelines to construct your metric names.

The overall structure of a metric name is generally *library_name_unit_suffix*.

Characters

Prometheus metric names should start with a letter, and can be followed with any number of letters, numbers, and underscores.

While `[a-zA-Z_:][a-zA-Z0-9_:]*` is a regular expression for valid metric names for Prometheus, you should avoid some of the valid values. You should not use colons in instrumentation as they are reserved for user use in recording rules, as discussed in "Naming of Recording Rules" on page 284. Underscores at the start of metric names are reserved for internal Prometheus use.

snake_case

The convention with Prometheus is to use snake case for metric names; that is, each component of the name should be lowercase and separated by an underscore.

Metric suffixes

The _total, the _count, _sum, and _bucket suffixes are used by the counter, summary, and histogram metrics. Aside from always having a _total suffix on counters, you should avoid putting these suffixes on the end of your metric names to avoid confusion.

Units

You should prefer using unprefixed base units such as seconds, bytes, and ratios.[15] This is because Prometheus uses seconds in functions such as time, and it avoids ugliness such as kilomicroseconds.

---

15 As a general rule, ratios typically go from 0...1 and percentages go from 0...100.

Using only one unit avoids confusion as to whether this particular metric is seconds or milliseconds.[16] To avoid this confusion you should always include the unit of your metric in the name. For example, `mymetric_seconds_total` for a counter with a unit of seconds.

There is not always an obvious unit for a metric, so don't worry if your metric name is missing a unit. You should avoid `count` as a unit, as aside from clashing with summarys and histograms, most metrics are counts of something so it doesn't tell you anything. Similarly with `total`.

Name

The meat of a metric name is, um, the name. The name of a metric should give someone who has no knowledge of the subsystem the metric is from a good idea of what it means. `requests` is not very insightful, `http_requests` is better, and `http_requests_authenticated` is better again. The metric description can expand further, but often the user will only have the metric name to go on.

As you can see from the preceding examples, a name may have several underscore-separated components. Try to have the same prefix on related metrics, so that it's easier to understand their relationship. `queue_size` and `queue_limit` are more useful than `size_queue` and `limit_queue`. You might even have `items` and `items_limit`. Names generally go from less to more specific as you go from left to right.

Do not put what should be labels (covered in Chapter 5) in metric names. When implementing direct instrumentation you should never procedurally generate metrics or metric names.

You should avoid putting the names of labels that a metric has into a metric's name because it will be incorrect when that label is aggregated away with PromQL.

Library

As metrics names are effectively a global namespace, it is important to both try to avoid collisions between libraries and indicate where a metric is coming from. A metric name is ultimately pointing you to a specific line of code in a specific file in a specific library. A library could be a stereotypical library that you have pulled in as a dependency, a subsystem in your application, or even the main function of the application itself.

---

16 At one point Prometheus itself was using seconds, milliseconds, microseconds, and nanoseconds for metrics.

You should provide sufficient distinction in the library part of the metric name to avoid confusion, but there's no need to include complete organisation names and paths in source control. There is a balance between succinctness and full qualification.

For example, Cassandra is a well-established application so it would be appropriate for it to use just `cassandra` as the library part of its metric names. On the other hand, using `db` for my company's internal database connection pool library would be unwise, as database libraries and database connection pool libraries are both quite common. You might even have several inside the same application. `robustpercep tion_db_pool` or `rp_db_pool` would be better choices there.

Some library names are already established. The `process` library exposes process-level metrics such as CPU and memory usage, and is standardised across client libraries. Thus you should not expose additional metrics with this prefix. Client libraries also expose metrics relating to their runtime. Python metrics use `python`, Java Virtual Machine (JVM) metrics use `jvm`, and Go uses `go`.

Combining these steps produces metric names like `go_memstats_heap_inuse_bytes`. This is from the `go_memstats` library, memory statistics from the Go runtime. `heap_inuse` indicates the metric is related to the amount of heap being used, and `bytes` tells us that it is measured in bytes. From just the name you can tell that it is the amount of the heap memory[17] that Go is currently using. While the meaning of a metric will not always be this obvious from the name, it is something to strive for.

 You should not prefix all metric names coming from an application with the name of the application. `process_cpu_seconds_total` is `process_cpu_seconds_total` no matter which application exposes it. The way to distinguish metrics from different applications is with target labels, not metric names. See "Target Labels" on page 139.

Now that you have instrumented your application, let's look at how you can expose those metrics to Prometheus.

---

17 The heap is memory of your process that is dynamically allocated. It is used for memory allocation by functions such as `malloc`.

Exposition

In Chapter 3 I mainly focused on adding instrumentation to your code. But all the instrumentation in the world isn't much use if the metrics produced don't end up in your monitoring system. The process of making metrics available to Prometheus is known as *exposition*.

Exposition to Prometheus is done over HTTP. Usually you expose metrics under the /metrics path, and the request is handled for you by a client library. Prometheus uses a human-readable text format, so you also have the option of producing the exposition format by hand. You may choose to do this if there is no suitable library for your language, but it is recommended you use a library as it'll get all the little details like escaping correct.

Exposition is typically done either in your main function or another top-level function and only needs to be configured once per application.

Metrics are usually registered with the *default registry* when you define them. If one of the libraries you are depending on has Prometheus instrumentation, the metrics will be in the default registry and you will gain the benefit of that additional instrumentation without having to do anything. Some users prefer to explicitly pass a registry all the way down from the main function, so you'd have to rely on every library between your application's main function and the Prometheus instrumentation being aware of the instrumentation. This presumes that every library in the dependency chain cares about instrumentation and agrees on the choice of instrumentation libraries.

This design allows for instrumentation for Prometheus metrics with no exposition at all. In that case, aside from still paying the (tiny) resource cost of instrumentation, there is no impact on your application. If you are the one writing a library you can add instrumentation for your users using Prometheus without requiring extra effort for your users who don't monitor. To better support this use case, the instrumentation parts of client libraries try to minimise their dependencies.

Let's take a look at exposition in some of the popular client libraries. I am going to presume here that you know how to install the client libraries and any other required dependencies.

Python

You have already seen `start_http_server` in Chapter 3. It starts up a background thread with a HTTP server that only serves Prometheus metrics.

```
from prometheus_client import start_http_server

if __name__ == '__main__':
    start_http_server(8000)
    // Your code goes here.
```

`start_http_server` is very convenient to get up and running quickly. But it is likely that you already have a HTTP server in your application that you would like your metrics to be served from.

In Python there are various ways this can be done depending on which frameworks you are using.

WSGI

Web Server Gateway Interface (WSGI) is a Python standard for web applications. The Python client provides a WSGI app that you can use with your existing WSGI code. In Example 4-1 the `metrics_app` is delegated to by `my_app` if the /metrics path is requested; otherwise, it performs its usual logic. By chaining WSGI applications you can add middleware such as authentication, which client libraries do not offer out of the box.

Example 4-1. Exposition using WSGI in Python

```
from prometheus_client import make_wsgi_app
from wsgiref.simple_server import make_server

metrics_app = make_wsgi_app()

def my_app(environ, start_fn):
    if environ['PATH_INFO'] == '/metrics':
        return metrics_app(environ, start_fn)
    start_fn('200 OK', [])
    return [b'Hello World']

if __name__ == '__main__':
```

```
httpd = make_server('', 8000, my_app)
httpd.serve_forever()
```

Does It Have to Be /metrics?

/metrics is the HTTP path where Prometheus metrics are served by convention, but it's just a convention, so you can put the metrics on other paths. For example, if /metrics is already in use in your application or you want to put administrative endpoints under a /admin/ prefix.

Even if it is on another path, it is still common to refer to such an endpoint as your /metrics.

Twisted

Twisted is a Python event-driven network engine. It supports WSGI so you can plug in make_wsgi_app, as shown in Example 4-2.

Example 4-2. Exposition using Twisted in Python

```
from prometheus_client import make_wsgi_app
from twisted.web.server import Site
from twisted.web.wsgi import WSGIResource
from twisted.web.resource import Resource
from twisted.internet import reactor

metrics_resource = WSGIResource(
        reactor, reactor.getThreadPool(), make_wsgi_app())

class HelloWorld(Resource):
    isLeaf = False
    def render_GET(self, request):
        return b"Hello World"

root = HelloWorld()
root.putChild(b'metrics', metrics_resource)

reactor.listenTCP(8000, Site(root))
reactor.run()
```

Multiprocess with Gunicorn

Prometheus assumes that the applications it is monitoring are long-lived and multi-threaded. But this can fall apart a little with runtimes such as CPython.[1] CPython is effectively limited to one processor core due to the Global Interpreter Lock (GIL). To work around this, some users spread the workload across multiple processes using a tool such as Gunicorn.

If you were to use the Python client library in the usual fashion, each worker would track its own metrics. Each time Prometheus went to scrape the application, it would randomly get the metrics from only one of the workers, which would be only a fraction of the information and would also have issues such as counters appearing to be going backwards. Workers can also be relatively short-lived.

The solution to this problem offered by the Python client is to have each worker track its own metrics. At exposition time all the metrics of all the workers are combined in a way that provides the semantics you would get from a multithreaded application. There are some limitations to the approach used, the process_ metrics and custom collectors will not be exposed, and the Pushgateway cannot be used.[2]

Using Gunicorn, you need to let the client library know when a worker process exits.[3] This is done in a config file like the one in Example 4-3.

Example 4-3. Gunicorn config.py to handle worker processes exiting

```
from prometheus_client import multiprocess

def child_exit(server, worker):
    multiprocess.mark_process_dead(worker.pid)
```

You will also need an application to serve the metrics. Gunicorn uses WSGI, so you can use make_wsgi_app. You must create a *custom registry* containing only a Multi ProcessCollector for exposition, so that it does not include both the multiprocess metrics and metrics from the local default registry (Example 4-4).

Example 4-4. Gunicorn application in app.py

```
from prometheus_client import multiprocess, make_wsgi_app, CollectorRegistry
from prometheus_client import Counter, Gauge
```

---

1 CPython is the official name of the standard Python implementation. Do not confuse it with Cython, which can be used to write C extensions in Python.

2 The Pushgateway is not suitable for this use case, so this is not a problem in practice.

3 child_exit was added in Gunicorn version 19.7 released in March 2017.

```
REQUESTS = Counter("http_requests_total", "HTTP requests")
IN_PROGRESS = Gauge("http_requests_inprogress", "Inprogress HTTP requests",
        multiprocess_mode='livesum')

@IN_PROGRESS.track_inprogress()
def app(environ, start_fn):
    REQUESTS.inc()
    if environ['PATH_INFO'] == '/metrics':
        registry = CollectorRegistry()
        multiprocess.MultiProcessCollector(registry)
        metrics_app = make_wsgi_app(registry)
        return metrics_app(environ, start_fn)
    start_fn('200 OK', [])
    return [b'Hello World']
```

As you can see in Example 4-4, counters work normally, as do summarys and histograms. For gauges there is additional optional configuration using multiprocess_mode. You can configure the gauge based on how you intended to use the gauge, as follows:

all

The default, it returns a time series from each process, whether it is alive or dead. This allows you to aggregate the series as you wish in PromQL. They will be distinguished by a pid label.

liveall

Returns a time series from each alive process.

livesum

Returns a single time series that is the sum of the value from each alive process. You would use this for things like in-progress requests or resource usage across all processes. A process might have aborted with a nonzero value, so dead processes are excluded.

max

Returns a single time series that is the maximum of the value from each alive or dead process. This is useful if you want to track the last time something happened such as a request being processed, which could have been in a process that is now dead.

min

Returns a single time series that is the minimum of the value from each alive or dead process.

There is a small bit of setup before you can run Gunicorn as shown in Example 4-5. You must set an environment variable called prometheus_multiproc_dir. This points to an empty directory the client library uses for tracking metrics. Before starting the application, you should always wipe this directory to handle any potential changes to your instrumentation.

Example 4-5. Preparing the environment before starting Gunicorn with two workers

```
hostname $ export prometheus_multiproc_dir=$PWD/multiproc
hostname $ rm -rf $prometheus_multiproc_dir
hostname $ mkdir -p $prometheus_multiproc_dir
hostname $ gunicorn -w 2 -c config.py app:app
[2018-01-07 19:05:30 +0000] [9634] [INFO] Starting gunicorn 19.7.1
[2018-01-07 19:05:30 +0000] [9634] [INFO] Listening at: http://127.0.0.1:8000 (9634)
[2018-01-07 19:05:30 +0000] [9634] [INFO] Using worker: sync
[2018-01-07 19:05:30 +0000] [9639] [INFO] Booting worker with pid: 9639
[2018-01-07 19:05:30 +0000] [9640] [INFO] Booting worker with pid: 9640
```

When you look at the /metrics you will see the two defined metrics, but python_info and the process_ metrics will not be there.

Multiprocess Mode Under the Covers

Performance is vital for client libraries. This excludes designs where work processes send UDP packets or any other use of networks, due to the system call overhead it would involve. What is needed is something that is about as fast as normal instrumentation, which means something that is as fast as local process memory but can be accessed by other processes.

The approach taken is to use mmap. Each process has its own set of mmaped files where it tracks its own metrics. At exposition time all the files are read and the metrics combined. There is no locking between the instrumentation writing to the files and the exposition reading it to ensure isolation metric values are aligned in memory and a two phase write is used when adding a new time series.

Counters (including summarys and histograms) must not go backwards, so files relating to counters are kept after a worker exits. Whether this makes sense for a gauge depends on how it is used. For a metric like in-progress requests, you only want it from live processes, whereas for the last time a request was processed, you want the maximum across both live and dead processes. This can be configured on a per-gauge basis.

Each process creates several files that must be read at exposition time in `prometheus_multiproc_dir`. If your workers stop and start a lot, this can make exposition slow when you have thousands of files.

It is not safe to delete individual files as that could cause counters to incorrectly go backwards, but you can either try to reduce the churn (for example, by increasing or removing a limit on the number of requests workers handle before exiting[4]), or regularly restarting the application and wiping the files.

These steps are for Gunicorn. The same approach also works with other Python multiprocesses setups, such as using the `multiprocessing` module.

Go

In Go, `http.Handler` is the standard interface for providing HTTP handlers, and `promhttp.Handler` provides that interface for the Go client library. You should place the code in Example 4-6 in a file called *example.go*.

Example 4-6. A simple Go program demonstrating instrumentation and exposition

```go
package main

import (
  "log"
  "net/http"

  "github.com/prometheus/client_golang/prometheus"
  "github.com/prometheus/client_golang/prometheus/promauto"
  "github.com/prometheus/client_golang/prometheus/promhttp"
)

var (
  requests = promauto.NewCounter(
    prometheus.CounterOpts{
      Name: "hello_worlds_total",
      Help: "Hello Worlds requested.",
    })
)

func handler(w http.ResponseWriter, r *http.Request) {
  requests.Inc()
  w.Write([]byte("Hello World"))
}
```

---

4 Gunicorn's `--max-requests` flag is one example of such a limit.

```
func main() {
  http.HandleFunc("/", handler)
  http.Handle("/metrics", promhttp.Handler())
  log.Fatal(http.ListenAndServe(":8000", nil))
}
```

You can fetch dependencies and run this code in the usual way.

```
hostname $ go get -d -u github.com/prometheus/client_golang/prometheus
hostname $ go run example.go
```

This example uses promauto, which will automatically register your metric with the default registry. If you do not wish to do so you can use prometheus.NewCounter instead and then use MustRegister in an init function:

```
func init() {
  prometheus.MustRegister(requests)
}
```

This is a bit more fragile, as it is easy for you to create and use the metric but forget the MustRegister call.

Java

The Java client library is also known as the *simpleclient*. It replaced the *original client*, which was developed before many of the current practices and guidelines around how to write a client library were established. The Java client should be used for any instrumentation for languages running on a Java Virtual Machine (JVM).

HTTPServer

Similar to start_http_server in Python, the HTTPServer class in the Java client gives you an easy way to get up and running (Example 4-7).

Example 4-7. A simple Java program demonstrating instrumentation and exposition

```
import io.prometheus.client.Counter;
import io.prometheus.client.hotspot.DefaultExports;
import io.prometheus.client.exporter.HTTPServer;

public class Example {
  private static final Counter myCounter = Counter.build()
      .name("my_counter_total")
      .help("An example counter.").register();

  public static void main(String[] args) throws Exception {
    DefaultExports.initialize();
    HTTPServer server = new HTTPServer(8000);
```

```
    while (true) {
      myCounter.inc();
      Thread.sleep(1000);
    }
  }
}
```

You should generally have Java metrics as class static fields, so that they are only registered once.

The call to `DefaultExports.initialize` is needed for the various `process` and `jvm` metrics to work. You should generally call it once in all of your Java applications, such as in the main function. However, `DefaultExports.initialize` is idempotent and thread-safe, so additional calls are harmless.

In order to run the code in Example 4-7 you will need the simpleclient dependencies. If you are using Maven, Example 4-8 is what the `dependencies` in your *pom.xml* should look like.

Example 4-8. pom.xml dependencies for Example 4-7

```
<dependencies>
  <dependency>
    <groupId>io.prometheus</groupId>
    <artifactId>simpleclient</artifactId>
    <version>0.3.0</version>
  </dependency>
  <dependency>
    <groupId>io.prometheus</groupId>
    <artifactId>simpleclient_hotspot</artifactId>
    <version>0.3.0</version>
  </dependency>
  <dependency>
    <groupId>io.prometheus</groupId>
    <artifactId>simpleclient_httpserver</artifactId>
    <version>0.3.0</version>
  </dependency>
</dependencies>
```

Servlet

Many Java and JVM frameworks support using subclasses of *HttpServlet* in their HTTP servers and middleware. Jetty is one such server, and you can see how to use the Java client's `MetricsServlet` in Example 4-9.

Example 4-9. A Java program demonstrating exposition using MetricsServlet and Jetty

```java
import io.prometheus.client.Counter;
import io.prometheus.client.exporter.MetricsServlet;
import io.prometheus.client.hotspot.DefaultExports;
import javax.servlet.http.HttpServlet;
import javax.servlet.http.HttpServletRequest;
import javax.servlet.http.HttpServletResponse;
import javax.servlet.ServletException;
import org.eclipse.jetty.server.Server;
import org.eclipse.jetty.servlet.ServletContextHandler;
import org.eclipse.jetty.servlet.ServletHolder;
import java.io.IOException;


public class Example {
  static class ExampleServlet extends HttpServlet {
    private static final Counter requests = Counter.build()
        .name("hello_worlds_total")
        .help("Hello Worlds requested.").register();

    @Override
    protected void doGet(final HttpServletRequest req,
        final HttpServletResponse resp)
        throws ServletException, IOException {
      requests.inc();
      resp.getWriter().println("Hello World");
    }
  }

  public static void main(String[] args) throws Exception {
      DefaultExports.initialize();

      Server server = new Server(8000);
      ServletContextHandler context = new ServletContextHandler();
      context.setContextPath("/");
      server.setHandler(context);
      context.addServlet(new ServletHolder(new ExampleServlet()), "/");
      context.addServlet(new ServletHolder(new MetricsServlet()), "/metrics");

      server.start();
      server.join();
  }
}
```

You will also need to specify the Java client as a dependency. If you are using Maven, this will look like Example 4-10.

Example 4-10. pom.xml dependencies for Example 4-9

```
<dependencies>
  <dependency>
    <groupId>io.prometheus</groupId>
    <artifactId>simpleclient</artifactId>
    <version>0.3.0</version>
  </dependency>
  <dependency>
    <groupId>io.prometheus</groupId>
    <artifactId>simpleclient_hotspot</artifactId>
    <version>0.3.0</version>
  </dependency>
  <dependency>
    <groupId>io.prometheus</groupId>
    <artifactId>simpleclient_servlet</artifactId>
    <version>0.3.0</version>
  </dependency>
  <dependency>
    <groupId>org.eclipse.jetty</groupId>
    <artifactId>jetty-servlet</artifactId>
    <version>8.2.0.v20160908</version>
  </dependency>
</dependencies>
```

Pushgateway

Batch jobs are typically run on a regular schedule, such as hourly or daily. They start up, do some work, and then exit. As they are not continuously running, Prometheus can't exactly scrape them.[5] This is where the *Pushgateway* comes in.

The Pushgateway[6] is a metrics cache for service-level batch jobs. Its architecture is shown in Figure 4-1. It remembers only the last push that you make to it for each batch job. You use it by having your batch jobs push their metrics just before they exit. Prometheus scrapes these metrics from your Pushgateway and you can then alert and graph them. Usually you run a Pushgateway beside a Prometheus.

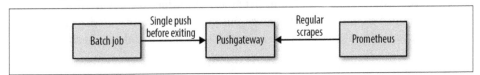

Figure 4-1. The Pushgateway architecture

---

5 Though for batch jobs that take more than a few minutes to run, it may also make sense to scrape them normally over HTTP to help debug performance issues.

6 You may see it referenced as *pgw* in informal contexts.

A service-level batch job is one where there isn't really an instance label to apply to it. That is to say it applies to all of one of your services, rather than being innately tied to one machine or process instance.[7] If you don't particularly care where a batch job runs but do care that it happens (even if it happens to currently be set up to run via cron on one machine), it is a service-level batch job. Examples include a per-datacenter batch job to check for bad machines, or one that performs garbage collection across a whole service.

 The Pushgateway is not a way to convert Prometheus from pull to push. If, for example, there are several pushes between one Prometheus scrape and the next, the Pushgateway will only return the last push for that batch job. This is discussed further in "Networks and Authentication" on page 342.

You can download the Pushgateway from the Prometheus download page. It is an exporter that runs by default on port 9091, and Prometheus should be set up to scrape it. However, you should also provide the honor_labels: true setting in the *scrape config* as shown in Example 4-11. This is because the metrics you push to the Pushgateway should not have an instance label, and you do not want the Pushgateway's own instance target label to end up on the metrics when Prometheus scrapes them.[8] honor_labels is discussed in "Label Clashes and honor_labels" on page 151.

Example 4-11. prometheus.yml scrape config for a local Pushgateway

```
scrape_configs:
 - job_name: pushgateway
   honor_labels: true
   static_configs:
    - targets:
      - localhost:9091
```

You can use client libraries to push to the Pushgateway. Example 4-12 shows the structure you would use for a Python batch job. A *custom registry* is created so that only the specific metrics you choose are pushed. The duration of the batch job is always pushed,[9] and only if the job is successful is the time it ended at pushed.

---

7 For batch jobs such as database backups that are tied to a machine's lifecycle, the node exporter textfile collector is a better choice. This is discussed in "Textfile Collector" on page 122.

8 The Pushgateway explicitly exports empty instance labels for metrics without an instance label. Combined with honor_labels: true, this results in Prometheus not applying an instance label to these metrics. Usually, empty labels and missing labels are the same thing in Prometheus, but this is the exception.

9 Just like summarys and histograms, gauges have a *time* function decorator and context manager. It is intended only for use in batch jobs.

There are three different ways you can write to the Pushgateway. In Python these are the push_to_gateway, pushadd_to_gateway, and delete_from_gateway functions.

push

> Any existing metrics for this job are removed and the pushed metrics added. This uses the PUT HTTP method under the covers.

pushadd

> The pushed metrics override existing metrics with the same metric names for this job. Any metrics that previously existed with different metric names remain unchanged. This uses the POST HTTP method under the covers.

delete

> The metrics for this job are removed. This uses the DELETE HTTP method under the covers.

As Example 4-12 is using pushadd_to_gateway, the value of my_job_duration_sec onds will always get replaced. However, my_job_last_success_seconds will only get replaced if there are no exceptions; it is added to the registry and then pushed.

Example 4-12. Instrumenting a batch job and pushing its metrics to a Pushgateway

```
from prometheus_client import CollectorRegistry, Gauge, pushadd_to_gateway

registry = CollectorRegistry()
duration = Gauge('my_job_duration_seconds',
        'Duration of my batch job in seconds', registry=registry)
try:
    with duration.time():
        # Your code here.
        pass

    # This only runs if there wasn't an exception.
    g = Gauge('my_job_last_success_seconds',
            'Last time my batch job successfully finished', registry=registry)
    g.set_to_current_time()
finally:
    pushadd_to_gateway('localhost:9091', job='batch', registry=registry)
```

You can see pushed data on the status page, as Figure 4-2 shows. An additional metric push_time_seconds has been added by the Pushgateway because Prometheus will always use the time at which it scrapes as the timestamp of the Pushgateway metrics. push_time_seconds gives you a way to know the actual time the data was last pushed.

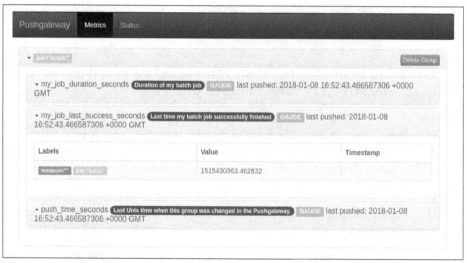

Figure 4-2. The Pushgateway status page showing metrics from a push

You might have noticed that the push is referred to as a *group*. You can provide labels in addition to the job label when pushing, and all of these labels are known as the *grouping key*. In Python this can be provided with the grouping_key keyword argument. You would use this if a batch job was sharded or split up somehow. For example, if you have 30 database shards and each had its own batch job, you might distinguish them with a shard label.

> Once pushed, groups stay forever in the Pushgateway. You should avoid using grouping keys that vary from one batch job run to the next, as this will make the metrics difficult to work with and cause performance issues. When decommissioning a batch job, don't forget to delete its metrics from the Pushgateway.

Bridges

Prometheus client libraries are not limited to outputting metrics in the Prometheus format. There is a separation of concerns between instrumentation and exposition so that you can process the metrics in any way you like.

For example, the Go, Python, and Java clients each include a *Graphite bridge*. A bridge takes metrics output from the client library registry and outputs it to something other than Prometheus. So the Graphite bridge will convert the metrics into a form that Graphite can understand[10] and write them out to Graphite as shown in Example 4-13.

Example 4-13. Using the Python GraphiteBridge to push to Graphite every 10 seconds

```
import time
from prometheus_client.bridge.graphite import GraphiteBridge

gb = GraphiteBridge(['graphite.your.org', 2003])
gb.start(10)
while True:
    time.sleep(1)
```

This works because the registry has a method that allows you to get a snapshot of all the current metrics. This is `CollectorRegistry.collect` in Python, `CollectorRegis try.metricFamilySamples` in Java, and `Registry.Gather` in Go. This is the method that HTTP exposition uses, and you can use it too. For example, you could use this method to feed data into another non-Prometheus instrumentation library.[11]

 If you ever want to hook into direct instrumentation you should instead use the metrics output by a registry. Wanting to know every time a counter is incremented does not make sense in terms of a metrics-based monitoring system. However the count of increments is already provided for you by `CollectorRegistry.collect` and works for custom collectors.

Parsers

In addition to a client library's registry allowing you to access metric output, the Go[12] and Python clients also feature a parser for the Prometheus exposition format. Example 4-14 only prints the samples, but you could feed Prometheus metrics into other monitoring systems or into your local tooling.

---

10 The labels are flattened into the metric name. Tag (i.e., label) support for Graphite was only recently added in 1.1.0.

11 This works both ways. Other instrumentation libraries with an equivalent feature can have their metrics fed into a Prometheus client library. This is discussed in "Custom Collectors" on page 201.

12 The Go client's parser is the reference implementation.

Example 4-14. Parsing the Prometheus text format with the Python client

```
from prometheus_client.parser import text_string_to_metric_families

for family in text_string_to_metric_families(u"counter_total 1.0\n"):
  for sample in family.samples:
    print("Name: {0} Labels: {1} Value: {2}".format(*sample))
```

DataDog, InfluxDB, Sensu, and Metricbeat[13] are some of the monitoring systems that have components that can parse the text format. Using one of these monitoring systems, you could take advantage of the Prometheus ecosystem without ever running the Prometheus server. I personally believe that this is a good thing, as there is currently a lot of duplication of effort between the various monitoring systems. Each of them has to write similar code to support the myriad of custom metric outputs provided by the most commonly used software. A project called OpenMetrics aims to work from the Prometheus exposition format and standardise it. Developers from various monitoring systems, including myself, are involved with the OpenMetrics effort.

Exposition Format

The Prometheus text exposition format is relatively easy to produce and parse. Although you should almost always rely on a client library to hande it for you, there are cases such as with the Node exporter textfile collector (discussed in "Textfile Collector" on page 122) where you may have to produce it yourself.

I will be showing you version 0.0.4 of the text format, which has the content type header

```
Content-Type: text/plain; version=0.0.4; charset=utf-8
```

In the simplest cases, the text format is just the name of the metric followed by a 64-bit floating-point number. Each line is terminated with a line-feed character (\n).

```
my_counter_total 14
a_small_gauge 8.3e-96
```

In Prometheus 1.0, a protocol buffer format was also supported as it was slightly (2-3%) more efficient. Only a literal handful of exporters ever exposed just the protocol buffer format. The Prometheus 2.0 storage and ingestion performance improvements are tied to the text format, so it is now the only format.

---

13 Part of the Elasticsearch stack.

Metric Types

More complete output would include the HELP and TYPE of the metrics as shown in Example 4-15. HELP is a description of what the metric is, and should not generally change from scrape to scrape. TYPE is one of counter, gauge, summary, histogram, or untyped. untyped is used when you do not know the type of the metric, and is the default if no type is specified. Prometheus currently throws away HELP and TYPE, but they will be made available to tools like Grafana in the future to aid in writing queries. It is invalid for you to have a duplicate metric, so make sure all the time series that belong to a metric are grouped together.

Example 4-15. Exposition format for a gauge, counter, summary, and histogram

```
# HELP example_gauge An example gauge
# TYPE example_gauge gauge
example_gauge -0.7
# HELP my_counter_total An example counter
# TYPE my_counter_total counter
my_counter_total 14
# HELP my_summary An example summary
# TYPE my_summary summary
my_summary_sum 0.6
my_summary_count 19
# HELP my_histogram An example histogram
# TYPE my_histogram histogram
latency_seconds_bucket{le="0.1"} 7
latency_seconds_bucket{le="0.2"} 18
latency_seconds_bucket{le="0.4"} 24
latency_seconds_bucket{le="0.8"} 28
latency_seconds_bucket{le="+Inf"} 29
latency_seconds_sum 0.6
latency_seconds_count 29
```

For histograms, the _count must match the +Inf bucket, and the +Inf bucket must always be present. Buckets should not change from scrape to scrape, as this will cause problems for PromQL's histogram_quantile function. The le labels have floating-point values and must be sorted. You should note how the histogram buckets are cumulative, as le stands for less than or equal to.

Labels

The histogram in the preceding example also shows how labels are represented. Multiple labels are separated by commas, and it is okay to have a trailing comma before the closing brace.

The ordering of labels does not matter, but it is a good idea to have the ordering consistent from scrape to scrape. This will make writing your unit tests easier, and consistent ordering ensures the best ingestion performance in Prometheus.

```
# HELP my_summary An example summary
# TYPE my_summary summary
my_summary_sum{foo="bar",baz="quu"} 1.8
my_summary_count{foo="bar",baz="quu"} 453
my_summary_sum{foo="blaa",baz=""} 0
my_summary_count{foo="blaa",baz="quu"} 0
```

It is possible to have a metric with no time series, if no children have been initialised, as discussed in "Child" on page 85.

```
# HELP a_counter_total An example counter
# TYPE a_counter_total counter
```

Escaping

The format is encoded in UTF-8, and full UTF-8[14] is permitted in both HELP and label values. Thus you need to use backslashes to escape characters that would cause issues using backslashes. For HELP this is line feeds and backslashes. For label values this is line feeds, backslashes, and double quotes.[15] The format ignores extra whitespace.

```
# HELP escaping A newline \\n and backslash \\ escaped
# TYPE escaping gauge
escaping{foo="newline \n backslash \\ double quote \" "} 1
```

Timestamps

It is possible to specify a timestamp on a time series. It is an integer value in milliseconds since the Unix epoch,[16] and it goes after the value. Timestamps in the exposition format should generally be avoided as they are only applicable in certain limited use cases (such as federation) and come with limitations. Timestamps for scrapes are usually applied automatically by Prometheus. It is not defined as to what happens if you specify multiple lines with the same name and labels but different timestamps.

```
# HELP foo I'm trapped in a client library
# TYPE foo gauge
foo 1 15100992000000
```

---

14 The null byte is a valid UTF-8 character.

15 Yes, there are two different sets of escaping rules within the format.

16 Midnight January 1st 1970 UTC.

check metrics

Prometheus 2.0 uses a custom parser for efficiency. So just because a /metrics can be scraped doesn't mean that the metrics are compliant with the format.

Promtool is a utility included with Prometheus that among other things can verify that your metric output is valid and perform lint checks.

```
curl http://localhost:8000/metrics | promtool check-metrics
```

Common mistakes include forgetting the line feed on the last line, using carriage return and line feed rather than just line feed,[17] and invalid metric or label names. As a brief reminder, metric and label names cannot contain hyphens, and cannot start with a number.

You now have a working knowledge of the text format. The full specification can be found in the official Prometheus documentation.

I have mentioned labels a few times now. In the following chapter you'll learn what they are in detail.

---

17 \r\n is the line ending on Windows, while on Unix, \n is used. Prometheus has a Unix heritage, so it uses \n.

Labels

Labels are a key part of Prometheus, and one of the things that make it powerful. In this chapter you will learn what labels are, where they come from, and how you can add them to your own metrics.

What Are Labels?

Labels are key-value pairs associated with time series that, in addition to the metric name, uniquely identify them. That's a bit of a mouthful, so let's look at an example.

If you had a metric for HTTP requests that was broken out by path, you might try putting the path in the metric name, such as is common in Graphite:[1]

```
http_requests_login_total
http_requests_logout_total
http_requests_adduser_total
http_requests_comment_total
http_requests_view_total
```

These would be difficult for you to work with in PromQL. In order to calculate the total requests you would either need to know every possible HTTP path or do some form of potentially expensive matching across all metric names. Accordingly, this is an antipattern you should avoid. Instead, to handle this common use case, Prometheus has labels. In the preceding case you might use a `path` label:

```
http_requests_total{path="/login"}
http_requests_total{path="/logout"}
http_requests_total{path="/adduser"}
```

---

1 Graphite would use periods rather than underscores.

```
http_requests_total{path="/comment"}
http_requests_total{path="/view"}
```

You can then work with the `http_requests_total` metric with all its `path` labels as one. With PromQL you could get an overall aggregated request rate, the rate of just one of the paths, or what proportion each request is of the whole.

You can also have metrics with more than one label. There is no ordering on labels, so you can aggregate by any given label while ignoring the others, or even aggregate by several of the labels at once.

Instrumentation and Target Labels

Labels come from two sources, *instrumentation labels* and *target labels*. When you are working in PromQL there is no difference between the two, but it's important to distinguish between them in order to get the most benefits from labels.

Instrumentation labels, as the name indicates, come from your instrumentation. They are about things that are known inside your application or library, such as the type of HTTP requests it receives, which databases it talks to, and other internal specifics.

Target labels identify a specific monitoring target; that is, a target that Prometheus scrapes. A target label relates more to your architecture and may include which application it is, what datacenter it lives in, if it is in a development or production environment, which team owns it, and of course, which exact instance of the application it is. Target labels are attached by Prometheus as part of the process of scraping metrics.

Different Prometheus servers run by different teams may have different views of what a "team," "region," or "service" is, so an instrumented application should not try to expose such labels itself. Accordingly, you will not find any features in client libraries to add labels[2] across all metrics of a target. Target labels come from service discovery and relabelling[3] and are discussed further in Chapter 8.

---

2 Or prefixes to metric names.

3 When using the Pushgateway, target labels may come from the application, as each Pushgateway group is in a way a monitoring target. Depending on who you ask, this is either a feature or a limitation of push-based monitoring.

Instrumentation

Let's extend Example 3-3 to use a label. In Example 5-1 you can see `label names=['path']` in the definition,[4] indicating that your metric has a single label called `path`. When using the metric in instrumentation you must add a call to the `labels` method with an argument for the label value.[5]

Example 5-1. A Python application using a label for a counter metric

```python
import http.server
from prometheus_client import start_http_server, Counter

REQUESTS = Counter('hello_worlds_total',
        'Hello Worlds requested.',
        labelnames=['path'])

class MyHandler(http.server.BaseHTTPRequestHandler):
    def do_GET(self):
        REQUESTS.labels(self.path).inc()
        self.send_response(200)
        self.end_headers()
        self.wfile.write(b"Hello World")

if __name__ == "__main__":
    start_http_server(8000)
    server = http.server.HTTPServer(('localhost', 8001), MyHandler)
    server.serve_forever()
```

If you visit *http://localhost:8001/* and *http://localhost:8001/foo*, then on the /metrics page at *http://localhost:8000/metrics* you will see the time series for each of the paths:

```
# HELP hello_worlds_total Hello Worlds requested.
# TYPE hello_worlds_total counter
hello_worlds_total{path="/favicon.ico"} 6.0
hello_worlds_total{path="/"} 4.0
hello_worlds_total{path="/foo"} 1.0
```

Label names are limited in terms of what characters you can use. They should begin with a letter (a-z or A-Z) and be followed with letters, numbers, and underscores. This is the same as for metric names, except without colons.

Unlike metric names, label names are not generally namespaced. However, you should take care when defining instrumentation labels to avoid labels likely to be

---

4 In Python be careful not to do `labelnames='path'`, which is the same as `labelnames=['p', 'a', 't', 'h']`. This is one of the more common gotchas in Python.

5 In Java the method is also `labels` and the Go equivalent is `WithLabelValues`.

used as target labels, such as env, cluster, service, team, zone, and region. I also recommend avoiding type as a label name, as it is very generic. Snake case is the convention for label names.

Label values can be any UTF-8 characters. You can also have an empty label value, but this can be a little confusing in the Prometheus server as at first glance it looks the same as not having that label.

Reserved Labels and __name__

Labels can start with underscores, but you should avoid such labels. Label names beginning with a double underscore __ are reserved.

Internally in Prometheus the metric name is just another label called __name__.[6] The expression up is syntactic sugar for {__name__="up"}, and there are also special semantics with PromQL operators as discussed in "Vector Matching" on page 245.

Metric

As you may have noticed by now, the word *metric* is a bit ambiguous and means different things depending on context. It could refer to a metric family, a child, or a time series:

```
# HELP latency_seconds Latency in seconds.
# TYPE latency_seconds summary
latency_seconds_sum{path="/foo"} 1.0
latency_seconds_count{path="/foo"} 2.0
latency_seconds_sum{path="/bar"} 3.0
latency_seconds_count{path="/bar"} 4.0
```

latency_seconds_sum{path="/bar"} is a time series, distinguished by a name and labels. This is what PromQL works with.

latency_seconds{path="/bar"} is a child, and is what the return value of labels() in the Python client represents. For a summary it contains both the _sum and _count time series with those labels.

latency_seconds is a metric family. It is only the metric name and its associated type. This is the metric definition when using a client library.

For a gauge metric with no labels, the metric family, child, and time series are the same.

---

6 This is different from the __name__ in the Python code examples.

Multiple Labels

You can specify any number of labels when defining a metric, and then the values in the same order in the `labels` call (Example 5-2).

Example 5-2. hello_worlds_total has path and method labels

```
REQUESTS = Counter('hello_worlds_total',
        'Hello Worlds requested.',
        labelnames=['path', 'method'])

class MyHandler(http.server.BaseHTTPRequestHandler):
    def do_GET(self):
        REQUESTS.labels(self.path, self.command).inc()
        self.send_response(200)
        self.end_headers()
        self.wfile.write(b"Hello World")
```

Python and Go also allow you to supply a map with both label names and values, though the label names must still match those in the metric definitions. This can make it harder to mix up the order of your arguments, but if that is a real risk, then you may have too many labels.

It is not possible to have varying label names for a metric, and client libraries will prevent it. When working with metrics it is important that you know what labels you have in play, so you must know your label names in advance when doing direct instrumentation. If you don't know your labels, you probably want a logs-based monitoring tool for that specific use case instead.

Child

The value returned to you by the `labels` method in Python is called a *child*. You can store this child for later use, which saves you from having to look it up at each instrumentation event, saving time in performance critical code that is called hundreds of thousands of times a second. In benchmarks with the Java client, I have found that with no contention the child lookup took 30 ns while the actual increment took 12 ns.[7]

A common pattern is, when an object refers to only one child of a metric, to call `labels` once and then store that in the object, as shown in Example 5-3.

---

7 For this reason you should also resist the temptation to write a facade or wrapper around a Prometheus client library that takes the metric name as an argument, as that would also incur this lookup cost. It is cheaper, simpler, and better semantically to have a file-level variable track the address of the metric object rather than having to look it up all the time.

Example 5-3. A simple Python cache that stores the child in each named cache

```python
from prometheus_client import Counter

FETCHES = Counter('cache_fetches_total',
        'Fetches from the cache.',
        labelnames=['cache'])

class MyCache(object):
    def __init__(self, name):
        self._fetches = FETCHES.labels(name)
        self._cache = {}

    def fetch(self, item):
        self._fetches.inc()
        return self._cache.get(item)

    def store(self, item, value):
        self._cache[item] = value
```

Another place where you will run into children is in initialising them. Children only appear on the /metrics after you call labels.[8] This can cause issues in PromQL as time series that appear and disappear can be very challenging to work with. Accordingly, where possible you should initialise children at startup, such as in Example 5-4, although if you follow the pattern in Example 5-3, you get this for free.

Example 5-4. Initialising children of a metric at application startup

```python
from prometheus_client import Counter

REQUESTS = Counter('http_requests_total',
        'HTTP requests.',
        labelnames=['path'])
REQUESTS.labels('/foo')
REQUESTS.labels('/bar')
```

When using Python decorators, you may also use labels without immediately calling a method on the return value, as shown in Example 5-5.

Example 5-5. Using a decorator with labels in Python

```python
from prometheus_client import Summary

LATENCY = Summary('http_requests_latency_seconds',
        'HTTP request latency.',
        labelnames=['path'])
```

---

8 This happens automatically for metrics with no labels.

```
foo = LATENCY.labels('/foo')
@foo.time()
def foo_handler(params):
    pass
```

 Client libraries usually offer methods to remove children from a
metric. You should only consider using these for unit tests. From a
PromQL semantic standpoint, once a child exists it should continue to exist until the process dies, otherwise functions such as
rate may return undesirable results. These methods also invalidate
previous values returned from labels.

Aggregating

Now that your instrumentation is bursting with labels, let's actually use them in
PromQL. I'll be going into more detail in Chapter 14, but want to give you a taste of
the power of labels now.

In Example 5-2, hello_worlds_total has path and method labels. As
hello_worlds_total is a counter, you must first use the rate function. Table 5-1 is
one possible output, showing results for two application instances with different
HTTP paths and methods.

Table 5-1. Output of rate(hello_worlds_total[5m])

{job="myjob",instance="localhost:1234",path="/foo",method="GET"}	1
{job="myjob",instance="localhost:1234",path="/foo",method="POST"}	2
{job="myjob",instance="localhost:1234",path="/bar",method="GET"}	4
{job="myjob",instance="localhost:5678",path="/foo",method="GET"}	8
{job="myjob",instance="localhost:5678",path="/foo",method="POST"}	16
{job="myjob",instance="localhost:5678",path="/bar",method="GET"}	32

This can be a little hard for you to consume, especially if you have far more time series than in this simple example. Let's start by aggregating away the path label. This is
done using the sum aggregation as you want to add samples together. The without
clause indicates what label you want to remove. This gives you the expression sum
without(path)(rate(hello_worlds_total[5m])) that produces the output in
Table 5-2.

Table 5-2. Output of sum without(path)(rate(hello_worlds_total[5m]))

{job="myjob",instance="localhost:1234",method="GET"}	5
{job="myjob",instance="localhost:1234",method="POST"}	2

```
{job="myjob",instance="localhost:5678",method="GET"}    40
{job="myjob",instance="localhost:5678",method="POST"}   16
```

It is not uncommon for you to have tens or hundreds of instances, and in my experience, looking at individual instances on dashboards breaks down somewhere around three to five. You can expand the `without` clause to include the `instance` label, which gives the output shown in Table 5-3. As you would expect from the values in Table 5-1, 1 + 4 + 8 + 32 = 45 requests per second for GET and 2 + 16 = 18 requests per second for POST.

Table 5-3. Output of sum without(path, instance)(rate(hello_worlds_total[5m]))

```
{job="myjob",method="GET"}    45
{job="myjob",method="POST"}   18
```

Labels are not ordered in any way, so just as you can remove `path` you can also remove `method` as seen in Table 5-4.

Table 5-4. Output of sum without(method, instance)(rate(hello_worlds_total[5m]))

```
{job="myjob",path="/foo"}   27
{job="myjob",path="/bar"}   36
```

> There is also a by clause that keeps only the labels you specify. `without` is preferred because if there are additional labels such as `env` or `region` across all of a job, they will not be lost. This helps when you are sharing your rules with others.

Label Patterns

Prometheus only supports 64-bit floating-point numbers as time series values, not any other data types such as strings. But label values are strings, and there are certain limited use cases where it is okay to (ab)use them without getting too far into logs-based monitoring.

Enum

The first common case for strings is *enums*. For example, you may have a resource that could be in exactly one of the states of STARTING, RUNNING, STOPPING, or TERMINATED.

You could expose this as a gauge with STARTING being 0, RUNNING being 1, STOPPING being 2, and TERMINATED being 3.[9] But this is a bit tricky to work with in PromQL. The numbers 0–3 are a bit opaque, and there is not a single expression you can write to tell you what proportion of the time your resource spent STARTING.

The solution to this is to add a label for the state to the gauge, with each potential state becoming a child. When exposing a boolean value in Prometheus, you should use 1 for true and 0 for false. Accordingly, one of the children will have the value 1 and all the others 0, which would produce metrics like those in Example 5-6.

Example 5-6. An enum example; the blaa resource is in the RUNNING state

```
# HELP gauge The current state of resources.
# TYPE gauge resource_state
resource_state{resource_state="STARTING",resource="blaa"} 0
resource_state{resource_state="RUNNING",resource="blaa"} 1
resource_state{resource_state="STOPPING",resource="blaa"} 0
resource_state{resource_state="TERMINATED",resource="blaa"} 0
```

As the 0s are always present, the PromQL expression avg_over_time(resource_state[1h]) would give you the proportion of time spent in each state. You could also aggregate by resource_state using sum without(resource)(resource_state) to see how many resources are in each state.

To produce such metrics you could use set on a gauge, but that would bring with it race conditions. A scrape might see a 1 on either zero or two of the states, depending on when exactly it happened. You need some isolation so that the gauge isn't exposed in the middle of an update.

The solution to this is to use a *custom collector*, which will be discussed further in "Custom Collectors" on page 201. To give you an idea of how to go about this, you can find a basic implementation in Example 5-7. In reality you would usually add code like this into an existing class rather than having a standalone class.[10]

Example 5-7. A custom collector for a gauge used as an enum

```
from threading import Lock
from prometheus_client.core import GaugeMetricFamily, REGISTRY

class StateMetric(object):
    def __init__(self):
```

---

9 Which is how an enum in a language like C works.

10 It is likely that future versions of the client libraries will offer you utilities to make working with enums easier. OpenMetrics for example currently plans on having a *state set* type, of which enums are a special case.

```
        self._resource_states = {}
        self._STATES = ["STARTING", "RUNNING", "STOPPING", "TERMINATED",]
        self._mutex = Lock()

    def set_state(self, resource, state):
        with self._mutex:
            self._resource_states[resource] = state

    def collect(self):
        family = GaugeMetricFamily("resource_state",
                "The current state of resources.",
                labels=["resource_state", "resource"])
        with self._mutex:
            for resource, state in self._resource_states.items():
                for s in self._STATES:
                    family.add_metric([s, resource], 1 if s == state else 0)
        yield family

sm = StateMetric()
REGISTRY.register(sm)

# Use the StateMetric.
sm.set_state("blaa", "RUNNING")
```

Enum gauges are normal gauges that follow all the usual gauge semantics, so no special metric suffix is needed.

Note that there are limits to this technique that you should be aware of. If your number of states combined with the number of other labels gets too high, performance issues due to the volume of samples and time series can result. You could try combining similar states together, but in the worst case you may have to fall back to using a gauge with values such as 0–3 to represent the enum, and deal with the complexity that brings to PromQL. This is discussed further in "Cardinality" on page 93.

Info

The second common case for strings are *info metrics*, which you may also find called the *machine roles approach* for historical reasons.[11] Info metrics are useful for annotations such as version numbers and other build information that would be useful to query on, but it doesn't make sense to use them as target labels, which apply to all metrics from a target (discussed in "Target Labels" on page 139) that applies to every metric from a target.

The convention that has emerged is to use a gauge with the value 1 and all the strings you'd like to have annotating the target as labels. The gauge should have the suffix

---

11 My article *https://www.robustperception.io/how-to-have-labels-for-machine-roles/* was the first place this technique was documented.

_info. This was shown in Figure 3-2 with the `python_info` metric, which would look something like Example 5-8 when exposed.

Example 5-8. The python_info metric the Python client exposes by default

```
# HELP python_info Python platform information
# TYPE python_info gauge
python_info{implementation="CPython",major="3",minor="5",patchlevel="2",
        version="3.5.2"} 1.0
```

To produce this in Python you could use either direct instrumentation or a custom collector. Example 5-9 takes the direct instrumentation route, and also takes advantage of the ability to pass in labels as keyword arguments with the Python client.

Example 5-9. An info metric using direct instrumentation

```
from prometheus_client import Gauge

version_info = {
    "implementation": "CPython",
    "major": "3",
    "minor": "5",
    "patchlevel": "2",
    "version": "3.5.2",
}

INFO = Gauge("my_python_info", "Python platform information",
        labelnames=version_info.keys())
INFO.labels(**version_info).set(1)
```

An info metric can be joined to any other metric using the multiplication operator and the `group_left` modifier. Any operator can be used to join the metrics, but as the value of the info metric is 1, multiplication won't change the value of the other metric.[12]

To add the `version` label from `python_info` to all up metrics you would use the PromQL expression:

```
up
* on (instance, job) group_left(version)
  python_info
```

---

12 More formally, 1 is the identity element for multiplication.

The `group_left(version)` indicates that this is a many-to-one match[13] and that the `version` label should be copied over from `python_info` into all up metrics that have the same `job` and `instance` labels. I'll look at `group_left` in more detail in "Many-to-One and group_left" on page 248.

You can tell from looking at this expression that the output will have the labels of the up metric, with a `version` label added. Adding all the labels from `python_info` is not possible, as you could potentially have unknown labels from both sides of the expression,[14] which is not workable semantically. It is important to always know what labels are in play.

Breaking Changes and Labels

If you add or remove a label from instrumentation, it is always a breaking change. Removing a label removes a distinction a user may have been depending on. Adding a label breaks aggregation that uses the `without` clause.

The one exception to this is for info metrics. For those, the PromQL expressions are constructed such that extra labels aren't a problem, so it's safe for you to add labels to info metrics.

Info metrics also have a value of 1 so it is easy to calculate how many time series have each label value using `sum`. The number of application instances running each version of Python would be `sum by (version)(python_version)`. If it were a different value such as 0, a mix of `sum` and `count` would be required in your aggregation hierarchy, which would be both more complicated and error prone.

When to Use Labels

For a metric to be useful, you need to be able to aggregate it somehow. The rule of thumb is that either summing or averaging across a metric should produce a meaningful result. For a counter of HTTP requests split by path and method, the sum is the total number of requests. For a queue, combining the items in it and its size limit into one metric would not make sense, as neither summing nor averaging it produces anything useful.

---

13 In this case it is only one-to-one as there is only one up time series per `python_info`; however, you could use same expression for metrics with multiple time series per target.

14 Target labels for up and any additional instrumentation labels added to `python_info` in the future.

One hint that an instrumentation label is not useful is if any time you use the metric you find yourself needing to specify that label in PromQL. In such a case you should probably move the label to be in the metric name instead.

Another thing to avoid is having a time series that is a total of the rest of the metric such as:

```
some_metric{label="foo"} 7
some_metric{label="bar"} 13
some_metric{label="total"} 20
```

or:

```
some_metric{label="foo"} 7
some_metric{label="bar"} 13
some_metric{} 20
```

Both of these break aggregation with sum in PromQL as you'd be double counting. PromQL already provides you with the ability to calculate this aggregate.

Table Exception

Astute readers probably noticed that summary metric quantiles break the rule about the sum or average being meaningful because you can't do math on quantiles.

This is what I call the *table exception*, where even though you can't do math across a metric, it's better to (ab)use a label than to have to do regexes against a metric name. Regexes on metric names are a very bad smell, and should never be used in graphs or alerts.

For you this exception should only ever come up when writing exporters, never for direct instrumentation. For example, you might have an unknown mix of voltages, fan speeds, and temperatures coming from hardware sensors. As you lack the information needed to split them into different metrics, the only thing you can really do is shove them all into one metric and leave it to the person consuming the metric to interpret it.

 The label names used for a metric should not change during the lifetime of an application process. If you feel the need for this, you probably want a logs-based monitoring solution for that use case.

Cardinality

Don't go too far when using labels. Monitoring is a means to an end, so more time series and more monitoring aren't always better. For a monitoring system, whether you run it yourself on-premises or pay a company to run it for you in the cloud, every time series and sample has both a resource cost and a human cost in terms of ongoing operations to keep the monitoring system up and running.

In this context I would like to talk about cardinality, which in Prometheus is the number of time series you have. If your Prometheus is provisioned to handle, say, ten million time series,[15] how would you best spend those? At what point do you move certain use cases to logs-based monitoring instead?

The way I look at it is to assume that someone running your code has a large setup with a thousand instances of a particular application.[16] Adding a simple counter metric to an obscure subsystem will add a thousand time series to your Prometheus, which is 0.01% of its capacity. That is basically free, and it might help you debug a weird problem one day. Across all of the application and its libraries you might have a hundred of these obscure metrics, which total to 1% of your monitoring capacity and is still quite cheap even given the rarity that you'll likely use any one of them.

Now consider a metric with a label with 10 values and in addition was a histogram that by default has 12 time series.[17] That is a 120 series, or 1.2% of your monitoring capacity. That this is a good tradeoff is less clear. It might be okay to have a handful of these, but you might also consider switching to a quantile-less summary metric instead.[18]

The next stage is where things get a little troublesome. If a label already has a cardinality of 10, there is a good chance that it will only increase over time as new features are introduced to your application. A cardinality of 10 today might be 15 next year, and 200 might change to 300. Increased traffic from users usually means more application instances. If you have more than one of these expanding labels on a metric, the impact is compounded, resulting in a combinatorial explosion of time series. And this is just one of the ever-growing applications that Prometheus is monitoring.

In this way cardinality can sneak up on you. It is usually obvious that email addresses, customers, and IP addresses are poor choices for label values on cardinality grounds. It is less clear that the HTTP path is going to be a problem. Given that the HTTP request metric is regularly used, removing labels from it, switching away from a histogram, or even reducing the number of buckets in the histogram can be challenging politically.

---

15 This is the approximate practical performance limit of Prometheus 1.x.

16 It is possible to have more, but it's a reasonably conservative upper bound.

17 Ten buckets, plus the _sum and _count.

18 With only the _sum and _count time series, quantileless summary metrics are a very cheap way to get an idea of latency.

The rule of thumb I use is that the cardinality of an arbitrary metric on one application instance should be kept below 10. It is also okay to have a handful of metrics that have a cardinality around 100, but you should be prepared to reduce metric cardinality and rely on logs as that cardinality grows.

 The handful of a 100 cardinality metrics per Prometheus presumes a thousand instances. If you are 100% certain that you will not reach these numbers, such as with applications you will run exactly one of, you can adjust the rule of thumb accordingly.

There is a common pattern that I have seen when Prometheus is introduced to an organisation. Initially, no matter how hard you try to convince your users to use Prometheus, they won't see the point. Then at some point it clicks, and they start to grasp the power of labels. It usually follows quickly after that your Prometheus has performance issues due to label cardinality. I advise talking about the limitations of cardinality with your users early on and also consider using `sample_limit` as an emergency safety valve (see "Reducing Load" on page 350).

The ten biggest metrics in a Prometheus commonly constitute over half of its resource usage, and this is almost always due to label cardinality. There is sometimes confusion that if the issue is the number of label values, if you were to move the label value into the metric name wouldn't that fix the problem? As the underlying resource constraint is actually time series cardinality (which manifests due to label values), moving label values to the metric name doesn't change the cardinality, it just makes the metrics harder to use.[19]

Now that you can add metrics to your applications and know some basic PromQL expressions, in the following chapter I'll show you how you can create dashboards in Grafana.

---

19 It would also make it harder to pinpoint the metrics responsible for your resource usage.

Dashboarding with Grafana

When you get an alert or want to check on the current performance of your systems, dashboards will be your first port of call. The expression browser that you have seen up to now is fine for ad hoc graphing and when you need to debug your PromQL, but it's not designed to be used as a dashboard.

What do I mean by dashboard? A set of graphs, tables, and other visualisations of your systems. You might have a dashboard for global traffic, which services are getting how much traffic and with what latency. For each of those services you would likely have a dashboard of its latency, errors, request rate, instance count, CPU usage, memory usage, and service-specific metrics. Drilling down, you could have a dashboard for particular subsystems or each service, or a garbage collection dashboard that can be used with any Java application.

Grafana is a popular tool with which you can build such dashboards for many different monitoring and nonmonitoring systems, including Graphite, InfluxDB, Elasticsearch, and PostgreSQL. It is the recommended tool for you to create dashboards when using Prometheus, and is continuously improving its Prometheus support.

In this chapter I introduce using Grafana with Prometheus, extending the Prometheus and Node exporter you set up in Chapter 2.

Promdash and Console Templates

Originally the Prometheus project had its own dashboarding tool called *Promdash*. Even though Promdash was better at the time for Prometheus use cases, the Prometheus developers decided to rally around Grafana rather than have to continue to work on their own dashboarding solution. These days Prometheus is a first-class plug-in in Grafana, and also one of the most popular.[1]

There is a feature included with Prometheus called *console templates* that can be used for dashboards. Unlike Promdash and Grafana, which store dashboards in relational databases, it is built right into Prometheus and is configured from the filesystem. It allows you to render web pages using Go's templating language[2] and easily keep your dashboards in source control. Console templates are a very raw feature upon which you could build a dashboard system, and as such it is recommended only for niche use cases and advanced users.

Installation

You can download Grafana from *https://grafana.com/grafana/download*. The site includes installation instructions, but if you're using Docker, for example, you would use:

```
docker run -d --name=grafana --net=host grafana/grafana:5.0.0
```

Note that this doesn't use a volume mount,[3] so it will store all state inside the container.

I use Grafana 5.0.0 here. You can use a newer version but be aware that what you see will likely differ slightly.

Once Grafana is running you should be able to access it in your browser at *http://localhost:3000/*, and you will see a login screen like the one in Figure 6-1.

---

1 Grafana by default reports anonymous usage statistics. This can be disabled with the `reporting_enabled` setting in its configuration file.

2 This is the same templating language that is used for alert templating, with some minor differences in available functionality.

3 A way to have filesystems shared across containers over time, as by default a Docker container's storage is specific to that container. Volume mounts can be specified with the `-v` flag to `docker run`.

Figure 6-1. Grafana login screen

Log in with the default username of **admin** and the default password, which is also **admin**. You should see the Home Dashboard as shown in Figure 6-2. I have switched to the Light theme in the Org Settings in order to make things easier to see in my screenshots.

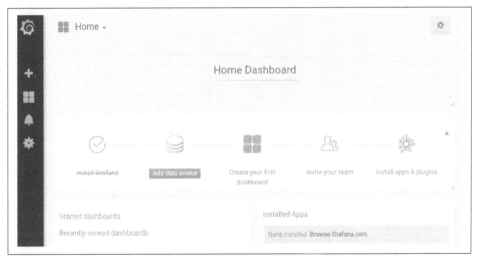

Figure 6-2. Grafana Home Dashboard on a fresh install

Data Source

Grafana uses *data sources* to fetch information used for graphs. There are a variety of types of data sources supported out of the box, including OpenTSDB, PostgreSQL, and of course, Prometheus. You can have many data sources of the same type, and usually you would have one per Prometheus running. A Grafana dashboard can have graphs from variety of sources, and you can even mix sources in a graph panel.

More recent versions of Grafana make it easy to add your first data source. Click on Add data source and add a data source with a Name of **Prometheus**, a Type of Prometheus, and a URL of *http://localhost:9090* (or whatever other URL your Prometheus from Chapter 2 is listening on). The form should look like Figure 6-3. Leave all other settings at their defaults, and finally click Save&Test. If it works you will get a message that the data source is working. If you don't, check that the Prometheus is indeed running and that it is accessible from Grafana.[4]

Figure 6-3. Adding a Prometheus data source to Grafana

---

4 The Access proxy setting has Grafana make the requests to your Prometheus. By contrast, the direct setting has your browser make the request.

Dashboards and Panels

Go again to *http://localhost:3000/* in your browser, and this time click New dashboard, which will bring you to a page that looks like Figure 6-4.

Figure 6-4. A new Grafana dashboard

From here you can select the first panel you'd like to add. Panels are rectangular areas containing a graph, table, or other visual information. You can add new panels beyond the first with the Add panel button, which is the button on the top row with the orange plus sign. As of Grafana 5.0.0, panels are organised within a grid system,[5] and can be rearranged using drag and drop.

 After making any changes to a dashboard or panels, if you want them to be remembered you must explicitly save them. You can do this with the save button at the top of the page or using the Ctrl-S keyboard shortcut.

You can access the dashboard settings, such as its name, using the gear icon up top. From the settings menu you can also duplicate dashboards using Save As, which is handy when you want to experiment with a dashboard.

---

5 Previously, Grafana panels were contained within rows.

Avoiding the Wall of Graphs

It is not unusual to end up with multiple dashboards per service you run. It is easy for dashboards to gradually get bloated with too many graphs, making it challenging for you to interpret what is actually going on. To mitigate this you should try to avoid dashboards that serve more than one team or purpose, and instead give them a dashboard each.

The more high-level a dashboard is, the fewer rows and panels it should have. A global overview should fit on one screen and be understandable at a distance. Dashboards commonly used for oncall might have a row or two more than that, whereas a dashboard for in-depth performance tuning by experts might run to several screens.

Why do I recommend that you limit the amount of graphs on each of your dashboards? The answer is that every graph, line, and number on a dashboard makes it harder to understand. This is particularly relevant when you are oncall and handling alerts. When you are stressed, need to act quickly, and are possibly only half-awake, having to remember the subtler points of what each graphs on your dashboard mean is not going to aid you in terms of either response time or taking an appropriate action.

To give an extreme example, one service I worked on had a dashboard (singular) with over 600 graphs.[6] This was hailed as superb monitoring, due to the vast wealth of data on display. The sheer volume of data meant I was never able to get my head around that dashboard, plus it took rather a long time to load. I like to call this style of dashboarding the Wall of Graphs antipattern.

You should not confuse having lots of graphs with having good monitoring. Monitoring is ultimately about outcomes, such as faster incident resolution and better engineering decisions, not pretty graphs.

Graph Panel

The Graph panel is the main panel you will be using. As the name indicates, it displays a graph. As seen in Figure 6-4, click the Graph button to add a graph panel. You now have a blank graph. To configure it, click Panel Title and then Edit as shown in Figure 6-5.[7]

---

6 The worst case of this I have heard of weighed in at over 1,000 graphs.

7 You can use the e keyboard shortcut to open the editor while hovering over the panel. You can press ? to view a full list of keyboard shortcuts.

Figure 6-5. Opening the editor for a graph panel

The graph editor will open on the Metrics tab. Enter `process_resident_memory_`
`bytes` for the query expression, in the text box beside A,[8] as shown in Figure 6-6, and
then click outside of the text box. You will see a graph of memory usage similar to
what Figure 2-7 showed when the same expression was used in the expression
browser.

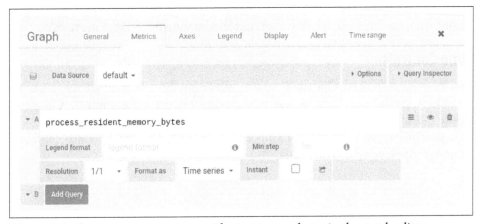

Figure 6-6. The expression process_resident_memory_bytes in the graph editor

---

8 The A indicates that it is the first query.

Grafana offers more than the expression browser. You can configure the legend to display something other than the full-time series name. Put {{job}} in the Legend Format text box. On the Axes tab, change the Left Y Unit to data/bytes. On the General tab, change the Title to Memory Usage. The graph will now look something like Figure 6-7, with a more useful legend, appropriate units on the axis, and a title.

Figure 6-7. Memory Usage graph with custom legend, title, and axis units configured

These are the settings you will want to configure on virtually all of your graphs, but this is only a small taste of what you can do with graphs in Grafana. You can configure colours, draw style, tool tips, stacking, filling, and even include metrics from multiple data sources.

Don't forget to save the dashboard before continuing! New dashboard is a special dashboard name for Grafana, so you should choose something more memorable.

Time Controls

You may have noticed Grafana's time controls on the top right of the page. By default, it should say "Last 6 hours." Clicking on the time controls will show Figure 6-8 from where you can choose a time range and how often to refresh. The time controls apply to an entire dashboard at once, though you can also configure some overrides on a per-panel basis.

Figure 6-8. Grafana's time control menu

Aliasing

As your graphs refresh you may notice that the shape can change, even though the underlying data hasn't changed. This is a signal processing effect called *aliasing*. You may already be familiar with aliasing from the graphics in first-person video games, where the rendering artifacts of a distant object change and may seem to flicker as you walk toward it.

The same thing is happening here. Each rendering of the data is at a slightly different time, so functions such as `rate` will calculate slightly different results. None of these results are wrong, they're just different approximations of what is going on.

This is a fundamental limitation of metrics-based monitoring, and any other system that takes samples, and is related to the *Nyquist-Shannon sampling theorem*. You can mitigate aliasing by increasing the frequency of your scrapes and evaluations, but ultimately to get a 100% accurate view of what is going on you need logs as logs have an exact record of every single event.

Singlestat Panel

The Singlestat panel displays the value of a single time series. More recent versions of Grafana can also show a Prometheus label value.

I will start this example by adding a time series value. Click on Back to dashboard (the back arrow in the top right) to return from the graph panel to the dashboard view. Click on the Add panel button and add a Singlestat panel. As you did for the previous panel, click on Panel Title and then Edit. For the query expression on the Metrics tab, use `prometheus_tsdb_head_series`, which is (roughly speaking) the number of different time series Prometheus is ingesting. By default the Singlestat panel will calculate the average of the time series over the dashboard's time range. This is often not what you want, so on the Options tab, change the Stat to Current.

The default text can be a bit small, so change the Font Size to 200%. On the General tab, change the Title to `Prometheus Time Series`. Finally, click Back to dashboard and you should see something like Figure 6-9.

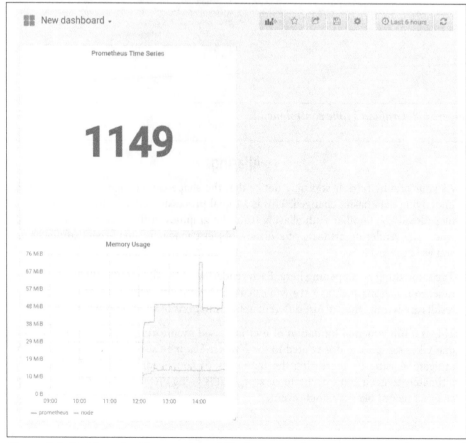

Figure 6-9. Dashboard with a graph and Singlestat panel

Displaying label values is handy for software versions on your graphs. Add another Singlestat panel; this time you will use the query expression `node_uname_info`, which contains the same information as the uname -a command. Set the Format as to Table, and on the Options tab set the Column to release. Leave the Font size as-is, as kernel versions can be relatively long. Under the General tab, the Title should be `Kernel version`. After clicking Back to dashboard and rearranging the panels using drag and drop, you should see something like Figure 6-10.

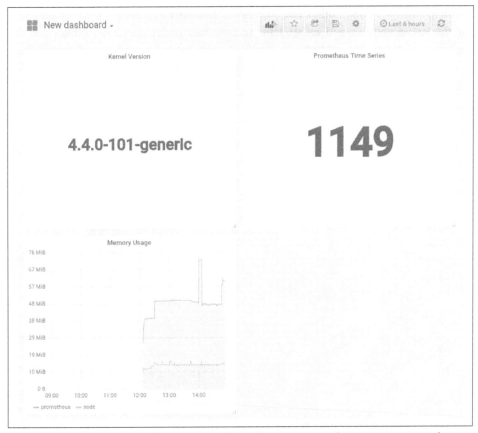

Figure 6-10. Dashboard with a graph and two Singlestat panels, one numeric and one text

The Singlestat panel has further features including different colours depending on the time series value, and displaying sparklines behind the value.

Table Panel

While the Singlestat panel can only display one time series at a time, the Table panel allows you to display multiple time series. Table panels tend to require more configuration than other panels, and all the text can look cluttered on your dashboards.

Add a new panel, this time a Table panel. As before, Click Panel Title and then Edit. Use the query expression **rate(node_network_receive_bytes_total[1m])** on the Metrics tab, and tick the Instant checkbox. There are more columns that you need here. On the Column styles tab, change the existing Time rule to have a Type of Hidden. Click +Add to add a new rule with Apply to columns named **job** with Type of

Hidden, and then add another rule hiding the **instance**. To set the unit, +Add a rule for the **Value** column and set its Unit to bytes/sec under data rate. Finally, on the General tab, set the title to **Network Traffic Received**. After all that, if you go Back to dashboard and rearrange the panels, you should see a dashboard like the one in Figure 6-11.

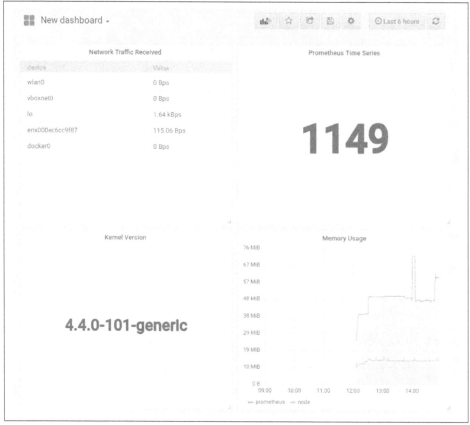

Figure 6-11. Dashboard with several panels, including a table for per-device network traffic

Template Variables

All the dashboard examples I have shown you so far have applied to a single Prometheus and a single Node exporter. This is fine for demonstration of the basics, but not great when you have hundreds or even tens of machines to monitor. The good news is that you don't have to create a dashboard for every individual machine. You can use Grafana's templating feature.

You only have monitoring for one machine set up, so for this example I will template based on network devices, as you should have at least two of those.[9]

To start with, create a new dashboard by clicking on the dashboard name and then +New dashboard at the bottom of the screen, as you can see in Figure 6-12.

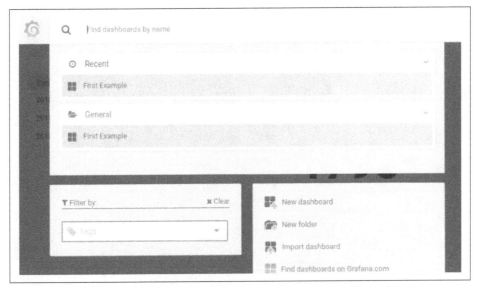

Figure 6-12. Dashboard list, including a button to create new dashboards

Click on the gear icon up top and then Variables.[10] Click +Add variable to add a template variable. The Name should be **Device**, and the Data source is Prometheus with a Refresh of On Time Range Change. The Query you will use is **node_net work_receive_bytes_total** with a Regex of **.*device="(.*?)".***, which will extract out the value of the device labels. The page should look like Figure 6-13. You can finally click Add to add the variable.

---

9 Loopback and your wired and/or WiFi device.

10 This was called templating in previous Grafana versions.

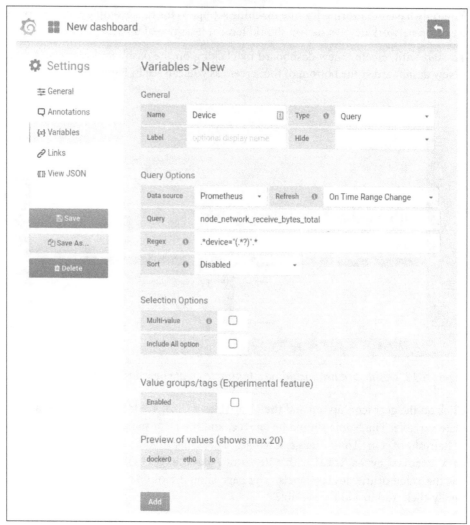

Figure 6-13. Adding a Device template variable to a Grafana dashboard

When you click Back to dashboard, a dropdown for the variable will now be available on the dashboard as seen in Figure 6-14.

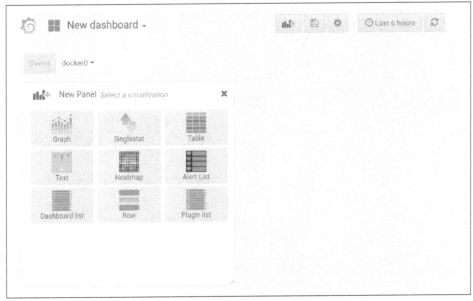

Figure 6-14. The dropdown for the Device template variable is visible

You now need to use the variable. Click the X to close the Templating section, then click the three dots, and add a new Graph panel. As before, click on Panel Title and then Edit. Configure the query expression to be **rate(node_network_receive_bytes_total{device="$Device"}[1m])**, and $Device will be substituted with the value of the template variable.[11] Set the Legend Format to **{{device}}**, the Title to **Bytes Received**, and the Unit to bytes/sec under data rate.

Go Back to the dashboard and click on the panel title, and this time click More and then Duplicate. This will create a copy of the existing panel. Alter the settings on this new panel to use the expression **rate(node_network_transmit_bytes_total {device=~"$Device"})[1m]** and the Title **Bytes Transmitted**. The dashboard will now have panels for bytes sent in both directions as shown in Figure 6-15, and you can look at each network device by selecting it in the dropdown.

---

11 If using the Multi-value option, you would use device=~"$Device" as the variable would be a regular expression in that case.

Figure 6-15. A basic network traffic dashboard using a template variable

In the real world you would probably template based on the instance label and display all the network related metrics for one machine at once. You might even have multiple variables for one dashboard. This is how a generic dashboard for Java garbage collection might work: one variable for the job, one for the instance, and one to select which Prometheus data source to use.

You may have noticed that as you change the value of the variable, the URL parameters change, and similarly if you use the time controls. This allows you to share dashboard links, or have your alerts link to a dashboard with just the right variable values as shown in "Notification templates" on page 317. There is a Share dashboard icon at the top of the page you can use to create the URLs and take snapshots of the data in the dashboard. Snapshots are perfect for postmortems and outage reports, where you want to preserve how the dashboard looked.

In the next chapter I will go into more detail on the Node exporter and some of the metrics it offers.

Infrastructure Monitoring

The entire world does not (yet) revolve around Prometheus, nor provide Prometheus metrics out of the box. Exporters are tools that let you translate metrics from other systems into a format that Prometheus understands.

In Chapter 7 one of the first exporters you will probably use, the Node exporter, is covered in detail.

In Chapter 8 you will learn how Prometheus knows what to pull metrics from and how to do so.

Chapter 9 dives into monitoring of container technologies such as Docker and Kubernetes.

There are literally hundreds of exporters in the Prometheus ecosystem. Chapter 10 shows you how to use various typical exporters.

As you may already have another metric-based monitoring system, Chapter 11 looks at how you can integrate those into Prometheus.

Exporters don't appear from thin air. If the exporter you want doesn't exist, you can use Chapter 12 to create one.

Node Exporter

The Node exporter[1] is likely one of the first exporters you will use, as already seen in Chapter 2. It exposes machine-level metrics, largely from your operating system's kernel, such as CPU, memory, disk space, disk I/O, network bandwidth, and motherboard temperature. The Node exporter is used with Unix systems; Windows users should use the wmi_exporter (*https://github.com/martinlindhe/wmi_exporter*) instead.

The Node exporter is intended only to monitor the machine itself, not individual processes or services on it. Other monitoring systems often have what I like to call an *uberagent*; that is, a single process that monitors everything on the machine. In the Prometheus architecture each of your services will expose its own metrics, using an exporter if needed, which is then directly scraped by Prometheus. This avoids you ending up with uberagent as either an operational or performance bottleneck, and enables you to think in terms more of dynamic services rather than machines.

The guidelines to use when you are creating metrics with direct instrumentation, such as those discussed in "What Should I Name My Metrics?" on page 58, are relatively black and white. This is not the case with exporters, where by definition the data is coming from a source not designed with the Prometheus guidelines in mind. Depending on the volume and quality of metrics, tradeoffs have to be made by the exporter developers between engineering effort and getting perfect metrics.

In the case of Linux, there are thousands of metrics on offer. Some are well documented and understood, such as CPU usage; others, like memory usage, have varied from kernel version to kernel version as the implementation has changed. You will

---

1 The Node exporter has nothing to do with Node.js, it's node in the sense of compute node.

even find metrics that are completely undocumented, where you would have to read the kernel source code to try and figure out what they do.

The Node exporter is designed to be run as a nonroot user, and should be run directly on the machine in the same way you run a system daemon like sshd or cron.

Docker and the Node Exporter

While all components of Prometheus can be run in containers, it is not recommended to run the Node exporter in Docker. Docker attempts to isolate a container from the inner workings of the machine, which doesn't work well with the Node exporter trying to get to those inner workings.

Unlike most other exporters, due to the broad variety of metrics available from operating systems, the Node exporter allows you to configure which categories of metrics it fetches. You can do this with command-line flags such as `--collector.wifi`, which would enable the WiFi collector, and `--no-collector.wifi`, which would disable it. There are reasonable defaults set, so this is not something you should worry about when starting out.

Different kernels expose different metrics, as for example Linux and FreeBSD do things in different ways. Metrics may move between collectors over time as the Node exporter is refactored. If you are using a different Unix system, you will find that the metrics and collectors on offer vary.

In this chapter I explain some of the key metrics Node exporter version 0.16.0 exposes with a 4.4.0 Linux kernel. This is not intended to be an exhaustive list of available metrics. As with most exporters and applications, you will want to look through the /metrics to see what is available. You can try out the example PromQL expressions using your setup from Chapter 2.

Changes in 0.16.0

As part of improving the metrics from the Node exporter, version 0.16.0 (which is used in this chapter) contained changes to the names of many commonly used metrics, such as `node_cpu` becoming `node_cpu_seconds_total`.

If you come across dashboards and tutorials from before this change, you will need to adjust accordingly.

CPU Collector

The main metric from the cpu collector is node_cpu_seconds_total, which is a counter indicating how much time each CPU spent in each mode. The labels are cpu and mode.

```
# HELP node_cpu_seconds_total Seconds the cpus spent in each mode.
# TYPE node_cpu_seconds_total counter
node_cpu_seconds_total{cpu="0",mode="idle"} 48649.88
node_cpu_seconds_total{cpu="0",mode="iowait"} 169.99
node_cpu_seconds_total{cpu="0",mode="irq"} 0
node_cpu_seconds_total{cpu="0",mode="nice"} 57.5
node_cpu_seconds_total{cpu="0",mode="softirq"} 8.05
node_cpu_seconds_total{cpu="0",mode="steal"} 0
node_cpu_seconds_total{cpu="0",mode="system"} 1058.32
node_cpu_seconds_total{cpu="0",mode="user"} 4234.94
node_cpu_seconds_total{cpu="1",mode="idle"} 9413.55
node_cpu_seconds_total{cpu="1",mode="iowait"} 57.41
node_cpu_seconds_total{cpu="1",mode="irq"} 0
node_cpu_seconds_total{cpu="1",mode="nice"} 46.55
node_cpu_seconds_total{cpu="1",mode="softirq"} 7.58
node_cpu_seconds_total{cpu="1",mode="steal"} 0
node_cpu_seconds_total{cpu="1",mode="system"} 1034.82
node_cpu_seconds_total{cpu="1",mode="user"} 4285.06
```

For each CPU, the modes will in aggregate increase by one second per second. This allows you to calculate the proportion of idle time across all CPUs using the PromQL expression:

```
avg without(cpu, mode)(rate(node_cpu_seconds_total{mode="idle"}[1m]))
```

This works as it calculates the idle time per second per CPU and then averages that across all the CPUs in the machine.

You could generalise this to calculate the proportion of time spent in each mode for a machine using:

```
avg without(cpu)(rate(node_cpu_seconds_total[1m]))
```

CPU usage by guests (i.e., virtual machines running under the kernel) is already included in the user and nice modes. You can see guest time separately in the node_cpu_guest_seconds_total metric.

Filesystem Collector

The filesystem collector unsurprisingly collects metrics about your *mounted* filesystems, just as you would obtain from the df command. The --collector.filesystem.ignored-mount-points and --collector.filesystem. ignored-fs-types flags allow restricting which filesystems are included (the defaults exclude various pseudo filesystems). As you will not have Node exporter running as root, you will need to ensure that file permissions allow it to use the statfs system call on mountpoints of interest to you.

All metrics from this collector are prefixed with node_filesystem_ and have device, fstype, and mountpoint labels.

```
# HELP node_filesystem_size_bytes Filesystem size in bytes.
# TYPE node_filesystem_size_bytes gauge
node_filesystem_size_bytes{device="/dev/sda5",fstype="ext4",mountpoint="/"} 9e+10
```

The filesystem metrics are largely self-evident. The one subtlety you should be aware of is the difference between node_filesystem_avail_bytes and node_filesystem_free_bytes. On Unix filesystems some space is reserved for the root user, so that they can still do things when users fill up all available space. node_filesystem_avail_bytes is the space available to users, and when trying to calculate used disk space you should accordingly use:

```
  node_filesystem_avail_bytes
/
  node_filesystem_size_bytes
```

node_filesystem_files and node_filesystem_files_free indicate the number of inodes and how many of them are free, which are roughly speaking the number of files your filesystem has. You can also see this with df -i.

Diskstats Collector

The diskstats collector exposes disk I/O metrics from /proc/diskstats. By default, the --collector.diskstats.ignored-devices flag attempts to exclude things that are not real disks, such as partitions and loopback devices:

```
# HELP node_disk_io_now The number of I/Os currently in progress.
# TYPE node_disk_io_now gauge
node_disk_io_now{device="sda"} 0
```

All metrics have a device label, and almost all are counters, as follows:

node_disk_io_now
  The number of I/Os in progress.

node_disk_io_time_seconds_total
  Incremented when I/O is in progress.

node_disk_read_bytes_total
  Bytes read by I/Os.

node_disk_read_time_seconds_total
  The time taken by read I/Os.

```
node_disk_reads_completed_total
```
The number of complete I/Os.

```
node_disk_written_bytes_total
```
Bytes written by I/Os.

```
node_disk_write_time_seconds_total
```
The time taken by write I/Os.

```
node_disk_writes_completed_total
```
The number of complete write I/Os.

These mostly mean what you think, but take a look at the kernel documentation (*https://www.kernel.org/doc/Documentation/iostats.txt*)[2] for more details.

You can use `node_disk_io_time_seconds_total` to calculate disk I/O utilisation, as would be shown by `iostat -x`:

```
rate(node_disk_io_time_seconds_total[1m])
```

You can calculate the average time for a read I/O with:

```
    rate(node_disk_read_time_seconds_total[1m])
/
    rate(node_disk_reads_completed_total[1m])
```

Netdev Collector

The netdev collector exposes metrics about your network devices with the prefix `node_network_` and a device label.

```
# HELP node_network_receive_bytes_total Network device statistic receive_bytes.
# TYPE node_network_receive_bytes_total counter
node_network_receive_bytes_total{device="lo"} 8.3213967e+07
node_network_receive_bytes_total{device="wlan0"} 7.0854462e+07
```

`node_network_receive_bytes_total` and `node_network_transmit_bytes_total` are the main metrics you will care about as you can calculate network bandwidth in and out with them.

```
rate(node_network_receive_bytes_total[1m])
```

You may also be interested in `node_network_receive_packets_total` and `node_net work_transmit_packets_total`, which track packets in and out, respectively.

---

2 A sector is always 512 bytes in `/proc/diskstats`; you do not need to worry if your disks are using larger sector sizes. This is an example of something that is only apparent from reading the Linux source code.

Meminfo Collector

The meminfo collector has all your standard memory-related metrics with a
`node_memory_` prefix. These all come from your `/proc/meminfo`, and this is the first
collector where semantics get a bit muddy. The collector does convert kilobytes to
preferred bytes, but beyond that it's up to you to know enough from the documentation (*https://www.kernel.org/doc/Documentation/filesystems/proc.txt*) and experience
with Linux internals to understand what these metrics mean:

```
# HELP node_memory_MemTotal_bytes Memory information field MemTotal.
# TYPE node_memory_MemTotal_bytes gauge
node_memory_MemTotal_bytes 8.269582336e+09
```

For example, `node_memory_MemTotal_bytes` is the total[3] amount of physical memory
in the machine—nice and obvious. But note that there is no used memory metric, so
you have to somehow calculate it and thus how much memory is not used from other
metrics.

`node_memory_MemFree_bytes` is the amount of memory that isn't used by anything,
but that doesn't mean it is all the memory you have to spare. In theory your page
cache (`node_memory_Cached_bytes`) can be reclaimed, as can your write buffers
(`node_memory_Buffers_bytes`), but that could adversely affect performance for some
applications.[4] In addition, there are various other kernel structures using memory
such as slab and page tables.

`node_memory_MemAvailable` is a heuristic from the kernel for how much memory is
really available, but was only added in version 3.14 of Linux. If you are running a new
enough kernel, this is a metric you could use to detect memory exhaustion.

Hwmon Collector

When on bare metal, the hwmon collector provides metrics such as temperature and
fan speeds with a `node_hwmon_` prefix. This is the same information you can obtain
with the `sensors` command:

```
# HELP node_hwmon_sensor_label Label for given chip and sensor
# TYPE node_hwmon_sensor_label gauge
node_hwmon_sensor_label{chip="platform_coretemp_0",
    label="core_0",sensor="temp2"} 1
node_hwmon_sensor_label{chip="platform_coretemp_0",
    label="core_1",sensor="temp3"} 1
# HELP node_hwmon_temp_celsius Hardware monitor for temperature (input)
```

---

3 Almost.

4 Prometheus 2.0, for example, relies on page cache.

```
# TYPE node_hwmon_temp_celsius gauge
node_hwmon_temp_celsius{chip="platform_coretemp_0",sensor="temp1"} 42
node_hwmon_temp_celsius{chip="platform_coretemp_0",sensor="temp2"} 42
node_hwmon_temp_celsius{chip="platform_coretemp_0",sensor="temp3"} 41
```

node_hwmon_temp_celsius is the temperature of various of your components, which may also have sensor labels[5] exposed in node_hwmon_sensor_label.

While it is not the case for all hardware, for some[6] you will need the sensor label to understand what the sensor is. In the preceding metrics, temp3 represents CPU core number 1.

You can join the label label from node_hwmon_sensor_label to node_hwmon_temp_celsius using group_left, which is further discussed in "Many-to-One and group_left" on page 248:

```
  node_hwmon_temp_celsius
* ignoring(label) group_left(label)
  node_hwmon_sensor_label
```

Stat Collector

The stat collector is a bit of a mix, as it provides metrics from /proc/stat.[7]

node_boot_time_seconds is when the kernel started, from which you can calculate how long the kernel has been up:

```
time() - node_boot_time_seconds
```

node_intr_total indicates the number of hardware interrupts you have had. It isn't called node_interrupts_total, as that is used by the interrupts collector, which is disabled by default due to high cardinality.

The other metrics relate to processes. node_forks_total is a counter for the number of fork syscalls, node_context_switches_total is the number of context switches, while node_procs_blocked and node_procs_running indicate the number of processes that are blocked or running.

---

5 *Labels* here does not mean Prometheus labels; they are sensor labels and come from files such as /sys/devi ces/platform/coretemp.0/hwmon/hwmon1/temp3_label.

6 Such as my laptop, which the above metric output is from.

7 It used to also provide CPU metrics, which have now been refactored into the cpu collector.

Uname Collector

The uname collector exposes a single metric `node_uname_info`, which you already saw in "Singlestat Panel" on page 105:

```
# HELP node_uname_info Labeled system information as provided by the uname
    system call.
# TYPE node_uname_info gauge
node_uname_info{domainname="(none)",machine="x86_64",nodename="kozo",
    release="4.4.0-101-generic",sysname="Linux",
    version="#124-Ubuntu SMP Fri Nov 10 18:29:59 UTC 2017"} 1
```

The `nodename` label is the hostname of the machine, which may differ from the `instance` target label (see "Target Labels" on page 139) or any other names, such as in DNS, that you may have for it.

To count how many machines run which kernel version you could use:

```
count by(release)(node_uname_info)
```

Loadavg Collector

The loadavg collector provides the 1-, 5-, and 15-minute load averages as `node_load1`, `node_load5`, and `node_load15`, respectively.

The meaning of this metric varies across platforms, and may not mean what you think it does. For example, on Linux it is not just the number of processes waiting in the run queue, but also uninterruptible processes such as those waiting for I/O.

Load averages can be useful for a quick and dirty idea if a machine has gotten busier (for some definition of busier) recently, but they are not a good choice to alert on. For a more detailed look I recommend "Linux Load Averages: Solving the Mystery" (*http://www.brendangregg.com/blog/2017-08-08/linux-load-averages.html*).

> Its a silly number but people think its important.
>
> —A comment in the Linux loadavg.c

Textfile Collector

The textfile collector is a bit different from the collectors I have already shown you. It doesn't obtain metrics from the kernel, but rather from files that you produce.

The Node exporter is not meant to run as root, so metrics such as those from SMART[8] require root privileges to run the `smartctl` command.

---

8 Self-Monitoring, Analysis, and Reporting Technology, metrics from hard drives that can be useful to predict and detect failure.

In addition to metrics that require root, you can only obtain some information by running a command such as `iptables`. For reliability the Node exporter does not start processes.

To use the textfile collector you would create a cronjob that regularly runs commands such as `smartctl` or `iptables`, converts its output into the Prometheus text exposition format, and atomically writes it to a file in a specific directory. On every scrape, the Node exporter will read the files in that directory and include their metrics in its output.

You can use this collector to add in your own metrics via cronjobs, or you could have more static information that comes from files written out by your machine configuration management system to provide some info metrics (discussed in "Info" on page 90), such as which Chef roles it has, about the machine.

As with the Node exporter generally, the textfile collector is intended for metrics about a machine. For example, there might be some kernel metric that the Node exporter does not yet expose, or that requires root to access. You might want to track more operating system–level metrics such as if there are pending package updates or a reboot due. While it is technically a service rather than an operating system metric, recording when batch jobs such as backups last completed for the Cassandra[9] node running on the machine would also be a good use of the textfile collector, as your interest in whether the backups worked on that machine goes away when the machine does. That is to say the Cassandra node has the same lifecycle as the machine.[10]

The textfile collector should not be used to try and convert Prometheus to push. Nor should you use the textfile collector as a way to take metrics from other exporters and applications running on the machine and expose them all on the Node exporter's /metrics, but rather have Prometheus scrape each exporter and application individually.

Using the Textfile Collector

The textfile collector is enabled by default, but you must provide the `--collector.textfile.directory` command-line flag to the Node exporter for it to work. This should point to a directory that you use solely for this purpose to avoid mixups.

---

9 A distributed database.

10 If a metric about a batch job has a different lifecycle than the machine, it is likely a service-level batch job and you may wish to use the Pushgateway as discussed in "Pushgateway" on page 71.

To try this out you should create a directory, write out a simple file in the exposition format (as discussed in "Exposition Format" on page 76), and start the Node exporter with it configured to use this directory, as seen in Example 7-1. The textfile collector only looks at files with the *.prom* extension.

Example 7-1. Using the textfile collector with a simple example

```
hostname $ mkdir textfile
hostname $ echo example_metric 1 > textfile/example.prom
hostname $ ./node_exporter --collector.textfile.directory=$PWD/textfile
```

If you look at the Node exporter's /metrics you will now see your metric:

```
# HELP example_metric Metric read from /some/path/textfile/example.prom
# TYPE example_metric untyped
example_metric 1
```

 If no HELP is provided the textfile collector will provide one for you. If you are putting the same metric in multiple files (with different labels of course) you need to provide the same HELP for each, as otherwise the mismatched HELP will cause an error.

Usually you will create and update the *.prom* files with a cronjob. As a scrape can happen at any time, it is important that the Node exporter does not see partially written files. To this end you should write first to a temporary file in the same directory and then move the complete file to the final filename.[11]

Example 7-2 shows a cronjob that outputs to the textfile collector. It creates the metrics in a temporary file,[12] and renames them to the final filename. This is a trivial example that uses short commands, but in most real-world use cases you will want to create a script to keep things readable.

Example 7-2. /etc/crontab that exposes the number of lines in /etc/shadow as the shadow_entries metric using the textfile collector

```
TEXTFILE=/path/to/textfile/directory

# This must all be on one line
*/5 * * * * root (echo -n 'shadow_entries '; grep -c . /etc/shadow)
    > $TEXTFILE/shadow.prom.$$
    && mv $TEXTFILE/shadow.prom.$$ $TEXTFILE/shadow.prom
```

---

11 The rename system call is atomic, but can only be used on the same filesystem.

12 $$ in shell expands to the current process id (pid).

A number of example scripts for use with the textfile collector are available in the node exporter Github repository (*https://github.com/prometheus/node_exporter/tree/ master/text_collector_examples*).

Timestamps

While the exposition format supports timestamps, you cannot use them with the textfile collector. This is because it doesn't make sense semantically, as your metrics would not appear with the same timestamp as other metrics from the scrape.

Instead, the mtime[13] of the file is available to you in the `node_textfile_mtime_seconds` metric. You can use this to alert on your cronjobs not working, as if this value is from too long ago it can indicate a problem:

```
# HELP node_textfile_mtime_seconds Unixtime mtime of textfiles successfully read.
# TYPE node_textfile_mtime_seconds gauge
node_textfile_mtime_seconds{file="example.prom"} 1.516205651e+09
```

Now that you have the Node exporter running, let's look at how you can tell Prometheus about all the machines you have it running on.

---

13 The mtime is the last time the file was modified.

Service Discovery

Thus far you've had Prometheus find what to scrape using static configuration via `static_configs`. This is fine for simple use cases,[1] but having to manually keep your *prometheus.yml* up to date as machines are added and removed would get annoying, particularly if you were in a dynamic environment where new instances might be brought up every minute. This chapter will show you how you can let Prometheus know what to scrape.

You already know where all of your machines and services are, and how they are laid out. Service discovery (SD) enables you to provide that information to Prometheus from whichever database you store it in. Prometheus supports many common sources of service information, such as Consul, Amazon's EC2, and Kubernetes out of the box. If your particular source isn't already supported, you can use the file-based service discovery mechanism to hook it in. This could be by having your configuration management system, such as Ansible or Chef, write the list of machines and services they know about in the right format, or a script running regularly to pull it from whatever data source you use.

Knowing what your monitoring targets are, and thus what should be scraped, is only the first step. Labels are a key part of Prometheus (see Chapter 5), and assigning *target labels* to targets allows them to be grouped and organised in ways that make sense to you. Target labels allow you to aggregate targets performing the same role, that are in the same environment, or are run by the same team.

As target labels are configured in Prometheus rather than in the applications and exporters themselves, this allows your different teams to have label hierarchies that

---

1 My home Prometheus uses a hardcoded static configuration, for example, as I only have a handful of machines.

make sense to them. Your infrastructure team might care only about which rack and PDU[2] a machine is on, while your database team would care that it is the PostgreSQL master for their production environment. If you had a kernel developer who was investigating a rarely occurring problem, they might just care which kernel version was in use.

Service discovery and the pull model allow all these views of the world to coexist, as each of your teams can run their own Prometheus with the target labels that make sense to them.

Service Discovery Mechanisms

Service discovery is designed to integrate with the machine and service databases that you already have. Out of the box, Prometheus 2.2.1 has support for Azure, Consul, DNS, EC2, OpenStack, File, Kubernetes, Marathon, Nerve, Serverset, and Triton service discovery in addition to the static discovery you have already seen.

Service discovery isn't just about you providing a list of machines to Prometheus, or monitoring. It is a more general concern that you will see across your systems; applications need to find their dependencies to talk to, and hardware technicians need to know which machines are safe to turn off and repair. Accordingly, you should not only have a raw list of machines and services, but also conventions around how they are organised and their lifecycles.

A good service discovery mechanism will provide you with *metadata*. This may be the name of a service, its description, which team owns it, structured tags about it, or anything else that you may find useful. Metadata is what you will convert into target labels, and generally the more metadata you have, the better.

A full discussion of service discovery is beyond the scope of this book. If you haven't gotten around to formalising your configuration management and service databases yet, Consul tends to be a good place to start.

---

2 The Power Distribution Unit, part of the electrical system in a datacenter. PDUs usually feed a group of racks with electricity, and knowing the CPU load on each machine could be useful to ensure each PDU can provide the power required.

Static

You have already seen static configuration in Chapter 2, where targets are provided directly in the *prometheus.yml*. It is useful if you have a small and simple setup that rarely changes. This might be your home network, a scrape config that is only for a local Pushgateway, or even Prometheus scraping itself as in Example 8-1.

Example 8-1. Using static service discovery to have Prometheus scrape itself

```
scrape_configs:
 - job_name: prometheus
   static_configs:
    - targets:
     - localhost:9090
```

If you are using a configuration management tool such as Ansible, you could have its templating system write out a list of all the machines it knows about to have their Node exporters scraped, such as in Example 8-2.

Example 8-2. Using Ansible's templating to create targets for the Node exporter on all machines

```
scrape_configs:
 - job_name: node
   static_configs:
    - targets:
{% for host in groups["all"] %}
     - {{ host }}:9100
{% endfor %}
```

In addition to providing a list of targets, a static config can also provide labels for those targets in the `labels` field. If you find yourself needing this, then file SD, covered in "File" on page 130, tends to be a better approach.

The plural in `static_configs` indicates that it is a list, and you can specify multiple static configs in one scrape config, as shown in Example 8-3. While there is not much point to doing this for static configs, it can be useful with other service discovery mechanisms if you want to talk to multiple data sources. You can even mix and match service discovery mechanisms within a scrape config, though that is unlikely to result in a particularly understandable configuration.

Example 8-3. Two monitoring targets are provided, each in its own static config

```
scrape_configs:
 - job_name: node
   static_configs:
    - targets:
       - host1:9100
    - targets:
       - host2:9100
```

The same applies to `scrape_configs`, a list of scrape configs in which you can specify as many as you like. The only restriction is that the `job_name` must be unique.

File

File service discovery, usually referred to as *file SD*, does not use the network. Instead, it reads monitoring targets from files you provide on the local filesystem. This allows you to integrate with service discovery systems Prometheus doesn't support out of the box, or when Prometheus can't quite do the things you need with the metadata available.

You can provide files in either JSON or YAML formats. The file extension must be *.json* for JSON, and either *.yml* or *.yaml* for YAML. You can see a JSON example in Example 8-4, which you would put in a file called *filesd.json*. You can have as many or as few targets as you like in a single file.

Example 8-4. filesd.json with three targets

```
[
  {
    "targets": [ "host1:9100", "host2:9100" ],
    "labels": {
      "team": "infra",
      "job": "node"
    }
  },
  {
    "targets": [ "host1:9090" ],
    "labels": {
      "team": "monitoring",
```

```
        "job": "prometheus"
      }
    }
  }
]
```

 JSON

The JSON format is not perfect. One issue you will likely encounter here is that the last item in a list or hash cannot have a trailing comma. I would recommend using a JSON library to generate JSON files rather than trying to do it by hand.

Configuration in Prometheus uses `file_sd_configs` in your scrape config as shown in Example 8-5. Each file SD config takes a list of filepaths, and you can use globs in the filename.[3] Paths are relative to Prometheus's working directory, which is to say the directory you start Prometheus in.

Example 8-5. prometheus.yml using file service discovery

```
scrape_configs:
 - job_name: file
   file_sd_configs:
    - files:
       - '*.json'
```

Usually you would not provide metadata for use with relabelling when using file SD, but rather the ultimate target labels you would like to have.

If you visit *http://localhost:9090/service-discovery* in your browser[4] and click on show more, you will see Figure 8-1, with both `job` and `team` labels from *filesd.json*.[5] As these are made up targets, the scrapes will fail, unless you actually happen to have a `host1` and `host2` on your network.

---

3 You cannot, however, put globs in the directory, so `a/b/*.json` is fine, `a/*/file.json` is not.

4 This endpoint was added in Prometheus 2.1.0. On older versions you can hover over the Labels on the Targets page to see the metadata.

5 `job_name` is only a default, which I'll look at further in "Duplicate Jobs" on page 148. The other __ labels are special and will be covered in "How to Scrape" on page 146.

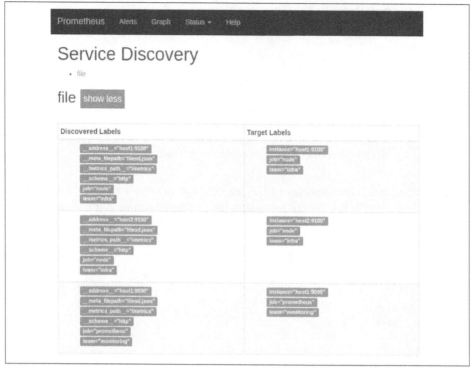

Figure 8-1. Service discovery status page showing three discovered targets from file SD

Providing the targets with a file means it could come from templating in a configuration management system, a daemon that writes it out regularly, or even from a web service via a cronjob using wget. Changes are picked up automatically using inotify, so it would be wise to ensure file changes are made atomically using rename, similarly to how you did in "Textfile Collector" on page 122.

Consul

Consul service discovery is a service discovery mechanism that uses the network, as almost all mechanisms do. If you do not already have a service discovery system within your organisation, Consul is one of the easier ones to get up and running. Consul has an agent that runs on each of your machines, and these gossip amongst themselves. Applications talk only to the local agent on a machine. Some number of agents are also servers, providing persistence and consistency.

To try it out, you can set up a development Consul agent by following Example 8-6. If you wish to use Consul in production, you should follow the official Getting Started (*https://www.consul.io/intro/getting-started/install.html*) guide.

Example 8-6. Setting up a Consul agent in development mode

```
hostname $ wget https://releases.hashicorp.com/consul/1.0.2/
    consul_1.0.2_linux_amd64.zip
hostname $ unzip consul_1.0.2_linux_amd64.zip
hostname $ ./consul agent -dev
```

The Consul UI should now be available in your browser on *http://localhost:8500/*. Consul has a notion of services, and in the development setup has a single service, which is Consul itself. Next, run a Prometheus with the configuration in Example 8-7.

Example 8-7. prometheus.yml using Consul service discovery

```
scrape_configs:
 - job_name: consul
   consul_sd_configs:
    - server: 'localhost:8500'
```

Go to *http://localhost:9090/service-discovery* in your browser and you will see Figure 8-2, showing that the Consul service discovery has discovered a single target with some metadata, which became a target with `instance` and `job` labels. If you had more agents and services, they would also show up here.

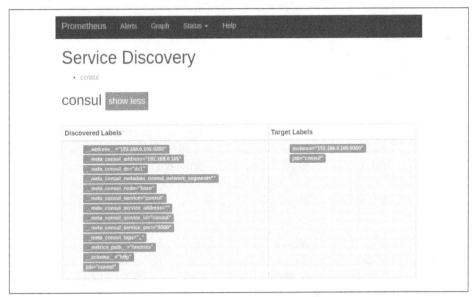

Figure 8-2. Service discovery status page showing one discovered target, its metadata, and target labels from Consul

Consul does not expose a /metrics, so the scrapes from your Prometheus will fail. But it does still provide enough to find all your machines running a Consul agent, and thus should be running a Node exporter that you can scrape. I will look at how in "Relabelling" on page 135.

 If you want to monitor Consul itself, there is a Consul exporter (*https://github.com/prometheus/consul_exporter*).

EC2

Amazon's Elastic Compute Cloud, more commonly known as EC2, is a popular provider of virtual machines. It is one of several cloud providers that Prometheus allows you to use out of the box for service discovery.

To use it you must provide Prometheus with credentials to use the EC2 API. One way you can do this is by setting up an IAM user with the AmazonEC2ReadOnlyAccess policy[6] and providing the access key and secret key in the configuration file, as shown in Example 8-8.

Example 8-8. prometheus.yml using EC2 service discovery

```
scrape_configs:
 - job_name: ec2
   ec2_sd_configs:
    - region: <region>
      access_key: <access key>
      secret_key: <secret key>
```

If you aren't already running some, start at least one EC2 instance in the EC2 region you have configured Prometheus to look at. If you go to *http://localhost:9090/service-discovery* in your browser, you can see the discovered targets and the metadata extracted from EC2. __meta_ec2_tag_Name="My Display Name", for example, is the Name tag on this instance, which is the name you will see in the EC2 Console (Figure 8-3).

You may notice that the instance label is using the private IP. This is a sensible default as it is presumed that Prometheus will be running beside what it is monitoring. Not all EC2 instances have public IPs, and there are network charges for talking to an EC2 instance's public IP.

---

6 Only the EC2:DescribeInstances permission is needed, but policies are generally easier for you to set up initially.

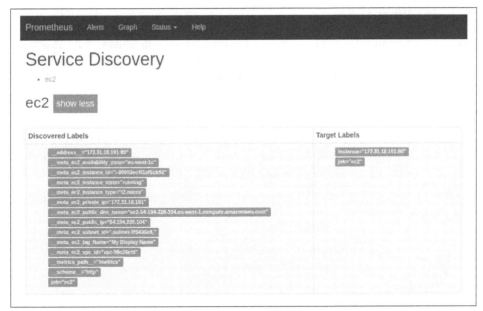

Figure 8-3. Service discovery status page showing one discovered target, its metadata, and target labels from EC2

You will find that service discovery for other cloud providers is broadly similar, but the configuration required and metadata returned vary.

Relabelling

As seen in the preceding examples of service discovery mechanisms, the targets and their metadata can be a little raw. You could integrate with file SD and provide Prometheus with exactly the targets and labels you want, but in most cases you won't need to. Instead, you can tell Prometheus how to map from metadata to targets using *relabelling*.

 Many characters, such as periods and asterisks, are not valid in Prometheus label names, so will be sanitised to underscore in service discovery metadata.

In an ideal world you will have service discovery and relabelling configured so that new machines and applications are picked up and monitored automatically. In the real world it is not unlikely that as your setup matures it will get sufficiently intricate that you have to regularly update the Prometheus configuration file, but by then you will likely also have the infrastructure where that is only a minor hurdle.

Choosing What to Scrape

The first thing you will want to configure is which targets you actually want to scrape. If you are part of one team running one service, you don't want your Prometheus to be scraping every target in the same EC2 region.

Continuing on from Example 8-5, what if you just wanted to monitor the infrastructure team's machines? You can do this with the keep *relabel action*, as shown in Example 8-9. The `regex` is applied to the values of the labels listed in `source_labels` (joined by a semicolon), and if the regex matches, the target is kept. As there is only one action here, this results in all targets with `team="infra"` being kept.

But for a target with a `team="monitoring"` label, the regex will not match, and the target will be dropped.

 Regular expressions in relabelling are *fully anchored*, meaning that the pattern `infra` will not match `fooinfra` or `infrabar`.

Example 8-9. Using a keep relabel action to only monitor targets with a team="infra" label

```
scrape_configs:
 - job_name: file
   file_sd_configs:
    - files:
       - '*.json'
   relabel_configs:
    - source_labels: [team]
      regex: infra
      action: keep
```

You can have multiple relabel actions in a `relabel_configs`; all of them will be processed in order unless either a `keep` or `drop` action drops the target. For example, Example 8-10 will drop all targets, as a label cannot have both `infra` and `monitoring` as a value.

Example 8-10. Two relabel actions requiring contradictory values for the team label

```
scrape_configs:
 - job_name: file
   file_sd_configs:
    - files:
       - '*.json'
   relabel_configs:
    - source_labels: [team]
```

```
      regex: infra
      action: keep
    - source_labels: [team]
      regex: monitoring
      action: keep
```

To allow multiple values for a label you would use | (the pipe symbol) for the alternation operator, which is a fancy way of saying one or the other. Example 8-11 shows the right way to keep only targets for either the infrastructure or monitoring teams.

Example 8-11. Using | to allow one label value or another

```
scrape_configs:
 - job_name: file
   file_sd_configs:
    - files:
       - '*.json'
   relabel_configs:
    - source_labels: [team]
      regex: infra|monitoring
      action: keep
```

In addition to the keep action that drops targets that do not match, you can also use the drop action to drop targets that do match. You can also provide multiple labels in source_labels; their values will be joined with a semicolon.[7] If you don't want to scrape the Prometheus jobs of the monitoring team, you can combine these as in Example 8-12.

Example 8-12. Using multiple source labels

```
scrape_configs:
 - job_name: file
   file_sd_configs:
    - files:
       - '*.json'
   relabel_configs:
    - source_labels: [job, team]
      regex: prometheus;monitoring
      action: drop
```

How you use relabelling is up to you. You should define some conventions. For example, EC2 instances should have a team tag with the name of the team that owns it, or all production services should have a production tag in Consul. Without con-

---

7 You can override the character used to join with the separator field.

ventions every new service will require special handling for monitoring, which is probably not the best use of your time.

If your service discovery mechanism includes health checking of some form, do not use this to drop unhealthy instances. Even when an instance is reporting as unhealthy it could be producing useful metrics, particularly around startup and shutdown.

 Prometheus needs to have a target for each of your individual application instances. Scraping through load balancers will not work, as you can hit a different instance on each scrape, which could, for example, make counters appear to go backwards.

Regular Expressions

Prometheus uses the *RE2* engine for regular expressions that comes with Go. RE2 is designed to be linear-time but does not support back references, lookahead assertions, and some other advanced features.

If you are not familiar with regular expressions, they let you provide a rule (called a *pattern*) that is then tested against text. The following table is a quick primer on regular expressions.

	Matches
a	The character a
.	Any single character
\.	A single period
.*	Any number of characters
.+	At least one character
a+	One or more a characters
[0-9]	Any single digit, 0-9
\d	Any single digit, 0-9
\d*	Any number of digits
[^0-9]	A single character that is not a digit
ab	The character a followed by the character b
a(b|c*)	An a, followed by a single b, or any number of c characters

In addition, parentheses create a capture group. So if you had the pattern (.)(\d+) and the text a123, then the first capture group would contain a and the second 123. Capture groups are useful to extract parts of a string for later use.

Target Labels

Target labels are labels that are added to the labels of every time series returned from a scrape. They are the identity of your targets,[8] and accordingly they should not generally vary over time as might be the case with version numbers or machine owners.

Every time your target labels change the labels of the scraped time series, their identities also change. This will cause discontinuities in your graphs, and can cause issues with rules and alerts.

So what does make a good target label? You have already seen job and instance, target labels all targets have. It is also common to add target labels for the broader scope of the application, such as whether it is in development or production, their region, datacenter, and which team manages them. Labels for structure within your application can also make sense, for example, if there is sharding.

Target labels ultimately allow you to select, group, and aggregate targets in PromQL. For example, you might want alerts for development to be handled differently to production, to know which shard of your application is the most loaded, or which team is using the most CPU time.

But target labels come with a cost. While it is quite cheap to add one more label in terms of resources, the real cost comes when you are writing PromQL. Every additional label is one more you need to keep in mind for every single PromQL expression you write. For example, if you were to add a host label which was unique per target, that would violate the expectation that only instance is unique per target, which could break all of your aggregation that used without(instance). This is discussed further in Chapter 14.

As a rule of thumb your target labels should be a hierarchy, with each one adding additional distinctiveness. For example, you might have a hierarchy where regions contain datacenters that contain environments that contain services that contain jobs that contain instances. This isn't a hard and fast rule; you might plan ahead a little and have a datacenter label even if you only have one datacenter today.[9]

For labels the application knows about but don't make sense to have as target labels, such as version numbers, you can expose them using info metrics as discussed in "Info" on page 90.

---

8 It is possible for two of your targets to have the same target labels, with other settings different, but this should be avoided because metrics such as up will clash.

9 On the other hand, don't try to plan too far in advance. It's not unusual that, as your architecture changes over the years, your target label hierarchy will need to change with it. Predicting exactly how it will change is usually impossible. Consider, for example, if you were moving from a traditional datacenter setup to a provider like EC2, which has availability zones.

If you find that you want every target in a Prometheus to share some labels such as region, you should instead use external_labels for them as discussed in "External Labels" on page 303.

Replace

So how do you use relabelling to specify your target labels? The answer is the *replace action*. The replace action allows you to copy labels around, while also applying regular expressions.

Continuing on from Example 8-5, let's say that the monitoring team was renamed to the monitor team and you can't change the file SD input yet so you want to use relabelling instead. Example 8-13 looks for a team label that matches the regular expression monitoring (which is to say, the exact string monitoring), and if it finds it, puts the replacement value metrics in the team label.

Example 8-13. Using a replace relabel action to replace team="monitoring" with team="monitor"

```
scrape_configs:
 - job_name: file
   file_sd_configs:
    - files:
       - '*.json'
   relabel_configs:
      source_labels: [team]
      regex: monitoring
      replacement: monitor
      target_label: team
      action: replace
```

That's fairly simple, but in practice having to specify replacement label values one by one would be a lot of work for you. Let's say it turns out that the problem was the ing in monitoring, and you wanted relabelling to strip any trailing "ings" in team names. Example 8-14 does this by applying the regular expression (.*)ing, which matches all strings that end with ing and puts the start of the label value in the first capture group. The replacement value consists of that first capture group, which will be placed in the team label.

Example 8-14. Using a replace relabel action to remove a trailing ing from the team label

```
scrape_configs:
 - job_name: file
   file_sd_configs:
    - files:
```

```
      - '*.json'
relabel_configs:
 - source_labels: [team]
   regex: '(.*)ing'
   replacement: '${1}'
   target_label: team
   action: replace
```

If one of your targets does not have a label value that matches, such as team="infra",
then the replace action has no effect on that target, as you can see in Figure 8-4.

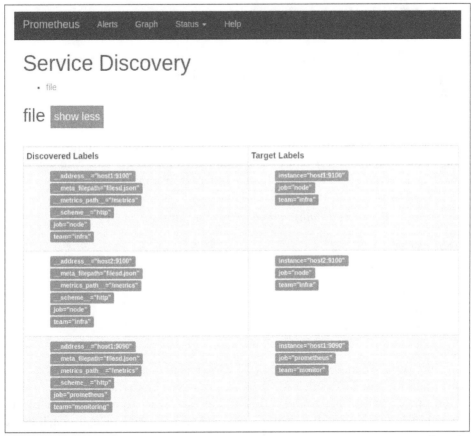

Figure 8-4. The ing is removed from monitoring, while the infra targets are unaffected

A label with an empty value is the same as not having that label, so if you wanted to
you could remove the team label using Example 8-15.

Example 8-15. Using a replace relabel action to remove the team label

```
scrape_configs:
 - job_name: file
   file_sd_configs:
    - files:
      - '*.json'
   relabel_configs:
    - source_labels: []
      regex: '(.*)'
      replacement: '${1}'
      target_label: team
      action: replace
```

 All labels beginning with __ are discarded at the end of relabelling for target labels, so you don't need to do this yourself.

Since performing a regular expression against the whole string, capturing it, and using it as the replacement is common, these are all defaults. Thus you can omit them,[10] and Example 8-16 will have the same effect as Example 8-15.

Example 8-16. Using the defaults to remove the team label succinctly

```
scrape_configs:
 - job_name: file
   file_sd_configs:
    - files:
       - '*.json'
   relabel_configs:
    - source_labels: []
      target_label: team
```

Now that you have more of a sense of how the replace action works, let's look at a more realistic example. Example 8-7 produced a target with port 80, but it'd be useful if you could change that to port 9100 where the Node exporter is running. In Example 8-17 I take the address from Consul and append :9100 to it, placing it in the __address__ label.

---

10 You could also omit source_labels: []. I left it in here to make it clearer that the label was being removed.

Example 8-17. Using the IP from Consul with port 9100 for the Node exporter

```
scrape_configs:
 - job_name: node
   consul_sd_configs:
    - server: 'localhost:8500'
   relabel_configs:
    - source_labels: [__meta_consul_address]
      regex: '(.*)'
      replacement: '${1}:9100'
      target_label: __address__
```

> If relabelling produces two identical targets from one of your scrape configs, they will be deduplicated automatically. So if you have many Consul services running on each machine, only one target per machine would result from Example 8-17.

job, instance, and __address__

In the preceding examples you may have noticed that there was an instance target label, but no matching instance label in the metadata. So where did it come from? The answer is that if your target has no instance label, it is defaulted to the value of the __address__ label.

instance along with job are two labels your targets will always have, job being defaulted from the job_name configuration option. The job label indicates a set of instances that serve the same purpose, and will generally all be running with the same binary and configuration.[11] The instance label identifies one instance within a job.

The __address__ is the host and port your Prometheus will connect to when scraping. While it provides a default for the instance label, it is separate so you can have a different value for it. For example, you may wish to use the Consul node name in the instance label, while leaving the address pointing to the IP address, as in Example 8-18. This is a better approach than adding an additional host, node, or alias label with a nicer name, as it avoids adding a second label unique to each target, which would cause complications in your PromQL.

---

11 A job could potentially be further divided into shards with another label.

Example 8-18. Using the IP from Consul with port 9100 as the address, with the node name in the instance label

```
scrape_configs:
 - job_name: consul
   consul_sd_configs:
     - server: 'localhost:8500'
   relabel_configs:
     - source_labels: [__meta_consul_address]
       regex: '(.*)'
       replacement: '${1}:9100'
       target_label: __address__
     - source_labels: [__meta_consul_node]
       regex: '(.*)'
       replacement: '${1}:9100'
       target_label: instance
```

> Prometheus will perform DNS resolution on the __address__, so one way you can have more readable instance labels is by providing host:port rather than ip:port.

Labelmap

The labelmap action is different from the drop, keep, and replace actions you have already seen in that it applies to label names rather than label values.

Where you might find this useful is if the service discovery you are using already has a form of key-value labels, and you would like to use some of those as target labels. This might be to allow configuration of arbitrary target labels, without having to change your Prometheus configuration every time there is a new label.

EC2's tags, for example, are key-value pairs. You might have an existing convention to have the name of the service go in the service tag and its semantics align with what the job label means in Prometheus. You might also declare a convention that any tags prefixed with monitor_ will become target labels. For example, an EC2 tag of monitor_foo=bar would become a Prometheus target label of foo="bar". Example 8-19 shows this setup, using a replace action for the job label and a label map action for the monitor_ prefix.

Example 8-19. Use the EC2 service tag as the job label, with all tags prefixed with
monitor_ as additional target labels

```
scrape_configs:
 - job_name: ec2
   ec2_sd_configs:
    - region: <region>
      access_key: <access key>
      secret_key: <secret key>
   relabel_configs:
    - source_labels: [__meta_ec2_tag_service]
      target_label: job
    - regex: __meta_ec2_public_tag_monitor_(.*)
      replacement: '${1}'
      action: labelmap
```

But you should be wary of blindly copying all labels in a scenario like this, as it is
unlikely that Prometheus is the only consumer of metadata such as this within your
overall architecture. For example, a new cost center tag might be added to all of your
EC2 instances for internal billing reasons. If that tag automatically became a target
label due to a labelmap action, that would change all of your target labels and likely
break graphing and alerting. Thus, using either well-known names (such as the
service tag here) or clearly namespaced names (such as monitor_) is wise.

Lists

Not all service discovery mechanisms have key-value labels or tags; some just have a
list of tags, with the canonical example being Consul's tags. While Consul is the most
likely place that you will run into this, there are various other places where a service
discovery mechanism must somehow convert a list into key-value metadata such as
the EC2 subnet ID.[12]

This is done by joining the items in the list with a comma and using the now-joined
items as a label value. A comma is also put at the start and the end of the value, to
make writing correct regular expressions easier.

As an example, say a Consul service had dublin and prod tags. The __meta_
consul_tags label could have the value ,dublin,prod, or ,prod,dublin, as tags are
unordered. If you wanted to only scrape production targets you would use a keep
action as shown in Example 8-20.

---

12 An EC2 instance can have multiple network interfaces, each of which could be in different subnets.

Example 8-20. Keeping only Consul services with the prod tag

```
scrape_configs:
 - job_name: node
   consul_sd_configs:
    - server: 'localhost:8500'
   relabel_configs:
    - source_labels: [__meta_consul_tag]
      regex:   '.*,prod,.*'
      action: keep
```

Sometimes you will have tags which are only the value of a key-value pair. You can convert such values to labels, but you need to know the potential values. Example 8-21 shows how a tag indicating the environment of a target can be converted into an env label.

Example 8-21. Using prod, staging, and dev tags to fill an env label

```
scrape_configs:
 - job_name: node
   consul_sd_configs:
    - server: 'localhost:8500'
   relabel_configs:
    - source_labels: [__meta_consul_tag]
      regex:   '.*,(prod|staging|dev),.*'
      target_label: env
```

> With sophisticated relabelling rules you may find yourself needing a temporary label to put a value in. The __tmp prefix is reserved for this purpose.

How to Scrape

You now have targets with their target labels and the __address__ to connect to. There are some additional things you may wish to configure, such as a path other than /metrics or client authentication.

Example 8-22 shows some of the more common options you can use. As these change over time, check the documentation (*http://bit.ly/2I7nQnt*) for the most up-to-date settings.

Example 8-22. A scrape config showing several of the available options

```
scrape_configs:
 - job_name: example
   consul_sd_configs:
    - server: 'localhost:8500'
   scrape_timeout: 5s
   metrics_path: /admin/metrics
   params:
     foo: [bar]
   scheme: https
   tls_config:
     insecure_skip_verify: true
   basic_auth:
     username: brian
     password: hunter2
```

`metrics_path` is only the path of the URL, and if you tried to put `/metrics?foo=bar`, for example, it would get escaped to `/metrics%3Ffoo=bar`. Instead, any URL paramaters should be placed in `params`, though you usually only need this for federation and the classes of exporters that include the SNMP and Blackbox exporters. It is not possible to add arbitrary headers, as that would make debugging more difficult. If you need flexibility beyond what is offered, you can always use a proxy server with `proxy_url` to tweak your scrape requests.

`scheme` can be `http` or `https`, and with `https` you can provide additional options including the `key_file` and `cert_file` if you wish to use TLS client authentication. `insecure_skip_verify` allows you to disable validation of a scrape target's TLS cert, which is not advisable security-wise.

Aside from TLS client authentication, HTTP Basic Authentication and HTTP Bearer Token Authentication are offered via `basic_auth` and `bearer_token`. The bearer token can also be read from a file, rather than from the configuration, using `bearer_token_file`. As the bearer tokens and basic auth passwords are expected to contain secrets, they will be masked on the status pages of Prometheus so that you don't accidentally leak them.

In addition to overriding the `scrape_timeout` in a scrape config, you can also override the `scrape_interval`, but in general you should aim for a single scrape interval in a Prometheus for sanity.

Of these scrape config settings, the scheme, path, and URL parameters are available to you and can be overridden by you via relabelling, with the label names `__scheme__`, `__metrics_path__`, and `__param_<name>`. If there are multiple URL parameters with the same name, only the first is available. It is not possible to relabel other settings for reasons varying from sanity to security.

Service discovery metadata is not considered security sensitive[13] and will be accessible to anyone with access to the Prometheus UI. As secrets can only be specified per scrape config, it is recommended that any credentials you use are made standard across your services.

Duplicate Jobs

While job_name must be unique, as it is only a default, you are not prevented from having different scrape configs producing targets with the same job label.

For example, if you had some jobs that required a different secret which were indicated by a Consul tag, you could segregate them using keep and drop actions, and then use a replace to set the job label:

```
- job_name: my_job
  consul_sd_configs:
   - server: 'localhost:8500'
  relabel
   - source_labels: [__meta_consul_tag]
     regex:  '.*,specialsecret,.*'
     action: drop
  basic_auth:
    username: brian
    password: normalSecret

- job_name: my_job_special_secret
  consul_sd_configs:
   - server: 'localhost:8500'
  relabel
   - source_labels: [__meta_consul_tag]
     regex:  '.*,specialsecret,.*'
     action: keep
   - replacement: my_job
     target_label: job
  basic_auth:
    username: brian
    password: specialSecret
```

---

metric_relabel_configs

In addition to relabelling being used for its original purpose of mapping service discovery metadata to target labels, relabelling has also been applied to other areas of Prometheus. One of those is metric relabelling: relabelling applied to the time series scraped from a target.

---

13 Nor are the service discovery systems typically designed to hold secrets.

The keep, drop, replace, and labelmap actions you have already seen can all be used in metric_relabel_configs as there are no restrictions on which relabel actions can be used where.[14]

 To help you remember which is which, relabel_configs occurs when figuring out what to scrape, metrics_relabel_configs happens after the scrape has occurred.

There are two cases where you might use metric relabelling: when dropping expensive metrics and when fixing bad metrics. While it is better to fix such problems at the source, it is always good to know that you have tactical options while the fix is in progress.

Metric relabelling gives you access to the time series after it is scraped but before it is written to storage. The keep and drop actions can be applied to the __name__ label (discussed in "Reserved Labels and __name__" on page 84) to select which time series you actually want to ingest. If, for example, you discovered that the http_request_size_bytes[15] metric of Prometheus had excessive cardinality and was causing performance issues, you could drop it as shown in Example 8-23. It is still being transferred over the network and parsed, but this approach can still offer you some breathing room.

Example 8-23. Dropping an expensive metric using metric_relabel_configs

```
scrape_configs:
 - job_name: prometheus
   static_configs:
    - targets:
       - localhost:9090
   metric_relabel_configs:
    - source_labels: [__name__]
      regex: http_request_size_bytes
      action: drop
```

The labels are also available, as mentioned in "Cumulative Histograms" on page 52, you can also drop certain buckets (but not +Inf) of histograms and you will still be able to calculate quantiles. Example 8-24 shows this with the prometheus_tsdb_compaction_duration_seconds histogram in Prometheus.

---

14 Which is not to say that all relabel actions make sense in all relabel contexts.

15 In Prometheus 2.3.0 this metric was changed to a histogram and renamed to prometheus_http_response_size_bytes.

Example 8-24. Dropping histogram buckets to reduce cardinality

```
scrape_configs:
 - job_name: prometheus
   static_configs:
    - targets:
       - localhost:9090
   metric_relabel_configs:
    - source_labels: [__name__, le]
      regex: 'prometheus_tsdb_compaction_duration_seconds_bucket;(4|32|256)'
      action: drop
```

 `metric_relabel_configs` only applies to metrics that you scrape from the target. It does not apply to metrics like up, which are about the scrape itself, and which will have only the target labels.

You could also use `metric_relabel_configs` to rename metrics, rename labels, or even extract labels from metric names.

labeldrop and labelkeep

There are two further relabel actions that are unlikely to be ever required for target relabelling, but that can come up in metric relabelling. Sometimes exporters can be overly enthusiastic in the labels they apply, or confuse instrumentation labels with target labels and return what they think should be the target labels in a scrape. The `replace` action can only deal with label names you know the name of in advance, which sometimes isn't the case.

This is where `labeldrop` and `labelkeep` come in. Similar to `labelmap`, they apply to label names rather than to label values. Instead of copying labels, `labeldrop` and `labelkeep` remove labels. Example 8-25 uses `labeldrop` to drop all labels with a given prefix.

*Example 8-25. Dropping all scraped labels that begin with node_*

```
scrape_configs:
 - job_name: misbehaving
   static_configs:
    - targets:
       - localhost:1234
   metric_relabel_configs:
    - regex: 'node_.*'
      action: labeldrop
```

When you have to use these actions, prefer using labeldrop where practical. With labelkeep you need to list every single label you want to keep, including __name__, le, and quantile.

Label Clashes and honor_labels

While labeldrop can be used when an exporter incorrectly presumes it knows what labels you want, there is a small set of exporters where the exporter does know the labels you want. For example, metrics in the Pushgateway should not have an instance label, as was mentioned in "Pushgateway" on page 71, so you need some way of not having the Pushgateway's instance target label apply.

But first let's look at what happens when there is a target label with the same name as an instrumentation label from a scrape. To avoid misbehaving applications interfering with your target label setup, it is the target label that wins. If you had a clash on the job label, for example, the instrumentation label would be renamed to exported_job.

If instead you want the instrumentation label to win and override the target label, you can set honor_labels: true in your scrape config. This is the one place in Prometheus where an empty label is not the same thing as a missing label. If a scraped metric explicitly has an instance="" label, and honor_labels: true is configured, the resultant time series will have no instance label. This technique is used by the Pushgateway.

Aside from the Pushgateway, honor_labels can also come up when ingesting metrics from other monitoring systems if you do not follow the recommendation in Chapter 11 to run one exporter per application instance.

 If you want more finegrained control for handling clashing target and instrumentation labels, you can use metric_relabel_configs to adjust the labels before the metrics are added to the storage. Handling of label clashes and honor_labels is performed before metric_relabel_configs.

Now that you understand service discovery, you're ready to look at monitoring containers and how service discovery can be used with Kubernetes.

Containers and Kubernetes

Container deployments are becoming more common with technologies such as Docker and Kubernetes—you may even already be using them. In this chapter I will cover exporters that you can use with containers, and explain how to use Prometheus with Kubernetes.

All Prometheus components run happily in containers, with the sole exception of the Node exporter as noted in Chapter 7.

cAdvisor

In the same way the Node exporter provides metrics about the machine, cAdvisor is an exporter that provides metrics about *cgroups*. Cgroups are a Linux kernel isolation feature that are usually used to implement containers on Linux, and are also used by runtime environments such as systemd.

You can run cAdvisor with Docker:

```
docker run \
  --volume=/:/rootfs:ro \
  --volume=/var/run:/var/run:rw \
  --volume=/sys:/sys:ro \
  --volume=/var/lib/docker/:/var/lib/docker:ro \
  --volume=/dev/disk/:/dev/disk:ro \
  --publish=8080:8080 \
  --detach=true \
  --name=cadvisor \
  google/cadvisor:v0.28.3
```

Due to issues with incorrect usage of the Prometheus Go client library, you should avoid versions of cAdvisor before 0.28.3.

If you visit *http://localhost:8080/metrics* you will see a long list of metrics, as Figure 9-1 shows.

The container metrics are prefixed with `container_`, and you will notice that they all have an `id` label. The `id` labels starting with `/docker/` are from Docker and its containers, and if you have `/user.slice/` and `/system.slice/`, they come from systemd running on your machine. If you have other software using cgroups, its cgroups will also be listed.

```
# HELP cadvisor_version_info A metric with a constant '1' value labeled by kernel
version, OS version, docker version, cadvisor version & cadvisor revision.
# TYPE cadvisor_version_info gauge
cadvisor_version_info{cadvisorRevision="1e567c2",cadvisorVersion="v0.28.3",dockerVersion=
"1.11.2",kernelVersion="4.4.0-101-generic",osVersion="Alpine Linux v3.4"} 1
# HELP container_cpu_load_average_10s Value of container cpu load average over the last
10 seconds.
# TYPE container_cpu_load_average_10s gauge
container_cpu_load_average_10s{id="/",image="",name=""} 0
container_cpu_load_average_10s{id="/docker",image="",name=""} 0
container_cpu_load_average_10s{id="/docker/2021405b75f2b12c8a8c6aa93e9c4b52f0a8f2ff3d5c92
2eefd9ae8e35e5d805",image="google/cadvisor:v0.28.3",name="cadvisor"} 0
container_cpu_load_average_10s{id="/init.scope",image="",name=""} 0
container_cpu_load_average_10s{id="/system.slice",image="",name=""} 0
container_cpu_load_average_10s{id="/system.slice/ModemManager.service",image="",name=""}
0
container_cpu_load_average_10s{id="/system.slice/NetworkManager-wait-
online.service",image="",name=""} 0
container_cpu_load_average_10s{id="/system.slice/NetworkManager.service",image="",name=""
} 0
container_cpu_load_average_10s{id="/system.slice/accounts-
daemon.service",image="",name=""} 0
container_cpu_load_average_10s{id="/system.slice/acpid.service",image="",name=""} 0
container_cpu_load_average_10s{id="/system.slice/alsa-restore.service",image="",name=""}
0
container_cpu_load_average_10s{id="/system.slice/apparmor.service",image="",name=""} 0
container_cpu_load_average_10s{id="/system.slice/apport.service",image="",name=""} 0
container_cpu_load_average_10s{id="/system.slice/avahi-daemon.service",image="",name=""}
0
container_cpu_load_average_10s{id="/system.slice/binfmt-
support.service",image="",name=""} 0
```

Figure 9-1. The start of a /metrics page from cAdvisor

These metrics can be scraped with a *prometheus.yml* such as:

```
scrape_configs:
 - job_name: cadvisor
   static_configs:
    - targets:
       - localhost:8080
```

CPU

You will find three metrics for container CPU: `container_cpu_usage_seconds_total`, `container_cpu_system_seconds_total`, and `container_cpu_user_seconds_total`.

`container_cpu_usage_seconds_total` is split out by CPU, but not by mode. `container_cpu_system_seconds_total` and `container_cpu_user_seconds_total` are the user and system modes, respectively, similar to the Node exporter's "CPU Collector" on page 117. These are all counters with which you can use the `rate` function.

 With many containers and CPUs in one machine, you may find that the aggregate cardinality of metrics from cAdvisor becomes a performance issue. You can use a `drop` relabel action as discussed in "metric_relabel_configs" on page 148 to drop less-valuable metrics at scrape time.

Memory

Similar to in the Node exporter, the memory usage metrics are less than perfectly clear and require digging through code and documentation (*http://bit.ly/2lijiBR*) to understand them.

`container_memory_cache` is the page cache used by the container, in bytes. `container_memory_rss` is the resident set size (RSS), in bytes. This is not the same RSS or physical memory used as a process would have, as it excludes the sizes of mapped files.[1] `container_memory_usage_bytes` is the RSS and the page cache, and is what is limited by `container_spec_memory_limit_bytes` if the limit is nonzero. `container_memory_working_set_bytes` is calculated by subtracting the inactive file-backed memory (`total_inactive_file` from the kernel) from `container_memory_usage_bytes`.

In practice, `container_memory_working_set_bytes` is the closest to RSS that is exposed, and you may also wish to keep an eye on `container_memory_usage_bytes` as it includes page cache.

In general, I would recommend relying on metrics such as `process_resident_memory_bytes` from the process itself rather than metrics from the cgroups. If your

---

1 Mapped files include both `mmap` and any libraries used by a process. This is exposed by the kernel as `file_mapped` but is not used by cAdvisor, thus the standard RSS is not available from cAdvisor.

applications do not expose Prometheus metrics, then cAdvisor is a good stopgap, and cAdvisor metrics are still important for debugging and profiling.

Labels

Cgroups are organised in a hierarchy, with the / cgroup at the root of the hierarchy. The metrics for each of your cgroups include the usage of the cgroups below it. This goes against the usual rule that within a metric the sum or average is meaningful, and is thus an example of the "Table Exception" on page 93.

In addition to the id label, cAdvisor adds in more labels about containers if it has them. For Docker containers there will always be the image and name labels, for the specific Docker image being run and Docker's name for the container.

Any metadata labels Docker has for a container will also be included with a container_label_ prefix. Arbitrary labels like these from a scrape can break your monitoring, so you may wish to remove them with a labeldrop as shown in Example 9-1, and as I talked about in "labeldrop and labelkeep" on page 150.[2]

Example 9-1. Using labeldrop to drop container_label_ labels from cAdvisor

```
scrape_configs:
 - job_name: cadvisor
   static_configs:
    - targets:
       - localhost:9090
   metric_relabel_configs:
    - regex: 'container_label_.*'
      action: labeldrop
```

Kubernetes

Kubernetes is a popular platform for orchestrating containers. Like Prometheus, the Kubernetes project is part of the Cloud Native Computing Foundation (CNCF). Here I am going to cover running Prometheus on Kubernetes and working with its service discovery.

As Kubernetes is a large and fast-moving target, I am not going to cover it in exhaustive detail. If you would like more depth, I would suggest the book *Kubernetes: Up and Running* by Joe Beda, Brendan Burns, and Kelsey Hightower (O'Reilly).

---

2 The behaviour of cAdvisor is the main reason the labeldrop and labelkeep relabel actions were added.

Running in Kubernetes

To demonstrate using Prometheus with Kubernetes, I will use Minikube (*https://github.com/kubernetes/minikube*), a tool used to run a single-node Kubernetes cluster inside a virtual machine.

Follow the steps in Example 9-2. I'm using a Linux amd64 machine with VirtualBox already installed. If you are running in a different environment, follow the Minikube installation documentation (*https://github.com/kubernetes/minikube#installation*). Here I am using Minikube 0.24.1 and Kubernetes 1.8.0.

Example 9-2. Downloading and running Minikube

```
hostname $ wget \
    https://storage.googleapis.com/minikube/releases/v0.24.1/minikube-linux-amd64
hostname $ mv minikube-linux-amd64 minikube
hostname $ chmod +x minikube
hostname $ ./minikube start
Starting local Kubernetes v1.8.0 cluster...
Starting VM...
Getting VM IP address...
Moving files into cluster...
Setting up certs...
Connecting to cluster...
Setting up kubeconfig...
Starting cluster components...
Kubectl is now configured to use the cluster.
Loading cached images from config file.
```

 `minikube dashboard --url` will provide you with a URL for the Kubernetes Dashboard, from which you can inspect your Kubernetes cluster.

You will also need to install `kubectl`, which is a command-line tool used to interact with Kubernetes clusters. Example 9-3 shows how to install it and confirm that it can talk to your Kubernetes cluster.

Example 9-3. Downloading and tesing kubectl

```
hostname $ wget \
    https://storage.googleapis.com/kubernetes-release/release/v1.9.2/bin/linux/amd64
    /kubectl
hostname $ chmod +x kubectl
hostname $ ./kubectl get services
NAME         TYPE        CLUSTER-IP    EXTERNAL-IP   PORT(S)    AGE
kubernetes   ClusterIP   10.96.0.1     >none<        443/TCP    44s
```

Example 9-4 shows how to get an example Prometheus running on Minikube. *prometheus-deployment.yml* contains permissions so that your Prometheus can access resources such as pods and nodes in the cluster, a *configMap* is created to hold the Prometheus configuration file, a *deployment* to run Prometheus, and a *service* to make it easier for you to access the Prometheus UI. The final command, the `./mini kube service`, will provide you with a URL where you can access the Prometheus UI.

Example 9-4. Setting up permissions and running Prometheus on Kubernetes

```
hostname $./kubectl apply -f prometheus-deployment.yml
hostname $./minikube service prometheus --url
http://192.168.99.100:30114
```

The target status page should look like Figure 9-2. You can find *prometheus-deployment.yml* on GitHub (*http://bit.ly/2N5kyFf*).

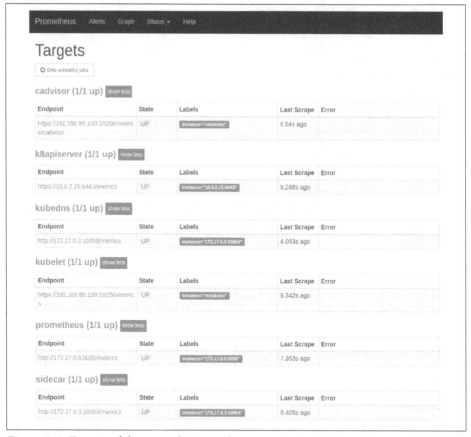

Figure 9-2. Targets of the example Prometheus running on Kubernetes

This is a basic Kubernetes setup to demonstrate the core ideas behind monitoring on Kubernetes, and it is not intended for you to use directly in production; for example, all data is lost every time Prometheus restarts.

Service Discovery

There are currently five different types of Kubernetes service discoveries you can use with Prometheus, namely *node*, *endpoints*, *service*, *pod*, and *ingress*. Prometheus uses the Kubernetes API to discover targets.

Node

Node service discovery is used to discover the nodes comprising the Kubernetes cluster, and you will use it to monitor the infrastructure around Kubernetes. The *Kubelet* is the name of the agent that runs on each node, and you should scrape it as part of monitoring the health of the Kubernetes cluster (Example 9-5).

Example 9-5. prometheus.yml fragment to scrape the Kubelet

```
scrape_configs:
- job_name: 'kubelet'
  kubernetes_sd_configs:
   - role: node
  scheme: https
  tls_config:
    ca_file: /var/run/secrets/kubernetes.io/serviceaccount/ca.crt
    insecure_skip_verify: true
```

Example 9-5 shows the configuration being used by Prometheus to scrape the Kubelet. I'm going to break down the scrape config:

```
job_name: 'kubelet'
```

A default job label is provided, and as there are no `relabel_configs`, `kubelet` will be the job label:[3]

```
kubernetes_sd_configs:
- role: node
```

A single Kubernetes service discovery is provided with the `node` role. The `node` role discovers one target for each of your Kubelets. As Prometheus is running inside the cluster, the defaults for the Kubernetes service discovery are already set up to authenticate with the Kubernetes API.

---

[3] I don't use `node` as the job label, as that's typically used for the Node exporter.

```
scheme: https
tls_config:
  ca_file: /var/run/secrets/kubernetes.io/serviceaccount/ca.crt
  insecure_skip_verify: true
```

The Kubelet serves its /metrics over HTTPS, so we must specify the scheme. Kubernetes clusters usually have their own *certificate authority* that are used to sign their TLS certs, and the ca_file provides that for the scrape. Unfortunately Minikube doesn't get this quite right, so insecure_skip_verify is required to bypass security checks.

The returned target points at the Kubelet, and authentication/authorisation is turned off in this Minikube setup, so no further configuration is needed.

The tls_config in the scrape config contains TLS settings for the scrape. kubernetes_sd_configs also has a tls_config that contains TLS settings for when service discovery talks to the Kubernetes API.

The metadata available includes node annotations and labels, as you can see in Figure 9-3. You could use this metadata with relabel_configs to add labels to distinguish interesting subsets of nodes, such as those with different hardware.

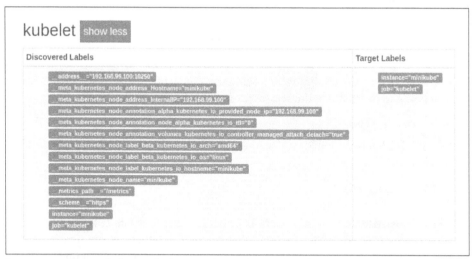

Figure 9-3. The Kubelet on the service discovery status page of Prometheus

The Kubelet's own /metrics only contain metrics about the Kubelet itself, not container-level information. The Kubelet has an embedded cAdvisor on its */metrics/cadvisor* endpoint. Scraping the embedded cAdvisor only requires adding a `metrics_path` to the scrape config used with the Kubelet, as shown in Example 9-6. The embedded cAdvisor includes labels for the Kubernetes `namespace` and `pod_name`.

Example 9-6. prometheus.yml fragment to scrape the Kubelet's embedded cAdvisor

```
scrape_configs:
- job_name: 'cadvisor'
  kubernetes_sd_configs:
    - role: node
  scheme: https
  tls_config:
    ca_file: /var/run/secrets/kubernetes.io/serviceaccount/ca.crt
    insecure_skip_verify: true
  metrics_path: /metrics/cadvisor
```

Node service discovery can be used for anything you want to monitor that runs on each machine in a Kubernetes cluster. If the Node exporter was running on your Minikube node you could scrape it by relabelling the port, for example.

Service

Node service discovery is useful for monitoring the infrastructure of and under Kubernetes, but not much use for monitoring your applications running on Kubernetes.

There are several ways that you can organise your applications on Kubernetes, and no single clear standard has emerged yet. But you are likely using *services*, which is how applications on Kubernetes find each other.

While there is a `service` role, it is not what you usually want. The service role returns a single target for each port[4] of your services. Services are basically load balancers, and scraping targets through load balancers is not wise as Prometheus can scrape a different application instance each time. However, the service role can be useful for blackbox monitoring, to check if the service is responding at all.

Endpoints

Prometheus should be configured to have a target for each application instance, and the `endpoints` role provides just that. Services are backed by *pods*. Pods are a group of tightly coupled containers that share network and storage. For each Kubernetes service port, the endpoints service discovery role returns a target for each pod backing that service. Additionally, any other ports of the pods will be returned as targets.

---

4 A service can have multiple ports.

That's a bit of a mouthful, so let's look at an example. One of the services that is running in your Minikube is the kubernetes service, which are the Kubernetes API servers. Example 9-7 is a scrape config that will discover and scrape the API servers.

Example 9-7. prometheus.yml fragment used to scrape the Kubernetes API servers

```
scrape_configs:
- job_name: 'k8apiserver'
  kubernetes_sd_configs:
   - role: endpoints
  scheme: https
  tls_config:
    ca_file: /var/run/secrets/kubernetes.io/serviceaccount/ca.crt
    insecure_skip_verify: true
  bearer_token_file: /var/run/secrets/kubernetes.io/serviceaccount/token
  relabel_configs:
   - source_labels:
      - __meta_kubernetes_namespace
      - __meta_kubernetes_service_name
      - __meta_kubernetes_endpoint_port_name
     action: keep
     regex: default;kubernetes;https
```

Breaking down this scrape config:

```
job_name: 'k8apiserver'
```

The job label is going to be k8apiserver, as there's no target relabelling to change it:

```
kubernetes_sd_configs:
- role: endpoints
```

There is a single Kubernetes service discovery using the endpoints role, which will return a target for every port of every pod backing each of your services:

```
scheme: https
tls_config:
  ca_file: /var/run/secrets/kubernetes.io/serviceaccount/ca.crt
  insecure_skip_verify: true
bearer_token_file: /var/run/secrets/kubernetes.io/serviceaccount/token
```

As with the Kubelet, the API servers are served over HTTPS. In addition, authentication is required, which is provided by the bearer_token_file:

```
relabel_configs:
- source_labels:
    - __meta_kubernetes_namespace
    - __meta_kubernetes_service_name
    - __meta_kubernetes_endpoint_port_name
   action: keep
   regex: default;kubernetes;https
```

This relabel configuration will only return targets that are in the `default` namespace, and are part of a service called `kubernetes` with a port called `https`.

You can see the resulting target in Figure 9-4. The API server is special, so there isn't much metadata. All the other potential targets were dropped.

Figure 9-4. The API server on the service discovery status page of Prometheus

While you will want to scrape the API servers, most of the time you'll be focused on your applications. Example 9-8 shows how you can automatically scrape the pods for all of your services.

Example 9-8. prometheus.yml fragment to scrape pods backing all Kubernetes services, except the API servers

```
scrape_configs:
 - job_name: 'k8services'
   kubernetes_sd_configs:
    - role: endpoints
   relabel_configs:
    - source_labels:
       - __meta_kubernetes_namespace
       - __meta_kubernetes_service_name
      regex: default;kubernetes
      action: drop
    - source_labels:
       - __meta_kubernetes_namespace
      regex: default
      action: keep
    - source_labels: [__meta_kubernetes_service_name]
      target_label: job
```

Once again I'll break it down:

```
job_name: 'k8services'
kubernetes_sd_configs:
 - role: endpoints
```

As with the previous example, this is providing a job name and the Kubernetes end points role, but this does not end up as the `job` label due to later relabelling.

There are no HTTPS settings, as I know the targets are all plain HTTP. There is no `bearer_token_file`, as no authentication is required, and sending a bearer token to all of your services could allow them to impersonate you:[5]

```
relabel_configs:
- source_labels:
    - __meta_kubernetes_namespace
    - __meta_kubernetes_service_name
  regex: default;kubernetes
  action: drop
- source_labels:
    - __meta_kubernetes_namespace
  regex: default
  action: keep
```

I excluded the API server, as there is already another scrape config handling it. I also only looked at the `default` namespace, which is where I am launching applications:[6]

```
- source_labels: [__meta_kubernetes_service_name]
  target_label: job
```

This relabel action takes the Kubernetes service name and uses it as the `job` label. The `job_name` I provided for the scrape config is only a default, and does not apply.

In this way you can have your Prometheus automatically pick up new services and start scraping them with a useful `job` label. In this case that's just Prometheus itself, as shown in Figure 9-5.

---

5 This is also the case with basic auth, but not for a challenge-response mechanism like TLS client certificate authentication.

6 And to not cause confusion with Example 9-10, as kube-dns is in the kube-system namespace.

Figure 9-5. Prometheus has automatically discovered itself using endpoint service discovery

You could go a step further and use relabelling to add additional labels from service or pod metadata, or even set __scheme__ or __metrics_path__ based on a Kubernetes annotation, as shown in Example 9-9. These would look for prometheus.io/scheme, prometheus.io/path, and prometheus.io/port service annotations,[7] and use them if present.

Example 9-9. Relabelling using Kubernetes service annotations to optionally configure the scheme, path, and port of targets

```
relabel_configs:
 - source_labels: [__meta_kubernetes_service_annotation_prometheus_io_scheme]
   regex: (.+)
   target_label: __scheme__
 - source_labels: [__meta_kubernetes_service_annotation_prometheus_io_path]
   regex: (.+)
   target_label: __metrics_path__
 - source_labels:
    - __address__
    - __meta_kubernetes_service_annotation_prometheus_io_port
   regex: ([^:]+)(:\d+)?;(\d+)
   replacement: ${1}:${3}
   target_label: __address__
```

---

7 Foward slashes are not valid in label names, so they are sanitised to underscores.

This is limited to monitoring only one port per service. You could have another scrape config using the `prometheus.io/port2` annotation, and so on for however many ports you need.

Pod

Discovering endpoints is great for monitoring the primary processes backing your services, but it won't discover pods that are not part of services.

The pod role discovers pods. It will return a target for each port of every one of your pods. As it works off pods, service metadata such as labels and annotations are not available as pods do not know which services they are members of. But you will have access to all pod metadata. How you use this boils down to a question of what conventions you want to use. The Kubernetes ecosystem is rapidly evolving, and there is no one standard yet.

You could create a convention that all pods must be part of a service, and then use the endpoint role in service discovery. You could have a convention that all pods have a label indicating the (single) Kubernetes service they are a part of, and use the pod role for service discovery. As all ports have names, you could base a convention off that and have ports named with a prefix of `prom-http` be scraped with HTTP, and `prom-https` be scraped with HTTPS.

One of the components that comes with Minikube is *kube-dns*, which provides DNS services. Its pod has multiple ports, including a port named `metrics` that serves Prometheus metrics. Example 9-10 shows how you could discover this port and use the name of the container as the `job` label, as Figure 9-6 shows.

Example 9-10. prometheus.yml to discover all pod ports with the name metrics and to use the container name as the job label

```
scrape_configs:
- job_name: 'k8pods'
  kubernetes_sd_configs:
   - role: pod
  relabel_configs:
   - source_labels: [__meta_kubernetes_pod_container_port_name]
     regex: metrics
     action: keep
   - source_labels: [__meta_kubernetes_pod_container_name]
     target_label: job
```

Figure 9-6. Two targets discovered using pod service discovery

 Another approach to managing what to monitor is the Prometheus Operator (*https://github.com/coreos/prometheus-operator*), which uses the *custom resource definition* feature of Kubernetes. The Operator also manages running Prometheus and the Alertmanager for you.

Ingress

An *ingress* is a way for a Kubernetes service to be exposed outside the cluster. As it is a layer on top of services, similar to the `service` role the `ingress` role is also basically a load balancer. If multiple pods backed the service and thus ingress, this would cause you problems when scraping with Prometheus. Accordingly, you should only use this role for blackbox monitoring.

kube-state-metrics

Using Kubernetes service discovery you can have Prometheus scrape your applications and Kubernetes infrastructure, but this will not include metrics about what Kubernetes knows about your services, pods, deployments, and other resources. This is because applications such as the Kubelet and Kubernetes API servers should expose information about their own performance, not dump their internal data structures.[8]

Instead, you would obtain such metrics from another endpoint,[9] or if that doesn't exist, have an exporter that extracts the relevant information. For Kubernetes, kube-state-metrics is that exporter.

To run kube-state-metrics you should follow the steps in Example 9-11 and then visit the /metrics on the returned URL in your browser. You can find *kube-state-metrics.yml* on GitHub (*http://bit.ly/2tE7K0j*).

Example 9-11. Running kube-state-metrics

```
hostname $./kubectl apply -f kube-state-metrics.yml
hostname $./minikube service kube-state-metrics --url
http://192.168.99.100:31774
```

Some useful metrics include kube_deployment_spec_replicas for the intended number of metrics in a deployment, kube_node_status_condition for node problems, and kube_pod_container_status_restarts_total for pod restarts.

> This kube-state-metrics will be automatically scraped by Prometheus due to the scrape config in Example 9-8.

kube-state-metrics features several examples of "Enum" on page 88 and "Info" on page 90 metrics, such as kube_node_status_condition and kube_pod_info, respectively.

Now that you have an idea about how to use Prometheus in container environments, let's look at some of the common exporters you will run into.

---

8 Put another way, a database exporter does not dump the contents of the database as metrics.

9 Such as the Kubelet exposing cAdvisor's metrics on another endpoint.

Common Exporters

You already saw the Node exporter in Chapter 7, and while it will likely be the first exporter you use, there are literally hundreds of other exporters you can use.

I'm not going to go through all of the ever-growing number of exporters out there, instead I will show you some examples of the types of things you will come across when using exporters. This will prepare you to use exporters in your own environment.

At the simplest, exporters Just Work, with no configuration required on your part, as you already saw for the Node exporter. Usually you will need to do minimal configuration to tell the exporter which application instance to scrape. At the far end, some exporters require extensive configuration as the data they are working with is very general.

You will generally have one exporter for every application instance that needs one. This is because the intended way to use Prometheus is for every application to have direct instrumentation and have Prometheus discover it and scrape it directly. When that isn't possible, exporters are used, and you want to keep to that architecture as much as possible. Having the exporter live right beside the application instance it is exporting from is easier to manage as you grow, and keeps your failure domains aligned. You will find that some exporters violate this guideline and offer the ability to scrape multiple instances, but you can still deploy them in the intended fashion and use the techniques shown in "metric_relabel_configs" on page 148 to remove any extraneous labels.

Consul

You already installed and ran Consul in "Consul" on page 132. Assuming it is still running, you can download and run the Consul exporter with the commands in

Example 10-1. Because Consul usually runs on port 8500, you don't need to do any extra configuration as the Consul exporter uses that port by default.

Example 10-1. Downloading and running the Consul exporter

```
hostname $ wget https://github.com/prometheus/consul_exporter/releases/
    download/v0.3.0/consul_exporter-0.3.0.linux-amd64.tar.gz
hostname $ tar -xzf consul_exporter-0.3.0.linux-amd64.tar.gz
hostname $ cd consul_exporter-0.3.0.linux-amd64/
hostname $ ./consul_exporter
INFO[0000] Starting consul_exporter (version=0.3.0, branch=master,
    revision=5f439584f4c4369186fec234d18eb071ec76fdde)
    source="consul_exporter.go:319"
INFO[0000] Build context (go=go1.7.5, user=root@4100b077eec6,
    date=20170302-02:05:48)  source="consul_exporter.go:320"
INFO[0000] Listening on :9107                     source="consul_exporter.go:339"
```

If you open *http://localhost:9107/metrics* in your browser you will see the metrics available.

The first metric you should make note of here is consul_up. Some exporters will return a HTTP error to Prometheus when fetching data fails, which results in up being set to 0 in Prometheus. But many exporters will still be successfully scraped in this scenario and use a metric such as consul_up to indicate if there was a problem. Accordingly, when alerting on Consul being down, you should check both up and consul_up. If you stop Consul and then check the /metrics you will see the value changes to 0, and back to 1 again when Consul is started again.

consul_catalog_service_node_healthy tells you about the health of the various services in the Consul node, similar to how kube-state-metrics (discussed in "kube-state-metrics" on page 168) tells you about the health of nodes and containers but across an entire Kubernetes cluster.

consul_serf_lan_members is the number of Consul agents in the cluster. You may wonder if this could come just from the *leader* of the Consul cluster, but remember that each agent might have a different view of how many members the cluster has if there is an issue such as a network partition. In general, you should expose metrics like this from every member of a cluster, and synthesise the value you want using aggregation in PromQL.

There are also metrics about your Consul exporter. consul_exporter_build_info is its build information, and there are a variety of process_ and go_ metrics about the process and the Go runtime. These are useful for debugging issues with the Consul exporter itself.

You can configure Prometheus to scrape the Consul exporter as shown in Example 10-2. Even though the scrape is going via an exporter, I used the job label of consul, as it is really Consul I am scraping.

 Exporters can be considered as a form of proxy. They take in a scrape request from Prometheus, fetch metrics from a process, munge them into a format that Prometheus can understand, and respond with them to Prometheus.

Example 10-2. prometheus.yml to scrape a local Consul exporter

```
global:
  scrape_interval: 10s
scrape_configs:
 - job_name: consul
   static_configs:
    - targets:
       - localhost:9107
```

HAProxy

The HAProxy exporter is a typical exporter. To demonstrate it you will first need to create a configuration file like the one shown in Example 10-3 called *haproxy.cfg*.

Example 10-3. haproxy.cfg proxying the Node exporter on port 1234, with port 1235 as a status port

```
defaults
  mode http
  timeout server 5s
  timeout connect 5s
  timeout client 5s

frontend frontend
  bind *:1234
  use_backend backend

backend backend
  server node_exporter 127.0.0.1:9100

frontend monitoring
  bind *:1235
  no log
  stats uri /
  stats enable
```

You can then run HAProxy:

```
docker run -v $PWD:/usr/local/etc/haproxy:ro haproxy:1.7
```

This configuration will proxy *http://localhost:1234* to your Node exporter (if it is still running). The important part of this configuration is:

```
frontend monitoring
  bind *:1235
  no log
  stats uri /
  stats enable
```

This opens a HAProxy frontend on *http://localhost:1235* with statistics reporting, and in particular, the comma-separated value (CSV) output on *http://localhost:1235/;csv* which the HAProxy exporter will use. Next, you should download and run the HAProxy exporter as shown in Example 10-4.

Example 10-4. Downloading and running the HAProxy exporter

```
hostname $ wget https://github.com/prometheus/haproxy_exporter/releases/download/
    v0.9.0/haproxy_exporter-0.9.0.linux-amd64.tar.gz
hostname $ tar -xzf haproxy_exporter-0.9.0.linux-amd64.tar.gz
hostname $ cd haproxy_exporter-0.9.0.linux-amd64/
hostname $ ./haproxy_exporter --haproxy.scrape-uri 'http://localhost:1235/;csv'
INFO[0000] Starting haproxy_exporter (version=0.9.0, branch=HEAD,
    revision=865ad4922f9ab35372b8a6d02ab6ef96805560fe)
    source=haproxy_exporter.go:495
INFO[0000] Build context (go=go1.9.2, user=root@4b9b5f43f4a2,
    date=20180123-18:27:27)  source=haproxy_exporter.go:496
INFO[0000] Listening on :9101                          source=haproxy_exporter.go:521
```

If you go to *http://localhost:9101/metrics* you will see the metrics being produced. Similar to the Consul exporter's consul_up, there is a haproxy_up metric, indicating if talking to HAProxy succeeded.

HAProxy has *frontends*, *backends*, and *servers*. They each have metrics with the prefixes haproxy_frontend_, haproxy_backend_, and haproxy_server_, respectively. For example, haproxy_server_bytes_out_total is a counter[1] with the number of bytes each server has returned.

Because a backend can have many servers, you may find the cardinality of the haproxy_server_ metrics causes issues. The --haproxy.server-metric-fields command-line flag allows you to limit which metrics are returned.

---

[1] In this version of the HAProxy exporter, the TYPE is incorrectly gauge. This sort of mismatch of types is not uncommon in exporters; it should be using counter or untyped.

This is an example of where a metric could have high cardinality and the exporter offers you a way to optionally tune it down. Other exporters, such as the MySQLd exporter, take the opposite approach, where most metrics are disabled by default.

Exporter Default Ports

You may have noticed that Prometheus, the Node exporter, Alertmanager, and other exporters in this chapter have similar port numbers.

Back when there were only a handful of exporters, many had the same default port number. Both the Node and HAProxy exporters used port 8080 by default, for example. This was annoying when trying out or deploying Prometheus, so a wiki page was started at *https://github.com/prometheus/prometheus/wiki/Default-port-allocations* to keep the official exporters on different ports.

This organically grew to being a comprehensive list of exporters, and aside from some users skipping over numbers, it now serves a purpose beyond its initial one.

Prior to 1.8.0, HAProxy could only use one CPU core, so to use multiple cores on older versions you have to run multiple HAProxy processes. Accordingly, you must also run one HAProxy exporter per HAProxy process.

The HAProxy exporter has one other notable feature that thus far few other exporters have implemented. In Unix it is common for daemons to have a *pid file* containing their processes ID, which is used by the *init system* to control the process. If you have such a file and pass it in the `--haproxy.pid-file` command-line flag, then the HAProxy exporter will include `haproxy_process_` metrics about the HAProxy process, even if scraping HAProxy itself fails. These metrics are the same as the `process_` metrics, except they refer to the HAProxy rather than the HAProxy exporter.

You can configure the HAProxy exporter to be scraped by Prometheus in the same way as any other exporter, as you can see in Example 10-5.

Example 10-5. prometheus.yml to scrape a local HAProxy exporter

```
global:
  scrape_interval: 10s
scrape_configs:
 - job_name: haproxy
   static_configs:
    - targets:
      - localhost:9101
```

Grok Exporter

Not all applications produce metrics in a form that can be converted into something that Prometheus understands using an exporter. But such applications may produce logs, and the Grok exporter (*https://github.com/fstab/grok_exporter*) can be used to convert those into metrics.[2] Grok is a way to parse unstructured logs that is commonly used with Logstash.[3] The Grok exporter reuses the same pattern language, allowing you to reuse patterns that you already have.

Say that you had a simple log that looks like:

```
GET /foo 1.23
GET /bar 3.2
POST /foo 4.6
```

which was in a file called *example.log*. You could convert these logs into metrics by using the Grok exporter. First, download the 0.2.3 Grok exporter Linux amd64 release (*http://bit.ly/2MBd6kK*) and unzip it. Next, create a file called *grok.yml* with the content in Example 10-6.

Example 10-6. grok.yml to parse a simple log file and produce metrics

```
global:
  config_version: 2
input:
  type: file
  path: example.log
  readall: true   # Use false in production
grok:
  additional_patterns:
  - 'METHOD [A-Z]+'
  - 'PATH [^ ]+'
  - 'NUMBER [0-9.]+'
metrics:
 - type: counter
   name: log_http_requests_total
   help: HTTP requests
   match: '%{METHOD} %{PATH:path} %{NUMBER:latency}'
   labels:
     path: '{{.path}}'
 - type: histogram
   name: log_http_request_latency_seconds_total
   help: HTTP request latency
   match: '%{METHOD} %{PATH:path} %{NUMBER:latency}'
   value: '{{.latency}}'
```

---

2 There is also *https://github.com/google/mtail* in this space.

3 The L in the ELK stack.

```
server:
  port: 9144
```

Finally, run the Grok exporter:

```
./grok_exporter -config grok.yml
```

I'll break this down. First there is some boilerplate:

```
global:
  config_version: 2
```

Next, you need to define the file to be read. Here I'm using `readall: true` so you will see the same results as in this example. In production you would leave it to the default of `false` so that the file is tailed:

```
input:
  type: file
  path: example.log
  readall: true  # Use false in production
```

Grok works with patterns based on regular expressions. I've defined all of my patterns here manually so you can better understand what's going on, but you can also reuse ones you already have:

```
grok:
  additional_patterns:
  - 'METHOD [A-Z]+'
  - 'PATH [^ ]+'
  - 'NUMBER [0-9.]+'
```

I have two metrics. The first is a counter called `log_http_requests_total`, which has a label `path`:

```
metrics:
- type: counter
  name: log_http_requests_total
  help: HTTP requests
  match: '%{METHOD} %{PATH:path} %{NUMBER:latency}'
  labels:
    path: '{{.path}}'
```

My second is a histogram called `log_http_request_latency_seconds_total`, which is observing the latency value, and has no labels:

```
- type: histogram
  name: log_http_request_latency_seconds_total
  help: HTTP request latency
  match: '%{METHOD} %{PATH:path} %{NUMBER:latency}'
  value: '{{.latency}}'
```

Finally, I define where I want the exporter to expose its metrics:

```
server:
    port: 9144
```

When you visit *http://localhost:9144*, amongst its output you will find the following metrics:

```
# HELP log_http_request_latency_seconds_total HTTP request latency
# TYPE log_http_request_latency_seconds_total histogram
log_http_request_latency_seconds_total_bucket{le="0.005"} 0
log_http_request_latency_seconds_total_bucket{le="0.01"} 0
log_http_request_latency_seconds_total_bucket{le="0.025"} 0
log_http_request_latency_seconds_total_bucket{le="0.05"} 0
log_http_request_latency_seconds_total_bucket{le="0.1"} 1
log_http_request_latency_seconds_total_bucket{le="0.25"} 2
log_http_request_latency_seconds_total_bucket{le="0.5"} 3
log_http_request_latency_seconds_total_bucket{le="1"} 3
log_http_request_latency_seconds_total_bucket{le="2.5"} 3
log_http_request_latency_seconds_total_bucket{le="5"} 3
log_http_request_latency_seconds_total_bucket{le="10"} 3
log_http_request_latency_seconds_total_bucket{le="+Inf"} 3
log_http_request_latency_seconds_total_sum 0.57
log_http_request_latency_seconds_total_count 3
# HELP log_http_requests_total HTTP requests
# TYPE log_http_requests_total counter
log_http_requests_total{path="/bar"} 1
log_http_requests_total{path="/foo"} 2
```

As you can see, the Grok exporter is more involved to configure than your typical exporter; it's closer to direct instrumentation in terms of effort, as you must individually define each metric you want to expose. You would generally run one per application instance that needs to be monitored, and scrape it with Prometheus in the usual way as shown in Example 10-7.

Example 10-7. prometheus.yml to scrape a local Grok exporter

```
global:
  scrape_interval: 10s
scrape_configs:
 - job_name: grok
   static_configs:
    - targets:
       - localhost:9144
```

Blackbox

While the recommended way to deploy exporters is to run one right beside each application instance, there are cases where this is not possible for technical reasons.[4] This is usually the case with blackbox monitoring—monitoring the system from the outside with no special knowledge of the internals. I like to think of blackbox monitoring as similar to smoketests when unit testing; their purpose is primarily to quickly tell you when things have gone hilariously wrong.

If you are monitoring whether a web service works from the standpoint of a user, you usually want to monitor that through the same load balancers and virtual IP (VIP) addresses the user is hitting. You can't exactly run an exporter on a VIP as it is, well, virtual. A different architecture is needed.

In Prometheus there is a class of exporters usually referred to as Blackbox-style or SNMP-style, after the two primary examples of exporters that cannot run beside an application instance. The Blackbox exporter by necessity usually needs to run somewhere else on the network, and there is no application instance to run on. For the SNMP[5] exporter, it's rare for you to be able to run your own code on a network device—and if you could, you would use the Node exporter instead.

So how are Blackbox-style or SNMP-style exporters different? Instead of you configuring them to talk to only one target, they instead take in the target as a URL parameter. Any other configuration is provided by you on the exporter side as usual. This keeps the responsibilities of service discovery and scrape scheduling with Prometheus, and the responsibility of translating metrics into a form understandable by Prometheus with your exporter.

The Blackbox exporter allows you to perform ICMP, TCP, HTTP, and DNS probing. I'll show you each in turn, but first you should get the blackbox exporter running as shown in Example 10-8.

Example 10-8. Downloading and running the Blackbox exporter

```
hostname $ wget https://github.com/prometheus/blackbox_exporter/releases/download/
    v0.12.0/blackbox_exporter-0.12.0.linux-amd64.tar.gz
hostname $ tar -xzf blackbox_exporter-0.12.0.linux-amd64.tar.gz
hostname $ cd blackbox_exporter-0.12.0.linux-amd64/
hostname $ sudo ./blackbox_exporter
level=info ... msg="Starting blackbox_exporter" version="(version=0.12.0,
    branch=HEAD, revision=4a22506cf0cf139d9b2f9cde099f0012d9fcabde)"
```

---

4 As distinct from cases where it's not possible for political reasons.

5 Simple Network Management Protocol, a standard for (among other things) exposing metrics on network devices. It can also sometimes be found on other hardware.

```
level=info ... msg="Loaded config file"
level=info ... msg="Listening on address" address=:9115
```

If you visit *http://localhost:9115/* in your browser you should see a status page like the one in Figure 10-1.

Blackbox Exporter

Probe prometheus.io for http_2xx

Debug probe prometheus.io for http_2xx

Metrics

Configuration

Recent Probes

Module	Target	Result	Debug

Figure 10-1. The Blackbox exporter's status page

ICMP

The Internet Control Message Protocol is a part of the Internet Protocol (IP). In the context of the Blackbox exporter it is the *echo reply* and *echo request* messages that are of interest to you, more commonly known as *ping*.[6]

 ICMP uses raw sockets so it requires more privileges than a typical exporter, which is why Example 10-8 uses sudo. On Linux you could instead give the Blackbox exporter the CAP_NET_RAW capability.

To start you should ask the Blackbox exporter to ping localhost by visiting *http://local host:9115/probe?module=icmp&target=localhost* in your browser, which should produce something like:

```
# HELP probe_dns_lookup_time_seconds Returns the time taken for probe dns lookup
    in seconds
# TYPE probe_dns_lookup_time_seconds gauge
probe_dns_lookup_time_seconds 0.000164439
# HELP probe_duration_seconds Returns how long the probe took to complete
    in seconds
# TYPE probe_duration_seconds gauge
```

---

6 Some pings can also work via UDP or TCP instead, but those are relatively rare.

```
probe_duration_seconds 0.000670403
# HELP probe_ip_protocol Specifies whether probe ip protocol is IP4 or IP6
# TYPE probe_ip_protocol gauge
probe_ip_protocol 4
# HELP probe_success Displays whether or not the probe was a success
# TYPE probe_success gauge
probe_success 1
```

The key metric here is `probe_success`, which is 1 if your probe succeeded and 0 otherwise. This is similar to `consul_up`, and you should check that neither up nor `probe_success` are 0 when alerting. There is an example of this in "for" on page 294.

The *metrics* of the Blackbox exporter provides metrics about the Blackbox exporter itself, such as how much CPU it has used. To perform blackbox probes, you use */probe*.

There are also other useful metrics that all types of probes produce. `probe_ip_proto col` indicates the IP protocol used, IPv4 in this case, and `probe_duration_seconds` is how long the entire probe took, including DNS resolution.

The name resolution used by Prometheus and the Blackbox exporter is DNS resolution, not the `gethostbyname` syscall. Other potential sources of name resolution, such as */etc/hosts* and *nsswitch.conf*, are not considered by the Blackbox exporter. This can lead to the `ping` command working, but the Blackbox exporter failing due to not being able to resolve its target via DNS.

If you look inside *blackbox.yml* you will find the `icmp` module:

```
icmp:
    prober: icmp
```

This says that there is a module called `icmp`, which you requested with the `?module=icmp` in the URL. This module uses the `icmp` prober, with no additional options specified. ICMP is quite simple, so only in niche use cases might you need to specify `dont_fragment` or `payload_size`.

You can also try other targets. For example, to probe *google.com* you can visit *http://localhost:9115/probe?module=icmp&target=www.google.com* in your browser. For the `icmp` probe, the `target` URL parameter is an IP address or hostname.

You may find that this probe fails, with output like:

```
# HELP probe_dns_lookup_time_seconds Returns the time taken for probe dns lookup
    in seconds
# TYPE probe_dns_lookup_time_seconds gauge
```

```
probe_dns_lookup_time_seconds 0.001169908
# HELP probe_duration_seconds Returns how long the probe took to complete
    in seconds
# TYPE probe_duration_seconds gauge
probe_duration_seconds 0.001397181
# HELP probe_ip_protocol Specifies whether probe ip protocol is IP4 or IP6
# TYPE probe_ip_protocol gauge
probe_ip_protocol 6
# HELP probe_success Displays whether or not the probe was a success
# TYPE probe_success gauge
probe_success 0
```

probe_success is 0 here, indicating the failure. Notice that probe_ip_protocol is also 6, indicating IPv6. In this case the machine I am using doesn't have a working IPv6 setup. Why is the Blackbox exporter using IPv6?

When resolving the Blackbox exporter, targets will prefer a returned IPv6 address if there is one; otherwise, it will use an IPv4 address. *google.com* has both, so IPv6 is chosen and fails on my machine.

You can see this in more detail if you add &debug=true on to the end of the URL, giving *http://localhost:9115/probe?module=icmp&target=www.google.com&debug= true*, which will produce output like:

```
Logs for the probe:
... module=icmp target=www.google.com level=info
        msg="Beginning probe" probe=icmp timeout_seconds=9.5
... module=icmp target=www.google.com level=info
        msg="Resolving target address" preferred_ip_protocol=ip6
... module=icmp target=www.google.com level=info
        msg="Resolved target address" ip=2a00:1450:400b:c03::63
... module=icmp target=www.google.com level=info
        msg="Creating socket"
... module=icmp target=www.google.com level=info
        msg="Creating ICMP packet" seq=10 id=3483
... module=icmp target=www.google.com level=info
        msg="Writing out packet"
... module=icmp target=www.google.com level=warn
        msg="Error writing to socket" err="write ip6 ::->2a00:1450:400b:c03::63:
        sendto: cannot assign requested address"
... module=icmp target=www.google.com level=error
        msg="Probe failed" duration_seconds=0.008982345

Metrics that would have been returned:
# HELP probe_dns_lookup_time_seconds Returns the time taken for probe dns lookup
    in seconds
# TYPE probe_dns_lookup_time_seconds gauge
probe_dns_lookup_time_seconds 0.008717006
# HELP probe_duration_seconds Returns how long the probe took to complete in
    seconds
# TYPE probe_duration_seconds gauge
probe_duration_seconds 0.008982345
```

```
# HELP probe_ip_protocol Specifies whether probe ip protocol is IP4 or IP6
# TYPE probe_ip_protocol gauge
probe_ip_protocol 6
# HELP probe_success Displays whether or not the probe was a success
# TYPE probe_success gauge
probe_success 0

Module configuration:
prober: icmp
```

The debug output is extensive, and by carefully reading through it you can understand exactly what the probe is doing. The error you see here is from the `sendto`
syscall, which cannot assign an IPv6 address. To prefer IPv4 instead, you can add a
new module with the `preferred_ip_protocol: ipv4` option to *blackbox.yml*:

```
icmp_ipv4:
  prober: icmp
  icmp:
    preferred_ip_protocol: ip4
```

After restarting the Blackbox exporter,[7] if you use this module via *http://localhost:
9115/probe?module=icmp_ipv4&target=www.google.com*, it will now work via IPv4.

TCP

The Transmission Control Protocol is the TCP in TCP/IP. Many standard protocols
use it, including websites (HTTP), email (SMTP), remote login (Telnet and SSH),
and chat (IRC). The `tcp` probe of the Blackbox exporter allows you to check TCP
services, and perform simple conversations for those that use line-based text protocols.

To start you can check if your local SSH server is listening on port 22 with *http://
localhost:9115/probe?module=tcp_connect&target=localhost:22*:

```
# HELP probe_dns_lookup_time_seconds Returns the time taken for probe dns lookup
    in seconds
# TYPE probe_dns_lookup_time_seconds gauge
probe_dns_lookup_time_seconds 0.000202381
# HELP probe_duration_seconds Returns how long the probe took to complete in
    seconds
# TYPE probe_duration_seconds gauge
probe_duration_seconds 0.000881654
# HELP probe_failed_due_to_regex Indicates if probe failed due to regex
# TYPE probe_failed_due_to_regex gauge
probe_failed_due_to_regex 0
# HELP probe_ip_protocol Specifies whether probe ip protocol is IP4 or IP6
```

---

7 Similar to Prometheus, you can also send a SIGHUP to the Blackbox exporter to have it reload its configuration.

```
# TYPE probe_ip_protocol gauge
probe_ip_protocol 4
# HELP probe_success Displays whether or not the probe was a success
# TYPE probe_success gauge
probe_success 1
```

This is quite similar to the metrics produced by the ICMP probe, and you can see that this probe succeeded as `probe_success` is 1. The definition of the `tcp_connect` module in *blackbox.yml* is:

```
tcp_connect:
  prober: tcp
```

This will try to connect to your target, and once it is connected immediately, it will close the connection. The `ssh_banner` module goes further, checking for a particular response from the remote server:

```
ssh_banner:
  prober: tcp
  tcp:
    query_response:
    - expect: "^SSH-2.0-"
```

As the very start of an SSH session is in plain text, you can check for this part of the protocol with the `tcp` probe. This is better than `tcp_connect` as you are not only checking that the TCP port is open, but that the server on the other end is responding with an SSH banner.

If your server returned something different, the `expect` regex will not match, and `probe_success` will be 0. In addition, `probe_failed_due_to_regex` would be 1. Since Prometheus is a metrics-based system, the full debug output cannot be saved, as that would be event logging.[8] However, the Blackbox exporter can provide a small number of metrics to help you to piece together what went wrong after the fact.

 If you find that every service needs a different module, consider standardising what your health checks look like across services. If a service exposes a /metrics, then there is not much need for basic connectivity checks with the Blackbox exporter, as Prometheus's scrapes will already provide that.

The `tcp` probe can also connect via TLS. Add a `tcp_connect_tls` to your *blackbox.yml* file with the following configuration:

---

8 However, the debug information for the most recent probes is available from the Blackbox exporter's status page.

```
tcp_connect_tls:
  prober: tcp
  tcp:
    tls: true
```

After restarting the Blackbox exporter, if you now visit *http://localhost:9115/probe? module=tcp_connect_tls&target=www.robustperception.io:443* you can check if my company website is contactable with HTTPS.[9] For the tcp prober, the target URL parameter is an IP address or hostname, followed by a colon, and then the port number.

You may notice among the metrics output:

```
# HELP probe_ssl_earliest_cert_expiry Returns earliest SSL cert expiry date
# TYPE probe_ssl_earliest_cert_expiry gauge
probe_ssl_earliest_cert_expiry 1.522039491e+09
```

probe_ssl_earliest_cert_expiry[10] is produced as a side effect of probing, indicating when your TLS/SSL certificate[11] will expire. You can use this to catch expiring certificates before they become outages.

While HTTP is a line-oriented text protocol[12] that you could use the tcp probe with, instead there is a http probe that is more suitable for this purpose.

HTTP

The HyperText Transfer Protocol is the basis for the modern web, and likely what most of the services you provide use. While most monitoring of web applications is best done by Prometheus scraping metrics over HTTP, sometimes you will want to perform blackbox monitoring of your HTTP services.

The http prober takes a URL[13] for the target URL parameter. If you visit *http://local host:9115/probe?module=http_2xx&target=https://www.robustperception.io* you can check my company's website over HTTPS using the http_2xx module,[14] producing output similar to:

```
# HELP probe_dns_lookup_time_seconds Returns the time taken for probe dns lookup
    in seconds
# TYPE probe_dns_lookup_time_seconds gauge
```

---

9 443 is the standard port for HTTPS.

10 This metric will likely be renamed at some point as it should have a unit of seconds.

11 More exactly, the first certifcate that will expire in your certificate chain.

12 At least for HTTP versions prior to 2.0.

13 You can even include URL parameters, if they are appropriately encoded.

14 The http_2xx module is incidentally the default module name if you don't provide one as a URL parameter.

```
probe_dns_lookup_time_seconds 0.00169128
# HELP probe_duration_seconds Returns how long the probe took to complete in
    seconds
# TYPE probe_duration_seconds gauge
probe_duration_seconds 0.191706498
# HELP probe_failed_due_to_regex Indicates if probe failed due to regex
# TYPE probe_failed_due_to_regex gauge
probe_failed_due_to_regex 0
# HELP probe_http_content_length Length of http content response
# TYPE probe_http_content_length gauge
probe_http_content_length -1
# HELP probe_http_duration_seconds Duration of http request by phase, summed over
    all redirects
# TYPE probe_http_duration_seconds gauge
probe_http_duration_seconds{phase="connect"} 0.018464759
probe_http_duration_seconds{phase="processing"} 0.132312499
probe_http_duration_seconds{phase="resolve"} 0.00169128
probe_http_duration_seconds{phase="tls"} 0.057145526
probe_http_duration_seconds{phase="transfer"} 6.0805e-05
# HELP probe_http_redirects The number of redirects
# TYPE probe_http_redirects gauge
probe_http_redirects 0
# HELP probe_http_ssl Indicates if SSL was used for the final redirect
# TYPE probe_http_ssl gauge
probe_http_ssl 1
# HELP probe_http_status_code Response HTTP status code
# TYPE probe_http_status_code gauge
probe_http_status_code 200
# HELP probe_http_version Returns the version of HTTP of the probe response
# TYPE probe_http_version gauge
probe_http_version 1.1
# HELP probe_ip_protocol Specifies whether probe ip protocol is IP4 or IP6
# TYPE probe_ip_protocol gauge
probe_ip_protocol 4
# HELP probe_ssl_earliest_cert_expiry Returns earliest SSL cert expiry in
    unixtime
# TYPE probe_ssl_earliest_cert_expiry gauge
probe_ssl_earliest_cert_expiry 1.522039491e+09
# HELP probe_success Displays whether or not the probe was a success
# TYPE probe_success gauge
probe_success 1
```

You can see probe_success, but also a number of other useful metrics for debugging, such as the status code, HTTP version, and timings for different phases of the request.

The http probe has many options to both affect how the request is made, and whether the response is considered successful. You can specify HTTP authentication, headers, POST body, and then in the response check that the status code, HTTP version, and body are acceptable.

For example, I may want to test that users to *http://www.robustperception.io* end up redirected to a HTTPS website, with a 200 status code, and that the word "Prometheus" is in the body. To do so you could create a module like:

```
http_200_ssl_prometheus:
  prober: http
  http:
    valid_status_codes: [200]
    fail_if_not_ssl: true
    fail_if_not_matches_regexp:
      - Prometheus
```

Visiting *http://localhost:9115/probe?module=http_200_ssl_prometheus&target=http:// www.robustperception.io* in your browser, you should see that this works as probe_success is 1. You could also use the same request against *http://prometheus.io* if you visit *http://localhost:9115/probe?module=http_200_ssl_prometheus&target= http://prometheus.io* in your browser.[15]

While the Blackbox exporter will follow HTTP redirects,[16] not all features work perfectly across redirects.

This example is a little contrived, but each module of the Blackbox exporter is a specific test that you can run against different targets by providing different target URL parameters as you did here with *http://www.robustperception.io* and *http://prometheus.io*. For example, you might check that each frontend application instance serving your website is returning the right result. If different services need different tests, then you can create modules for each of them. It is not possible to override modules via URL parameters, as that would lead to the Blackbox exporter being an open proxy[17] and would confuse the division of responsibilities between Prometheus and exporters.

The http probe is the most configurable of the Blackbox exporter's probes (the documentation (*http://bit.ly/2K9cm8l*) lists all of the options). While flexible, the Blackbox exporter cannot handle all possible use cases, as it is a relatively simple HTTP probe at the end of the day. If you need something more sophisticated, you may need to write your own exporter, or take advantage of existing exporters such as the Web-

---

15 Presuming you have a working IPv6 setup; if not, add preferred_ip_protocol: ip4.

16 Unless no_follow_redirects is configured.

17 Which would be unwise from a security standpoint.

Driver exporter (*https://github.com/mattbostock/webdriver_exporter*), which simulates a browser visiting a URL.

DNS

The dns probe is primarily for testing DNS servers. For example, checking that all of your DNS replicas are returning results.

If you wanted to test that your DNS servers were responding over TCP,[18] you could create a module in your *blackbox.yml* like this:

```
dns_tcp:
  prober: dns
  dns:
    transport_protocol: "tcp"
    query_name: "www.prometheus.io"
```

After restarting the Blackbox exporter, you can visit *http://localhost:9115/probe?module=dns_tcp&target=8.8.8.8* to check if Google's Public DNS service[19] works via TCP. Note that the target URL parameter is the DNS server that is talked to, and the query_name is the DNS request sent to the DNS server. This is the same as if you ran the command **dig -tcp @8.8.8.8 www.prometheus.io**.

For the dns prober, the target URL parameter is an IP address or hostname, followed by a colon, and then the port number. You can also provide just the IP address or hostname, in which case the standard DNS port of 53 will be used.

Aside from testing DNS servers, you could also use a dns probe to confirm that specific results are being returned by DNS resolution. But usually you want to go further and communicate to the returned service via HTTP, TCP, or ICMP, in which case one of those probes makes more sense as you get the DNS check for free.

An example of using the dns probe to check for specific results would be to check that your MX records[20] have not disappeared.

You could create a module in your *blackbox.yml* like this:

```
dns_mx_present_rp_io:
  prober: dns
  dns:
    query_name: "robustperception.io"
    query_type: "MX"
```

---

18 While DNS usually uses UDP, it can also use TCP in cases such as for large responses. Unfortunately, many site operators are not aware of this and block TCP on port 53, which is the DNS port.

19 Which is offered on the IPs 8.8.8.8, 8.8.4.4, 2001:4860:4860::8888, and 2001:4860:4860::8844.

20 Used for email, MX stands for Mail eXchanger.

```
validate_answer_rrs:
  fail_if_not_matches_regexp:
    - ".+"
```

After restarting the Blackbox exporter, you can visit *http://localhost:9115/probe?mod ule=dns_mx_present_rp_io&target=8.8.8.8* to check that robustperception.io has MX records. Note that as the query_name is specified per module, you will need a module for every domain that you want to check. I am using 8.8.8.8 here as Google's Public DNS is a public DNS resolver, but you could also use a local resolver.

The dns probe has more features intended to help check for aspects of DNS responses, such as authority and additional records, which you can find out more about in the documentation (*http://bit.ly/2JTOiqI*). For a better understanding of DNS I recommend RFCs 1034 (*https://www.ietf.org/rfc/rfc1034.txt*) and 1035 (*https://www.ietf.org/rfc/rfc1035.txt*),[21] or a book such as *DNS and BIND* by Paul Albitz and Cricket Liu (O'Reilly).

Prometheus Configuration

As you have seen, the Blackbox exporter takes a module and target URL parameter on the */probe* endpoint. Using the params and metrics_path as discussed in "How to Scrape" on page 146, you can provide these in a scrape config, but that would mean having a scrape config per target, which would be unwieldy as you could not take advantage of Prometheus's ability to do service discovery.

The good news is that you can take advantage of service discovery, as the __param_<name> label can be used to provide URL parameters in relabelling. In addition, the instance and __address__ labels are distinct as discussed in "job, instance, and __address__" on page 143, so you can have Prometheus talk to the Blackbox exporter while having an instance label of your actual target.

Example 10-9 shows an example of this in practice.

Example 10-9. prometheus.yml to check if several websites work

```
scrape_configs:
 - job_name: blackbox
   metrics_path: /probe
   params:
     module: [http_2xx]
   static_configs:
    - targets:
       - http://www.prometheus.io
       - http://www.robustperception.io
```

---

21 I learned DNS from these RFCs; they're a little outdated but still give a good sense of how DNS operates.

```
      - http://demo.robustperception.io
  relabel_configs:
  - source_labels: [__address__]
    target_label: __param_target
  - source_labels: [__param_target]
    target_label: instance
  - target_label: __address__
    replacement: 127.0.0.1:9115
```

To break it down:

```
- job_name: 'blackbox'
  metrics_path: /probe
  params:
    module: [http_2xx]
```

A default job label, custom path, and one URL parameter are specified:

```
static_configs:
  - targets:
    - http://www.prometheus.io
    - http://www.robustperception.io
    - http://demo.robustperception.io
```

There are three websites that you will be probing:

```
relabel_configs:
  - source_labels: [__address__]
    target_label: __param_target
  - source_labels: [__param_target]
    target_label: instance
  - target_label: __address__
    replacement: 127.0.0.1:9115
```

The relabel_configs is where the magic happens. First, the __address__ label becomes the target URL parameter and secondly also the instance label. At this point the instance label and target URL parameter have the value you want, but the __address__ is still a URL rather than the Blackbox exporter. The final relabelling action sets the __address__ to the host and port of the local Blackbox exporter.

If you run Prometheus with this configuration and look at the Target status page you will see something like Figure 10-2. The endpoint has the desired URL parameters, and the instance label is the URL.

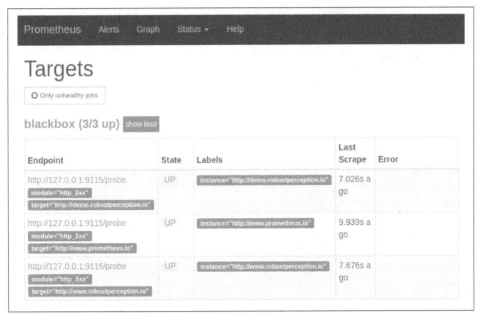

Figure 10-2. The Blackbox exporter's status page

That the State is UP for the Blackbox exporter does not mean that the probe was successful, merely that the Blackbox exporter was scraped successfully.[22] You need to check that probe_success is 1.

This approach is not limited to static_configs. You can use any other service discovery mechanism (as discussed in Chapter 8). For example, building on Example 8-17, which scraped the Node exporter for all nodes registered in Consul, Example 10-10 will check that SSH is responding for all nodes registered in Consul.

---

22 Indeed, in Figure 10-2 the probe of *http://www.prometheus.io* is failing, as my machine has a broken IPv6 setup.

Example 10-10. Checking SSH on all nodes registered in Consul

```
scrape_configs:
 - job_name: node
   metrics_path: /probe
   params:
     module: [ssh_banner]
   consul_sd_configs:
    - server: 'localhost:8500'
   relabel_configs:
    - source_labels: [__meta_consul_address]
      regex: '(.*)'
      replacement: '${1}:22'
      target_label: __param_target
    - source_labels: [__param_target]
      target_label: instance
    - target_label: __address__
      replacement: 127.0.0.1:9115
```

The power of this approach allows you to reuse service discovery for not just scraping of /metrics, but also to do blackbox monitoring of your applications.

Blackbox Timeouts

You may be wondering how to configure timeouts for your probes. The good news is that the Blackbox prober determines the timeout automatically based on the `scrape_timeout` in Prometheus.

Prometheus sends a HTTP header called `X-Prometheus-Scrape-Timeout-Seconds` with every scrape. The Blackbox exporter uses this for its timeouts, less a buffer.[23] The end result is that the Blackbox exporter will usually return with some metrics that will be useful in debugging in the event of the target being slow, rather than the scrape as a whole failing.

You can reduce the timeout further using the `timeout` field in *blackbox.yml*.

Now that you have an idea of the sorts of exporters you will run into, you're ready to learn how to pull metrics from your existing monitoring systems.

---

23 Specified by the `--timeout-offset` command-line flag.

Working with Other Monitoring Systems

In an ideal world all of your applications would be directly exposing Prometheus metrics, but this is unlikely to be the world you inhabit. You may have other monitoring systems already in use, and doing a big switchover one day to Prometheus is not practical.

The good news is that amongst the hundreds of exporters for Prometheus there are several that convert data from other monitoring systems into the Prometheus format. While your ideal end goal would be to move completely to Prometheus, exporters like the ones you'll learn about in this chapter are very helpful when you are still transitioning.

Other Monitoring Systems

Monitoring systems vary in how compatible they are with Prometheus; some require notable effort while others require close to none. For example, InfluxDB has a data model fairly similar to Prometheus, so you can have your application push the InfluxDB line protocol to the InfluxDB exporter (*http://bit.ly/2M5XpBb*), which can then be scraped by Prometheus.

Other systems like collectd do not have labels, but it is possible to automatically convert the metrics it outputs into an okay Prometheus metric with no additional configuration using the collectd exporter (*http://bit.ly/2MDIEq8*). As of version 5.7, collectd even includes this natively with the Write Prometheus plug-in (*http://bit.ly/2JPFy4I*).

But not all monitoring systems have data models that can be automatically converted into reasonable Prometheus metrics. Graphite does not traditionally support key-value labels,[1] and some configuration labels can be extracted from the dotted strings it uses using the Graphite exporter (*http://bit.ly/2M0Evvp*). StatsD has basically the same data model as Graphite; StatsD uses events rather than metrics so the StatsD exporter (*http://bit.ly/2t9v7i6*) aggregates the events into metrics, and can also extract labels.

In the Java/JVM space, JMX (Java Management eXtensions) is a standard often used for exposing metrics, but how it is used varies quite a bit from application to application. The JMX exporter (*http://bit.ly/2K3grrm*) has okay defaults, but given the lack of standardisation of the mBean structure, the only sane way to configure it is via regular expressions. The good news is that there are a variety of example configurations provided, and that the JMX exporter is intended to run as a Java agent so you don't have to manage a separate exporter process.

SNMP actually has a data model that is quite close to Prometheus's, and by using MIBs,[2] SNMP metrics can be automatically produced by the SNMP exporter (*http://bit.ly/2t8kiNe*). The bad news is twofold. First, MIBs from vendors are often not freely available, so you need to acquire the MIBs yourself and use the *generator* included with the SNMP exporter to convert the MIBs into a form the SNMP exporter can understand. Second, many vendors follow the letter of the SNMP specification but not the spirit so additional configuration and/or munging with PromQL is sometimes required. The SNMP exporter is a Blackbox/SNMP-style exporter as was discussed in "Blackbox" on page 177, so unlike almost all other exporters, you typically run one per Prometheus rather than one per application instance.

 SNMP is a very chatty network protocol. It is advisable to have SNMP exporters as close as you can on the network to the network devices they are monitoring to mitigate this. Furthermore, many SNMP devices can speak the SNMP protocol but not return metrics in anything resembling a reasonable timeframe. You may need to be judicious in what metrics you request and generous in your `scrape_interval`.

There are also exporters you can use to extract metrics from a variety of Software as a Service (SaaS) monitoring systems, including the CloudWatch exporter (*http://bit.ly/2t9AYEa*), NewRelic exporter (*http://bit.ly/2I3QyFJ*), and Pingdom exporter (*http://bit.ly/2MFOZkP*). One thing to watch with such exporters is that there may be rate limits and financial costs for using the APIs they access.

---

1 Though version 1.1.0 recently added *tags*, which are key-value labels.

2 Management Information Base, basically a schema for SNMP objects.

The NRPE exporter (*http://bit.ly/2yqJMKI*) is an SNMP/Blackbox-style exporter that allows you to run NRPE checks. NRPE stands for Nagios Remote Program Execution, a way to run Nagios checks on remote machines. While many existing checks in a Nagios-style monitoring setup can be replaced by metrics from the Node and other exporters, you may have some custom checks that are a bit harder to migrate. The NRPE exporter gives you a transition option here, allowing you to later convert these checks to another solution such as the textfile collector as discussed in "Textfile Collector" on page 122.

Integration with other monitoring systems isn't limited to running separate exporters; there are also integrations with popular instrumentation systems such as Dropwizard metrics.[3] The Java client (*http://bit.ly/2tmzNQK*) has an integration that can pull metrics from Dropwizard metrics using its reporting feature that will then appear alongside any direct instrumentation you have on /metrics.

 Dropwizard can also expose its metrics via JMX. If possible (i.e., you control the codebase) you should prefer using the Java client's Dropwizard integration over JMX, since going via JMX has higher overhead and requires more configuration.

InfluxDB

The InfluxDB exporter accepts the InfluxDB line protocol that was added in version 0.9.0 of InfluxDB. The protocol works over HTTP, so the same TCP port can be used both to accept writes and serve /metrics. To run the InfluxDB exporter you should follow the steps in Example 11-1.

Example 11-1. Downloading and running the InfluxDB exporter

```
hostname $ wget https://github.com/prometheus/influxdb_exporter/releases/download/
    v0.1.0/influxdb_exporter-0.1.0.linux-amd64.tar.gz
hostname $ tar -xzf influxdb_exporter-0.1.0.linux-amd64.tar.gz
hostname $ cd influxdb_exporter-0.1.0.linux-amd64/
hostname $ ./influxdb_exporter
INFO[0000] Starting influxdb_exporter (version=0.1.0, branch=HEAD,
    revision=4d30f926a4d82f9db52604b0e4d10396a2994360)  source="main.go:258"
INFO[0000] Build context (go=go1.8.3, user=root@906a0f6cc645,
    date=20170726-15:10:21)  source="main.go:259"
INFO[0000] Listening on :9122                          source="main.go:297"
```

---

3 Previously known as Yammer metrics.

You can then direct your existing applications that speak the InfluxDB line protocol to use the InfluxDB exporter. To send a metric by hand with labels you can do:

```
curl -XPOST 'http://localhost:9122/write' --data-binary \
    'example_metric,foo=bar value=43 1517339868000000000'
```

If you then visit *http://localhost:9122/metrics* in your browser, amongst the output you will see:

```
# HELP example_metric InfluxDB Metric
# TYPE example_metric untyped
example_metric{foo="bar"} 43
```

You may notice that the timestamp that you sent to the exporter is not exposed. There are very few valid use cases for /metrics to expose timestamps, as scrapes are meant to synchronously gather metrics representing the application state at scrape time. When working with other monitoring systems this is often not the case and using timestamps would be valid. At the time of writing only the Java client library supports timestamps for custom collectors. When metrics are exported without timestamps, Prometheus will use the time at which the scrape happens. The InfluxDB exporter will garbage collect the point after a few minutes and stop exposing it. These are the challenges you face when you convert from push to pull. On the other hand, converting from pull to push is quite simple, as seen in Example 4-13.

You can scrape the InfluxDB exporter like any other exporter, as shown in Example 11-2.

Example 11-2. prometheus.yml to scrape a local InfluxDB exporter

```
global:
  scrape_interval: 10s
scrape_configs:
 - job_name: application_name
   static_configs:
    - targets:
      - localhost:9122
```

StatsD

StatsD takes in events and aggregates them over time into metrics. You can think of sending an event to StatsD as being like calling inc on a counter or observe on a summary. The StatsD exporter does just that, converting your StatsD events into Prometheus client library metrics and instrumentation calls.

You can run the StatsD exporter by following the steps in Example 11-3.

Example 11-3. Downloading and running the StatsD exporter

```
hostname $ wget https://github.com/prometheus/statsd_exporter/releases/download/
    v0.6.0/statsd_exporter-0.6.0.linux-amd64.tar.gz
hostname $ tar -xzf statsd_exporter-0.6.0.linux-amd64.tar.gz
hostname $ cd statsd_exporter-0.6.0.linux-amd64/
hostname $ ./statsd_exporter
INFO[0000] Starting StatsD -> Prometheus Exporter (version=0.6.0, branch=HEAD,
    revision=3fd85c92fc0d91b3c77bcb1a8b2c7aa2e2a99d04)  source="main.go:149"
INFO[0000] Build context (go=go1.9.2, user=root@29b80e16fc07,
    date=20180117-17:45:48)  source="main.go:150"
INFO[0000] Accepting StatsD Traffic: UDP :9125, TCP :9125  source="main.go:151"
INFO[0000] Accepting Prometheus Requests on :9102          source="main.go:152"
```

As StatsD uses a custom TCP and UDP protocol, you need different ports for sending events than for scraping /metrics.

You can send a gauge by hand with:[4]

```
echo 'example_gauge:123|g' | nc localhost 9125
```

Which will appear on *http://localhost:9102/metrics* as:

```
# HELP example_gauge Metric autogenerated by statsd_exporter.
# TYPE example_gauge gauge
example_gauge 123
```

You can also send counter increments and summary/histogram observations:

```
echo 'example_counter_total:1|c' | nc localhost 9125
echo 'example_latency_total:20|ms' | nc localhost 9125
```

The StatsD protocol isn't fully specified; many implementations only support integer values. While the StatsD exporter does not have this limitation, note that many metrics will not be in the base units you are used to with Prometheus.

You can also extract labels, as StatsD is often used with the Graphite *dotted string* notation, where position indicates meaning. app.http.requests.eu-west-1./foo might, for example, mean what would be app_http_requests_total{region="eu-west-1",path="/foo"} in Prometheus. To be able to map from such a string you need to provide a mapping file in *mapping.yml*, such as:

```
mappings:
- match: app.http.requests.*.*
  name: app_http_requests_total
  labels:
    region: "${1}"
    path: "${2}"
```

---

4 nc is a handy networking utility whose full name is *netcat*. You may need to install it if you don't have it already.

and then run the StatsD exporter using it:

```
./statsd_exporter -statsd.mapping-config mapping.yml
```

If you now send requests following that pattern to the StatsD exporter, they will be appropriately named and labeled:

```
echo 'app.http.requests.eu-west-1./foo:1|c' | nc localhost 9125
echo 'app.http.requests.eu-west-1./bar:1|c' | nc localhost 9125
```

If you visit *http://localhost:9102/metrics* it will now contain:

```
# HELP app_http_requests_total Metric autogenerated by statsd_exporter.
# TYPE app_http_requests_total counter
app_http_requests_total{path="/bar",region="eu-west-1"} 1
app_http_requests_total{path="/foo",region="eu-west-1"} 1
```

The Graphite exporter has a similar mechanism to convert dotted strings into labels.

You may end up running the StatsD exporter even after you have completed your transition to Prometheus if you are using languages such as PHP and Perl for web applications. As mentioned in "Multiprocess with Gunicorn" on page 64, Prometheus presumes a multithreaded model with long-lived processes. You typically use languages like PHP in a way that is not only multiprocess, but also often with processes that only live for a single HTTP request. While an approach such as the Python client uses for multiprocess deployments is theoretically possible for typical PHP deployments, you may find that the StatsD exporter is more practical. There is also the prom-aggregation-gateway (*https://github.com/weaveworks/prom-aggregation-gateway*) in this space.

I would recommend that for exporters like the InfluxDB, Graphite, StatsD, and collectd exporters that convert from push to pull that you have one exporter per application instance and the same lifecycle as the application. You should start, stop, and restart the exporter at the same time as you start, stop, and restart the application instance. That way is easier to manage, avoids issues with labels changing, and keeps the exporter from becoming a bottleneck.[5]

While there are hundreds of exporters on offer, you may find yourself needing to write or extend one yourself. The next chapter will show you how to write exporters.

---

5 One of the reasons that Prometheus exists is due to scaling issues that SoundCloud had with many many applications sending to one StatsD.

Writing Exporters

Sometimes you will not be able to either add direct instrumentation to an application, nor find an existing exporter that covers it. This leaves you with having to write an exporter yourself. The good news is that exporters are relatively easy to write. The hard part is figuring out what the metrics exposed by applications mean. Units are often unknown, and documentation, if it exists at all, can be vague. In this chapter you will learn how to write exporters.

Consul Telemetry

I'm going to write a small exporter for Consul to demonstrate the process. While we already saw version 0.6.0 of the Consul exporter in "Consul" on page 169, that version is missing metrics from the newly added telemetry API.[1]

While you can write exporters in any programming language, the majority are written in Go, and that is the language I will use here. However, you will find a small number of exporters written in Python, and an even smaller number in Java.

If your Consul is not running, start it again following the instructions in Example 8-6. If you visit *http://localhost:8500/v1/agent/metrics* you will see the JSON output that you will be working with, which is similar to Example 12-1. Conveniently, Consul provides a Go library that you can use, so you don't have to worry about parsing the JSON yourself.

---

[1] These metrics will likely be in the 0.7.0 version of the Consul exporter.

Example 12-1. An abbreviated example output from a Consul agent's metrics output

```json
{
  "Timestamp": "2018-01-31 14:42:10 +0000 UTC",
  "Gauges": [
    {
      "Name": "consul.autopilot.failure_tolerance",
      "Value": 0,
      "Labels": {}
    }
  ],
  "Points": [],
  "Counters": [
    {
      "Name": "consul.raft.apply",
      "Count": 1,
      "Sum": 1, "Min": 1, "Max": 1, "Mean": 1, "Stddev": 0,
      "Labels": {}
    }
  ],
  "Samples": [
    {
      "Name": "consul.fsm.coordinate.batch-update",
      "Count": 1,
      "Sum": 0.13156799972057343,
      "Min": 0.13156799972057343, "Max": 0.13156799972057343,
      "Mean": 0.13156799972057343, "Stddev": 0,
      "Labels": {}
    }
  ]
}
```

You are in luck that Consul has split out the counters and gauges for you.[2] The Samples also look like you can use the Count and Sum in a summary metric. Looking at all the Samples again, I have a suspicion that they are tracking latency. Digging through the documentation (*https://www.consul.io/docs/agent/telemetry.html*) confirms that they are *timers*, which means a Prometheus Summary (see "The Summary" on page 48). The timers are also all in milliseconds, so we can convert them to seconds.[3] While the JSON has a field for labels, none are used, so you can ignore that. Aside from that, the only other thing you need to do is ensure any invalid characters in the metric names are sanitised.

---

2 Just because something is called a counter does not mean it is a counter. For example, Dropwizard has counters that can go down, so depending on how the counter is used in practice it may be a counter, gauge, or untyped in Prometheus terms.

3 If only some of the Samples were timers, you would have to choose between exposing them as-is or maintaining a list of which metrics are latencies and which weren't.

You now know the logic you need to apply to the metrics that Consul exposes, so you can write your exporter as in Example 12-2.

Example 12-2. consul_metrics.go, an exporter for Consul metrics written in Go

```go
package main

import (
  "log"
  "net/http"
  "regexp"

  "github.com/hashicorp/consul/api"
  "github.com/prometheus/client_golang/prometheus"
  "github.com/prometheus/client_golang/prometheus/promhttp"
)

var (
  up = prometheus.NewDesc(
    "consul_up",
    "Was talking to Consul successful.",
    nil, nil,
  )
  invalidChars = regexp.MustCompile("[^a-zA-Z0-9:_]")
)

type ConsulCollector struct {
}

// Implements prometheus.Collector.
func (c ConsulCollector) Describe(ch chan<- *prometheus.Desc) {
  ch <- up
}

// Implements prometheus.Collector.
func (c ConsulCollector) Collect(ch chan<- prometheus.Metric) {
  consul, err := api.NewClient(api.DefaultConfig())
  if err != nil {
    ch <- prometheus.MustNewConstMetric(up, prometheus.GaugeValue, 0)
    return
  }

  metrics, err := consul.Agent().Metrics()
  if err != nil {
    ch <- prometheus.MustNewConstMetric(up, prometheus.GaugeValue, 0)
    return
  }
  ch <- prometheus.MustNewConstMetric(up, prometheus.GaugeValue, 1)

  for _, g := range metrics.Gauges {
    name := invalidChars.ReplaceAllLiteralString(g.Name, "_")
```

```
    desc := prometheus.NewDesc(name, "Consul metric "+g.Name, nil, nil)
    ch <- prometheus.MustNewConstMetric(
        desc, prometheus.GaugeValue, float64(g.Value))
  }

  for _, c := range metrics.Counters {
    name := invalidChars.ReplaceAllLiteralString(c.Name, "_")
    desc := prometheus.NewDesc(name+"_total", "Consul metric "+c.Name, nil, nil)
    ch <- prometheus.MustNewConstMetric(
        desc, prometheus.CounterValue, float64(c.Count))
  }

  for _, s := range metrics.Samples {
    // All samples are times in milliseconds, we convert them to seconds below.
    name := invalidChars.ReplaceAllLiteralString(s.Name, "_") + "_seconds"
    countDesc := prometheus.NewDesc(
        name+"_count", "Consul metric "+s.Name, nil, nil)
    ch <- prometheus.MustNewConstMetric(
        countDesc, prometheus.CounterValue, float64(s.Count))
    sumDesc := prometheus.NewDesc(
        name+"_sum", "Consul metric "+s.Name, nil, nil)
    ch <- prometheus.MustNewConstMetric(
        sumDesc, prometheus.CounterValue, s.Sum/1000)
  }
}

func main() {
  c := ConsulCollector{}
  prometheus.MustRegister(c)
  http.Handle("/metrics", promhttp.Handler())
  log.Fatal(http.ListenAndServe(":8000", nil))
}
```

If you have a working Go development environment you can run the exporter with:

```
go get -d -u github.com/hashicorp/consul/api
go get -d -u github.com/prometheus/client_golang/prometheus
go run consul_metrics.go
```

If you visit *http://localhost:8000/metrics* you will see metrics like:

```
# HELP consul_autopilot_failure_tolerance Consul metric
    consul.autopilot.failure_tolerance
# TYPE consul_autopilot_failure_tolerance gauge
consul_autopilot_failure_tolerance 0
# HELP consul_raft_apply_total Consul metric consul.raft.apply
# TYPE consul_raft_apply_total counter
consul_raft_apply_total 1
# HELP consul_fsm_coordinate_batch_update_seconds_count Consul metric
    consul.fsm.coordinate.batch-update
# TYPE consul_fsm_coordinate_batch_update_seconds_count counter
consul_fsm_coordinate_batch_update_seconds_count 1
# HELP consul_fsm_coordinate_batch_update_seconds_sum Consul metric
```

```
  consul.fsm.coordinate.batch-update
# TYPE consul_fsm_coordinate_batch_update_seconds_sum counter
consul_fsm_coordinate_batch_update_seconds_sum 1.31567999720057343e-01
```

That's all well and good, but how does the code work? In the next section I'll show you how.

Custom Collectors

With direct instrumentation the client library takes in instrumentation events and tracks the values of the metrics over time. Client libraries provide the counter, gauge, summary, and histogram metrics for this, which are all examples of *collectors*. At scrape time each collector in a registry is *collected*, which is to say, asked for its metrics. These metrics will then be returned by the scrape of /metrics. Counters and the other three standard metric types only ever return one metric family.

If rather than using direct instrumentation you want to provide from some other source, you use a *custom collector*, which is any collector that is not one of the standard four. Custom collectors can return any number of metric families. Collection happens on every single scrape of a /metrics, where each collection is a consistent snapshot of the metrics from a collector.

In Go your collectors must implement the prometheus.Collector interface. That is to say the collectors must be objects with Describe and Collect methods with a specific signature.

The Describe method returns a description of the metrics it will produce, in particular the metric name, label names, and help string. The Describe method is called at registration time, and is used to avoid duplicate metric registration. There are two types of metrics an exporter can have, ones where it knows the names and labels in advance, and ones where they are only determined at scrape time. In this example, consul_up is known in advance so you can create its Desc once with NewDesc and provide it via Describe. All the other metrics are generated dynamically at scrape time, so cannot be included:

```go
var (
  up = prometheus.NewDesc(
    "consul_up",
    "Was talking to Consul successful.",
    nil, nil,
  )
)
// Implements prometheus.Collector.
func (c ConsulCollector) Describe(ch chan<- *prometheus.Desc) {
  ch <- up
}
```

The Go client requires that at least one `Desc` is provided by `Describe`. If all your metrics are dynamic, you can provide a dummy `Desc` to work around this.

At the core of a custom collector is the `Collect` method. In this method you fetch all the data you need from the application instance you are working with, munge it as needed, and then send the metrics back to the client library. Here you need to connect to Consul and then fetch its metrics. If an error occurs, `consul_up` is returned as 0; otherwise, once we know that the collection is going to be successful, it is returned as 1. Only returning a metric sometimes is difficult[4] to deal with in PromQL; having `consul_up` allows you to alert on issues talking to Consul so you'll know that something is awry.

To return `consul_up`, `prometheus.MustNewConstMetric` is used to provide a sample for just this scrape. It takes its `Desc`, type, and value:

```
// Implements prometheus.Collector.
func (c ConsulCollector) Collect(ch chan<- prometheus.Metric) {
  consul, err := api.NewClient(api.DefaultConfig())
  if err != nil {
    ch <- prometheus.MustNewConstMetric(up, prometheus.GaugeValue, 0)
    return
  }

  metrics, err := consul.Agent().Metrics()
  if err != nil {
    ch <- prometheus.MustNewConstMetric(up, prometheus.GaugeValue, 0)
    return
  }
  ch <- prometheus.MustNewConstMetric(up, prometheus.GaugeValue, 1)
```

There are three possible values: `GaugeValue`, `CounterValue`, and `UntypedValue`. Gauge and Counter you already know, and Untyped is for cases where you are not sure whether a metric is a counter or a gauge. This is not possible with direct instrumentation, but it is not unusual for the type of metrics from other monitoring and instrumentation systems to be unclear and impractical to determine.

Now that you have the metrics from Consul, you can process the gauges. Invalid characters in the metric name, such as dots and hyphens, are converted to underscores. A `Desc` is created on the fly, and immediately used in a `MustNewConstMetric`:

---

4 See "or operator" on page 251.

```
for _, g := range metrics.Gauges {
  name := invalidChars.ReplaceAllLiteralString(g.Name, "_")
  desc := prometheus.NewDesc(name, "Consul metric "+g.Name, nil, nil)
  ch <- prometheus.MustNewConstMetric(
      desc, prometheus.GaugeValue, float64(g.Value))
}
```

Processing of counters is similar, except that a _total suffix is added to the metric name:

```
for _, c := range metrics.Counters {
  name := invalidChars.ReplaceAllLiteralString(c.Name, "_")
  desc := prometheus.NewDesc(name+"_total", "Consul metric "+c.Name, nil, nil)
  ch <- prometheus.MustNewConstMetric(
      desc, prometheus.CounterValue, float64(s.Count))
}
```

The contents of metrics.Samples are more complicated. While the samples are a Prometheus summary, the Go client does not currently support those for MustNew ConstMetric. Instead, you can emulate it using two counters. _seconds is appended to the metric name, and the sum is divided by a thousand to convert from milliseconds to seconds:

```
for _, s := range metrics.Samples {
  // All samples are times in milliseconds, we convert them to seconds below.
  name := invalidChars.ReplaceAllLiteralString(s.Name, "_") + "_seconds"
  countDesc := prometheus.NewDesc(
      name+"_count", "Consul metric "+s.Name, nil, nil)
  ch <- prometheus.MustNewConstMetric(
      countDesc, prometheus.CounterValue, float64(s.Count))
  sumDesc := prometheus.NewDesc(
      name+"_sum", "Consul metric "+s.Name, nil, nil)
  ch <- prometheus.MustNewConstMetric(
      sumDesc, prometheus.CounterValue, s.Sum/1000)
}
```

 s.Sum here is a float64, but you must be careful when doing division with integers to ensure you don't unnecessarily lose precision. If sum were an integer, float64(sum)/1000 would convert to floating point first and then divide, which is what you want. On the other hand, float64(sum/1000) will first divide the integer value by 1000, losing three digits of precision.

Finally, the custom collector object is instantiated and registered with the default registry, in the same way you would one of the direct instrumentation metrics:

```
c := ConsulCollector{}
prometheus.MustRegister(c)
```

Exposition is performed in the usual way, which you already saw in "Go" on page 67:

```
http.Handle("/metrics", promhttp.Handler())
log.Fatal(http.ListenAndServe(":8000", nil))
```

This is, of course, a simplified example. In reality you would have some way to configure the Consul server to talk to, such as a command-line flag, rather than depending on the client's default. You would also reuse the client between scrapes, and allow the various authentication options of the client to be specified.

 The min, max, mean, and stddev were discarded as they are not very useful. You can calculate a mean using the sum and count. min, max, and stddev, on the other hand, are not aggregatable and you don't know over what time period they were measured.

As the default registry is being used, go_ and process_ metrics are included in the result. These provide you with information about the performance of the exporter itself, and are useful to detect issues such as file descriptor leaks using the process_open_fds. This saves you from having to scrape the exporter separately for these metrics.

The only time you might not use the default registry for an exporter is when writing a Blackbox/SNMP style exporter, where some interpretation of URL parameters needs to be performed as collectors have no access to URL parameters for a scrape. In that case, you would also scrape the /metrics of the exporter in order to monitor the exporter itself.

For comparison, the equivalent exporter written using Python 3 is shown in Example 12-3. This is largely the same as the one written in Go, the only notable difference is that a SummaryMetricFamily is available to represent a summary, instead of emulating it with two separate counters. The Python client does not have as many sanity checks as the Go client, so you need to be a little more careful with it.

Example 12-3. consul_metrics.py, an exporter for Consul metrics written in Python 3

```
import json
import re
import time
from urllib.request import urlopen

from prometheus_client.core import GaugeMetricFamily, CounterMetricFamily
from prometheus_client.core import SummaryMetricFamily, REGISTRY
from prometheus_client import start_http_server


def sanitise_name(s):
    return re.sub(r"[^a-zA-Z0-9:_]", "_", s)
```

```
class ConsulCollector(object):
  def collect(self):
    out = urlopen("http://localhost:8500/v1/agent/metrics").read()
    metrics = json.loads(out.decode("utf-8"))

    for g in metrics["Gauges"]:
      yield GaugeMetricFamily(sanitise_name(g["Name"]),
          "Consul metric " + g["Name"], g["Value"])

    for c in metrics["Counters"]:
      yield CounterMetricFamily(sanitise_name(c["Name"]) + "_total",
          "Consul metric " + c["Name"], c["Count"])

    for s in metrics["Samples"]:
      yield SummaryMetricFamily(sanitise_name(s["Name"]) + "_seconds",
          "Consul metric " + s["Name"],
          count_value=c["Count"], sum_value=s["Sum"] / 1000)

if __name__ == '__main__':
  REGISTRY.register(ConsulCollector())
  start_http_server(8000)
  while True:
    time.sleep(1)
```

Labels

In the preceding example you only saw metrics without labels. To provide labels you need to specify the label names in Desc and then the values in MustNewConstMetric.

To expose a metric with the time series example_gauge{foo="bar", baz="small"} and example_gauge{foo="quu", baz="far"} you could do:

```
func (c MyCollector) Collect(ch chan<- prometheus.Metric) {
  desc := prometheus.NewDesc(
    "example_gauge",
    "A help string.",
    []string{"foo", "baz"}, nil,
  )
  ch <- prometheus.MustNewConstMetric(
    desc, prometheus.GaugeValue, 1, "bar", "small")
  ch <- prometheus.MustNewConstMetric(
    desc, prometheus.GaugeValue, 2, "quu", "far")
}
```

with the Go Prometheus client library. First, you can provide each time series individually. The registry will take care of combining all the time series belonging to the same metric family together in the /metrics output.

The help strings of all metrics with the same name must be identical. Providing differing Descs will cause the scrape to fail.

The Python client works a little differently; you assemble the metric family and then return it. While that may sound like more effort, it usually works out to be the same level of effort in practice:

```
class MyCollector(object):
  def collect(self):
    mf = GaugeMetricFamily("example_gauge", "A help string.",
        labels=["foo", "baz"])
    mf.add_metric(["bar", "small"], 1)
    mf.add_metric(["quu", "far"], 2)
    yield mf
```

Guidelines

While direct instrumentation tends to be reasonably black and white, writing exporters tends to be murky and involve engineering tradeoffs. Do you want to spend a lot of ongoing effort to produce perfect metrics, or do something that's good enough and requires no maintenance? Writing exporters is more of an art than a science.

You should try to follow the metric naming practices, in particular, avoiding the _count, _sum, _total, _bucket, and _info suffixes unless the time series is part of a metric that is meant to contain such a time series.

It is often not possible or practical to determine whether a bunch of metrics are gauges, counters, or a mix of the two. In cases where there is a mix you should mark them as *untyped* rather than using gauge or counter, which would be incorrect. If a metric is a counter, don't forget to add the _total suffix.

Where practical you should try to provide units for your metrics, and at the very least try to ensure that the units are in the metric name. Having to determine what the units are from metrics as in Example 12-1 is not fun for anyone, so you should try to remove this burden from the users of your exporter. Seconds and bytes are always preferred.

In terms of using labels in exporters there are a few gotchas to look out for. As with direct instrumentation, cardinality is also a concern for exporters for the same reasons that were discussed in "Cardinality" on page 93. Metrics with high churn in their labels should be avoided.

Labels should create a partition across a metric, and if you take a sum or average across a metric it should be meaningful, as discussed in "When to Use Labels" on page 92. In particular, you should look out for any time series that are just totals of all the other values in a metric, and remove them. If you are ever unsure as to whether a label makes sense when writing an exporter then it is safest not to use one, though keep in mind "Table Exception" on page 93. As with direct instrumentation, you should not apply a label such as `env="prod"` to all metrics coming from your exporter, as that is what target labels are for, as discussed in "Target Labels" on page 139.

It is best to expose raw metrics to Prometheus, rather than doing calculations on the application side. For example, there is no need to expose a 5-minute rate when you have a counter, as you can use the `rate` function to calculate a rate over any period you like. Similarly with ratios, drop them in favour of the numerator and denominator. If you have a percentage without its constituent numerator and denominator, at the least convert it to a ratio.[5]

Beyond multiplication and division to standardise units, you should avoid math in exporters, as processing raw data in PromQL is preferred. Race conditions between metrics instrumentation events can lead to artifacts, particularly when you subtract one metric from another. Addition of metrics for the purposes of reducing cardinality can be okay, but if they're counters, make sure there will not be spurious resets due to some of them disappearing.

Some metrics are not particularly useful given how Prometheus is intended to be used. Many applications expose metrics such as machine RAM, CPU, and disk. You should not expose machine-level metrics in your exporter, as that is the responsibility of the Node exporter.[6] Minimums, maximums, and standard deviations cannot be sanely aggregated so should also be dropped.

You should plan on running one exporter per application instance,[7] and fetch metrics synchronously for each scrape without any caching. This keeps the responsibilities of service discovery and scrape scheduling with Prometheus. Note that you should be aware that concurrent scrapes can happen.

Just as Prometheus adds a `scrape_duration_seconds` metric when performing a scrape, you may also add a `myexporter_scrape_duration_seconds` metric for how long it takes your exporter to pull the data from its application. This helps in performance debugging, as you can see if it's the application or your exporter that is getting slow. Additional metrics such as the number of metrics processed can also be helpful.

---

5 And check that it is actually a ratio/percentage; it's not unknown for metrics to confuse the two.

6 Or WMI exporter for Windows users.

7 Unless writing a Blackbox/SNMP-style exporter, which is rare.

It can make sense for you to add direct instrumentation to exporters, in addition to the custom collectors that provide their core functionality. For example, the Cloud-Watch exporter has a `cloudwatch_requests_total` counter tracking the number of API calls it makes, as each API call costs money. But this is usually only something that you will see with Blackbox/SNMP-style exporters.

Now that you know how to get metrics out of both your applications and third-party code, in the next chapter I'll start covering PromQL, which allows you to work with these metrics.

PromQL

The Prometheus Query Language offers you the ability to do all sorts of aggregations, analysis, and arithmetic, allowing you to better understand the performance of your systems from your metrics.

In this part you will be reusing the Prometheus and Node exporter setup you created in Chapter 2, and using the expression browser to execute queries.

Chapter 13 covers the basics of PromQL, and how you can use the HTTP API to evaluate expressions.

Chapter 14 looks in depth into how aggregation works.

Chapter 15 covers operators such as addition and comparisons, and how you can join different metrics together.

Chapter 16 goes into the wide variety of functions that PromQL offers you, from knowing the time of day to predicting when your hard disk will fill up.

PromQL rules. Chapter 17 covers the recording rule feature of Prometheus, which allows you to precompute metrics for faster and more sophisticated querying with PromQL.

Introduction to PromQL

PromQL is the Prometheus Query Language. While it ends in *QL*, you will find that it is not an SQL-like language, as SQL languages tend to lack expressive power when it comes to the sort of calculations you would like to perform on time series.

Labels are a key part of PromQL, and you can use them not only to do arbitrary aggregations but also to join different metrics together for arithmetic operations against them. There are a wide variety of functions available to you from prediction to date and math functions.

This chapter will introduce you to the basic concepts of PromQL, including aggregation, basic types, and the HTTP API.

Aggregation Basics

Let's get started with some simple aggregation queries. These queries will likely cover most of your potential uses for PromQL. While PromQL is as powerful as it is possible to be,[1] most of the time your needs will be reasonably simple.

Gauge

Gauges are a snapshot of state, and usually when aggregating them you want to take a sum, average, minimum, or maximum.

---

[1] I have demonstrated PromQL to be Turing Complete in two (*https://youtu.be/lrfTpnzq3Kw*) different (*https://youtu.be/dyDmNd3qg_Q*) ways. Don't try this in production.

Consider the metric `node_filesystem_size_bytes` from your Node exporter, which reports the size of each of your mounted filesystems, and has `device`, `fstype`, and `mountpoint` labels. You can calculate total filesystem size on each machine with:

```
sum without(device, fstype, mountpoint)(node_filesystem_size_bytes)
```

This works as `without` tells the `sum` aggregator to sum everything up with the same labels, ignoring those three. So if you had the time series:

```
node_filesystem_free_bytes{device="/dev/sda1",fstype="vfat",
    instance="localhost:9100",job="node",mountpoint="/boot/efi"} 70300672
node_filesystem_free_bytes{device="/dev/sda5",fstype="ext4",
    instance="localhost:9100",job="node",mountpoint="/"} 30791843840
node_filesystem_free_bytes{device="tmpfs",fstype="tmpfs",
    instance="localhost:9100",job="node",mountpoint="/run"} 817094656
node_filesystem_free_bytes{device="tmpfs",fstype="tmpfs",
    instance="localhost:9100",job="node",mountpoint="/run/lock"} 5238784
node_filesystem_free_bytes{device="tmpfs",fstype="tmpfs",
    instance="localhost:9100",job="node",mountpoint="/run/user/1000"} 826912768
```

The result would be:

```
{instance="localhost:9100",job="node"} 32511390720
```

You will notice that the `device`, `fstype`, and `mountpoint` labels are now gone. The metric name is also no longer present, as this is no longer `node_filesys tem_free_bytes` as math has been performed on it. Since there is only one Node exporter being scraped by Prometheus there is only one result, but if you were scraping more then you would have a result for each of the Node exporters.

You could go a step further and remove the `instance` label with:

```
sum without(device, fstype, mountpoint, instance)(node_filesystem_size_bytes)
```

This as expected removes the `instance` label, but the value remains the same as the previous expression as there is only one Node exporter to aggregate metrics from:

```
{job="node"} 32511390720
```

You can use the same approach with other aggregations. `max` would tell you the size of the biggest mounted filesystem on each machine:

```
max without(device, fstype, mountpoint)(node_filesystem_size_bytes)
```

The outputted labels are exactly the same as when you aggregated using `sum`:

```
{instance="localhost:9100",job="node"} 30792601600
```

This predictability in what labels are returned is important for vector matching with operators, as will be discussed in Chapter 15.

You are not limited to aggregating metrics about one type of job. For example, to find the average number of file descriptors open across all your jobs you could use:

```
avg without(instance, job)(process_open_fds)
```

Counter

Counters track the number or size of events, and the value your applications expose on their /metrics is the total since it started. But that total is of little use to you on its own, what you really want to know is how quickly the counter is increasing over time. This is usually done using the `rate` function, though the `increase` and `irate` functions also operate on counter values.

For example, to calculate the amount of network traffic received per second you could use:

```
rate(node_network_receive_bytes_total[5m])
```

The [5m] says to provide `rate` with 5 minutes of data, so the returned value will be an average over the last 5 minutes:

```
{device="lo",instance="localhost:9100",job="node"}  1859.389655172414
{device="wlan0",instance="localhost:9100",job="node"} 1314.5034482758622
```

The values here are not integers, as the 5-minute window `rate` is looking at does not perfectly align with the samples that Prometheus has scraped. Some estimation is used to fill in the gaps between the data points you have and the boundaries of the range.

The output of `rate` is a gauge, so the same aggregations apply as for gauges. The `node_network_receive_bytes_total` metric has a `device` label, so if you aggregate it away you will get the total bytes received per machine per second:

```
sum without(device)(rate(node_network_receive_bytes_total[5m]))
```

Running this query will give you a result like:

```
{instance="localhost:9100",job="node"} 3173.8931034482762
```

You can filter down which time series to request, so you could only look at `eth0` and then aggregate it across all machines by aggregating away the `instance` label:

```
sum without(instance)(rate(node_network_receive_bytes_total{device="eth0"}[5m]))
```

When you run this query the `instance` label is gone, but the `device` label remains as you did not ask for it to be removed:

```
{device="eth0",job="node"} 3173.8931034482762
```

There is no ordering or hierarchy within labels, allowing you to aggregate by as many or as few labels as you like.

Summary

A summary metric will usually contain both a _sum and _count, and sometimes a time series with no suffix with a `quantile` label. The _sum and _count are both counters.

Your Prometheus exposes a `http_response_size_bytes` summary, for the amount of data some of its HTTP APIs return.[2] `http_response_size_bytes_count` tracks the number of requests, and as it is a counter you must use `rate` before aggregating away its `handler` label:

```
sum without(handler)(rate(http_response_size_bytes_count[5m]))
```

This gives you the total per-second HTTP request rate, and as the Node exporter also returns this metric you will see both jobs in the result:

```
{instance="localhost:9090",job="prometheus"} 0.26868836781609196
{instance="localhost:9100",job="node"} 0.1
```

Similarly, `http_response_size_bytes_sum` is a counter with the number of bytes each handle has returned, so the same pattern applies:

```
sum without(handler)(rate(http_response_size_bytes_sum[5m]))
```

This will return results with the same labels as the previous query, but the values are larger as responses tend to return many bytes:

```
{instance="localhost:9090",job="prometheus"} 796.0015958275862
{instance="localhost:9100",job="node"} 1581.6103448275862
```

The power of a summary is that it allows you to calculate the average size of an event, in this case the average amount of bytes that are being returned in each response. If you had three responses of size 1, 4, and 7, then the average would be their sum divided by their count, which is to say 12 divided by 3. The same applies to the summary. You divide the _sum by the _count (after taking a `rate`) to get an average over a time period:

```
  sum without(handler)(rate(http_response_size_bytes_sum[5m]))
/
  sum without(handler)(rate(http_response_size_bytes_count[5m]))
```

The division operator matches the time series with the same labels and divides, giving you the same two time series out but with the average response size over the past 5 minutes as a value:

```
{instance="localhost:9090",job="prometheus"} 2962.54580091246150133317
{instance="localhost:9100",job="node"} 15816.10344827586200000000
```

---

2 In Prometheus 2.3.0 this was renamed to `prometheus_http_response_size_bytes_count`.

When calculating an average, it is important that you first aggregate up the sum and count, and only as the last step perform the division. Otherwise, you could end up averaging averages, which is not statistically valid.

For example, if you wanted to get the average response size across all instances of a job, you could do:[3]

```
sum without(instance)(
  sum without(handler)(rate(http_response_size_bytes_sum[5m]))
)
/
  sum without(instance)(
  sum without(handler)(rate(http_response_size_bytes_count[5m]))
)
```

However, it'd be incorrect to do:

```
avg without(instance)(
  sum without(handler)(rate(http_response_size_bytes_sum[5m]))
  /
  sum without(handler)(rate(http_response_size_bytes_count[5m]))
)
```

It is incorrect to average an average, and both the division and avg would be calculating averages.

> It is not possible for you to aggregate the quantiles of a summary (the time series with the quantile label) from a statistical standpoint.

Histogram

Histogram metrics allow you to track the distribution of the size of events, allowing you to calculate quantiles from them. For example, you can use histograms to calculate the 0.9 quantile (which is also known as the 90th percentile) latency.

Prometheus 2.2.1 exposes a histogram metric called prometheus_tsdb_compaction_duration_seconds that tracks how many seconds compaction takes for the time series database. This histogram metric has time series with a _bucket suffix called prometheus_tsdb_compaction_duration_seconds_bucket. Each bucket has a le label, which is a counter of how many events have a size less than or equal to the bucket boundary. This is an implementation detail you largely need not worry about

---

3 This can of course be more simply calculated as sum without(instance, handler)(…), but with recording rules covered in Chapter 17, such an expression could end up split into several expressions.

as the `histogram_quantile` function takes care of this when calculating quantiles. For example, the 0.90 quantile would be:

```
histogram_quantile(
    0.90,
    rate(prometheus_tsdb_compaction_duration_seconds_bucket[1d]))
```

As `prometheus_tsdb_compaction_duration_seconds_bucket` is a counter you must first take a `rate`. Compaction usually only happens every two hours, so a one-day time range is used here so you will see a result in the expression browser such as:

```
{instance="localhost:9090",job="prometheus"} 7.720000000000001
```

This indicates that the 90th percentile latency of compactions is around 7.72 seconds. As there will usually only be 12 compactions in a day, the 90th percentile says that 10% of compactions take longer than this, which is to say one or two compactions. This is something to be aware of when using quantiles. For example, if you want to calculate a 0.999 quantile you should have several thousand data points to work with in order to produce a reasonably accurate answer. If you have fewer than that, single outliers could greatly affect the result, and you should consider using lower quantiles to avoid making statements about your system that you have insufficient data to back up.

 Usually you would use a 5- or 10-minute `rate` with histograms. All the bucket time series combined with any labels, and a long range on the `rate`, can make for a lot of samples that need to be processed. Be wary of PromQL expressions using ranges that are hours or days, as they can be relatively expensive to calculate.[4]

Similar to when taking averages, using `histogram_quantile` should be the last step in a query expression. Quantiles cannot be aggregated, or have arithmetic performed upon them, from a statistical standpoint. Accordingly, when you want to take a histogram of an aggregate, first aggregate up with `sum` and then use `histogram_quantile`:

```
histogram_quantile(
    0.90,
    sum without(instance)(rate(prometheus_tsdb_compaction_duration_bucket[1d])))
```

This calculates the 0.9 quantile compaction duration across all of your Prometheus servers, and will produce a result without an `instance` label:

```
{job="prometheus"} 7.720000000000001
```

---

4 The day-long range is only being used here due to the limited number of histograms that Prometheus and the Node exporter offer for me to use as examples.

Histogram metrics also include _sum and _count metrics, which work exactly the same as for the summary metric. You can use these to calculate average event sizes, such as the average compaction duration:

```
  sum without(instance)(rate(prometheus_tsdb_compaction_duration_sum[1d]))
/
  sum without(instance)(rate(prometheus_tsdb_compaction_duration_count[1d]))
```

This would produce a result like:

```
{job="prometheus"} 3.1766430400714287
```

Selectors

Working with all the different time series with different label values for a metric can be a bit overwhelming, and potentially confusing if a metric is coming from multiple different types of server.[5] Usually you will want to narrow down which time series you are working on. You almost always will want to limit by job label, and depending on what you are up to, you might want to only look at one instance or one handler, for example.

This limiting by labels is done using *selectors*. You have seen selectors in every example thus far, and now I'm going to explain them to you in detail. For example:

```
process_resident_memory_bytes{job="node"}
```

is a selector that will return all time series with the name process_resident_memory_bytes and a job label of node. This particular selector is most properly called a instant vector selector as it returns the values of the given time series at a given instant. *Vector* here basically means a one-dimensional list, as a selector can return zero or more time series, and each time series will have one sample.

The job="node" is called a *matcher*, and you can have many matchers in one selector that are ANDed together.

Matchers

There are four matchers (you have already seen the *equality matcher* which is also the most commonly used).

=

= is the *equality matcher*; for example, job="node". With this you can specify that the returned time series has a label name with exactly the given label value. As an

---

5 Such as process_cpu_seconds_total, which most exporters and client libraries will expose.

empty label, value is the same as not having that label, you could use `foo=""` to specify that the `foo` label not be present.

`!=`

    `!=` is the *negative equality matcher*; for example, `job!="node"`. With this you can specify that the returned time series do not have a label name with exactly the given label value.

`=~`

    `=~` is the *regular expression matcher*; for example, `job=~"n.*"`. With this you specify that for the returned time series the given label's value will be matched by the regular expression. The regular expression is fully anchored, which is to say that the regular expression a will only match the string a, and not xa or ax. You can prepend or suffix your regular expression with `.*` if you do not want this behaviour.[6] As with relabelling, the RE2 regular expression engine is used, as covered in "Regular Expressions" on page 138.

`!~`

    `!~` is the *negative regular expression matcher*. RE2 does not support negative lookahead expressions, so this provides you with an alternative way to exclude label values based on a regular expression.

You can have multiple matchers with the same label name in a selector, which can be a substitute for negative lookahead expressions. For example, to find the size of all filesystems mounted under `/run` but not `/run/user`, you could use:[7]

```
node_filesystem_size_bytes{job="node",mountpoint=~"/run/.*",
    mountpoint!~"/run/user/.*"}
```

Internally the metric name is stored in a label called `__name__` (as discussed in "Reserved Labels and `__name__`" on page 84), so `process_resident_mem ory_bytes{job="node"}` is syntactic sugar for `{__name__="process_resident_mem ory_bytes",job="node"}`. You can even do regular expressions on the metric name, but this is unwise outside of when you are debugging the performance of the Prometheus server.

---

6 It works this way to avoid accidentally overmatching. This way you usually get immediate feedback if your regular expression is under matching, while an unanchored expression might cause subtle issues down the line.

7 The Node exporter has a `--collector.filesystem.ignored-mount-points` flag you could use if you didn't want these filesystems exported in the first place.

Having to use regular expression matchers is a little bit of a smell. If you find yourself using them a lot on a given label, consider if you should instead combine the matched label values into one. For example, for HTTP status codes instead of doing `code~="4.."` to catch 401s, 404s, 405s, etc., you might instead combine them into a label value 4xx and use the equality matcher `code="4xx"`.

The selector `{}` returns an error, which is a safety measure to avoid accidentally returning all the time series inside the Prometheus server as that could be expensive. To be more precise, at least one of the matchers in a selector must not match the empty string. So `{foo=""}`, `{foo!=""}`, and `{foo=~".*"}` will return an error, while `{foo="",bar="x"}` or `{foo=~".+"}` are permitted.[8]

Instant Vector

An instant vector selector returns an `instant vector` of the most recent samples before the query evaluation time, which is to say a list of zero or more time series. Each of these time series will have one sample, and a sample contains both a value and a timestamp. While the instant vector returned by an instant vector selector has the timestamp of the original data,[9] any instant vectors returned by other operations or functions will have the timestamp of the query evaluation time for all of their values.

When you ask for current memory usage you do not want samples from an instance that was turned down days ago to be included, a concept known as *staleness*. In Prometheus 1.x this was handled by returning time series that had a sample no more than 5 minutes before the query evaluation time. This largely worked but had downsides such as double counting if an instance restarted with a new `instance` label within that 5-minute window.

Prometheus 2.x has a more sophisticated approach. If a time series disappears from one scrape to the next, or if a target is no longer returned from service discovery, a special type of sample called a *stale marker*[10] is appended to the time series. When evaluating an instant vector selector, all time series satisfying all the matchers are first found, and the most recent sample in the 5 minutes before the query evaluation time is still considered. If the sample is a normal sample, then it is returned in the instant

---

8 If you do want to return all time series you can use `{__name__=~".+"}`, but beware of the expense of this expression.

9 You can extract the samples' timestamps using the `timestamp` function.

10 Internally stale markers are a special type of NaN value. They are an implementation detail, and you cannot access them directly via any of the query APIs that use PromQL. But you could see them if you looked at the Prometheus server's storage directly, such as via Prometheus's remote read endpoint.

vector, but if it is a stale marker, then that time series will not be included in that instant vector.

The outcome of all of this is that when you use an instant vector selector, time series that have gone stale are not returned.

 If you have an exporter exposing timestamps, as described in "Timestamps" on page 78, then stale markers and the Prometheus 2.x staleness logic will not apply. The affected time series will work instead with the older logic that looks back 5 minutes.

Range Vector

There is a second type of selector you have already seen, called the *range vector selector*. Unlike an instant vector selector which returns one sample per time series, a range vector selector can return many samples for each time series.[11] Range vectors are always used with the rate function; for example:

```
rate(process_cpu_seconds_total[1m])
```

The [1m] turns the instant vector selector into a range vector selector, and instructs PromQL to return for all time series matching the selector all samples for the minute up to the query evaluation time. If you execute just process_cpu_seconds_total[1m] in the Console tab of the expression browser you will see something like Figure 13-1.

In this case each time series happens to have six samples in the past minute. You will notice that while the samples for each time series happen to be perfectly 10 seconds apart[12] in line with the scrape interval you configured, the two time series timestamps are not aligned with each other. One time series has a sample with a timestamp of 1517925155.087 and the other 1517925156.245.

---

11 You may also see it referred to as a *matrix* in places, as it is a two-dimensional data structure.

12 This is a very lightly loaded Prometheus, so there is no jitter.

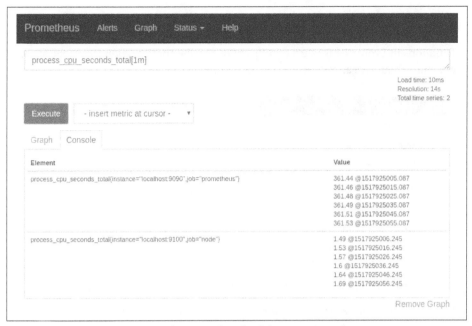

Figure 13-1. A range vector in the Console tab of the expression browser

This is because range vectors preserve the actual timestamps of the samples, and the scrapes for different targets are distributed in order to spread load more evenly. While you can control the frequency of scrapes and rule evaluations, you cannot control their phase or alignment. If you have a 10-second scrape interval and hundreds of targets, then all those targets will be scraped at different points in a given 10-second window. Put another way, your time series all have slightly different ages. This generally won't matter to you in practice, but can lead to artifacts as fundamentally metrics-based monitoring systems like Prometheus produce (quite good) estimates rather than exact answers.

You will very rarely look at range vectors directly. It only comes up when you need to see raw samples when debugging. Almost always you will use a range vector with a function such as `rate` or `avg_over_time` that takes a range vector as an argument.

Staleness and stale markers have no impact on range vectors; you will get all the normal samples in a given range. Any stale markers also in that range are not returned by a range vector selector.

Durations

Durations in Prometheus as used in PromQL and the configuration file support several units. You have already seen m for minute.

Suffix	Meaning
ms	Milliseconds
s	Seconds, which have 1,000 milliseconds
m	Minutes, which have 60 seconds
h	Hours, which have 60 minutes
d	Days, which have 24 hours
w	Weeks, which have 7 days
y	Years, which have 365 days

You can use one unit with integers, so 90m is valid but 1h30m and 1.5h are not.

Leap years and leap seconds are ignored, 1y is always 60*60*24*365 seconds.

Offset

There is a modifier you can use with either type of vector selector called offset. Offset allows you to take the evaluation time for a query, and on a per-selector basis put it further back in time. For example:

```
process_resident_memory_bytes{job="node"} offset 1h
```

would get memory usage an hour before the query evaluation time.

Offset is not used much in simple queries like this, as it would be easier to change the evaluation time for the whole query instead. Where this can be useful is when you only want to adjust one selector in a query expression. For example:

```
process_resident_memory_bytes{job="node"}
    -
process_resident_memory_bytes{job="node"} offset 1h
```

would give the change in memory usage in the Node exporter over the past hour.[13]

---

13 This is susceptible to outliers as it is using only two data points; the deriv function discussed in "deriv" on page 272 is more robust.

The same approach works with range vectors:

```
rate(process_cpu_seconds_total{job="node"}[5m])
-
rate(process_cpu_seconds_total{job="node"}[5m] offset 1h)
```

`offset` only allows you to look further back into the past. This is because having "historical" graphs change as new data comes in would be counterintuitive. If you wish to have a negative offset, you can instead move the query evaluation time forward and add offsets to all the other selectors in an expression.

 Grafana has a feature to time shift a panel to a different time range than the rest of the dashboard it is a part of. In Grafana 5.0.0 you can find this in the Time range tab of the panel editor.

HTTP API

Prometheus offers a number of HTTP APIs. The ones you will mostly interact with are `query` and `query_range`, which give you access to PromQL and can be used by dashboarding tools or custom reporting scripts.

All the endpoints of interest are under `/api/v1/`, and beyond executing PromQL you can also look up time series metadata and perform administrative actions such as taking snapshots and deleting time series. These other APIs are mainly of interest to dashboarding tools such as Grafana, which can use metadata to enhance its UI, and to those administering Prometheus, but are not relevant to PromQL execution.

query

The *query endpoint*, or more formally `/api/v1/query`, executes a PromQL expression at a given time and returns the result. For example, *http://localhost:9090/api/v1/query?query=process_resident_memory_bytes* will return results like:[14]

```
{
  "status": "success",
  "data": {
    "resultType": "vector",
    "result": [
      {
        "metric": {
          "__name__": "process_resident_memory_bytes",
          "instance": "localhost:9090",
          "job": "prometheus"
```

---

14 I have pretty printed these JSON results for readability.

```
      },
      "value": [1517929228.782, "91656192"]
    },
    {
      "metric": {
        "__name__": "process_resident_memory_bytes",
        "instance": "localhost:9100",
        "job": "node"
      },
      "value": [1517929228.782, "15507456"]
    }
  ]
  }
}
```

The status is success, meaning that the query worked. If it had failed, the status would be error, and an error field would provide more details.

This particular result is an instant vector, which you can tell from "resultType": "vector". For each of the samples in the result, the labels are in the metric map and the sample value is in the value list. The first number in the value list is the time-stamp of the sample, in seconds, and the second is the actual value of the sample. The value is inside a string as JSON cannot represent nonreal values such as NaN and +Inf.

The time of all the samples will be the query evaluation time, even if the expression consisted of only an instant vector selector. Here the query evaluation time defaulted to the current time, but you can specify a time with the time URL parameter, which can be a UNIX time, in seconds, or an RFC 3339 time. For example, *http://localhost:9090/api/v1/query?query=process_resident_memory_bytes&time=1514764800* would evaluate the query at midnight of January 1st, 2018.[15]

You can also use range vectors with the query endpoint, for example *http://localhost:9090/api/v1/query?query=prometheus_tsdb_head_samples_appended_total[1m]* will return results like:

```
{
  "status": "success",
  "data": {
    "resultType": "matrix",
    "result": [
      {
        "metric": {
          "__name__": "process_resident_memory_bytes",
          "instance": "localhost:9090",
          "job": "prometheus"
        },
```

---

15 Unless your Prometheus has been running since then, this will produce an empty result.

```
          "values": [
            [1518008453.662, "87318528"],
            [1518008463.662, "87318528"],
            [1518008473.662, "87318528"]
          ]
        },
        {
          "metric": {
            "__name__": "process_resident_memory_bytes",
            "instance": "localhost:9100",
            "job": "node"
          },
          "values": [
            [1518008444.819, "17043456"],
            [1518008454.819, "17043456"],
            [1518008464.819, "17043456"]
          ]
        }
      ]
    }
  }
}
```

This is different than the previous instant vector result as `resultType` is now `matrix`, and each time series has multiple values. When used with a range vector, the `query` endpoint returns the raw samples,[16] but be wary of asking for too much data at once because one end or the other may run out of memory.

There is one other type of result called a *scalar*. Scalars don't have labels, they are just numbers.[17] *http://localhost:9090/api/v1/query?query=42* would produce:

```
{
  "status": "success",
  "data": {
    "resultType": "scalar",
    "result": [1518008879.023, "42"]
  }
}
```

query_range

The *query range endpoint* at /api/v1/query_range is the main HTTP endpoint of Prometheus you will use, as it is the endpoint to use for graphing. Under the covers, `query_range` is syntactic sugar (plus some performance optimisations) for multiple calls to the `query` endpoint.

---

16 Excluding stale markers.

17 This is different from {}, which is the identity of a time series with no labels.

In addition to a query URL parameter, you provide `query_range` with a `start` time, end time, and a `step`. The query is first executed at the `start` time. Then it is executed `step` seconds after the start time. Then it is executed twice `step` seconds after the `start` time and so on, stopping when the query evaluation time would exceed the end time. All the instant vector[18] results from the different executions are combined into a range vector and returned.

For example, if you wanted to query the number of samples Prometheus ingested in the first 15 minutes of 2018, you could run the following: *http://localhost:9090/api/v1/ query_range?query=rate(prometheus_tsdb_head_samples_appended_total[5m])&start =1514764800&end=1514765700&step=60*, which would produce a result like:

```
{
  "status": "success",
  "data": {
    "resultType": "matrix",
    "result": [
      {
        "metric": {
          "instance": "localhost:9090",
          "job": "prometheus"
        },
        "values": [
          [1514764800, "85.07241379310345"],
          [1514764860, "102.6793103448276"],
          [1514764920, "120.30344827586208"],
          [1514764980, "137.93103448275863"],
          [1514765040, "146.7586206896552"],
          [1514765100, "146.7793103448276"],
          [1514765160, "146.8"],
          [1514765220, "146.8"],
          [1514765280, "146.8"],
          [1514765340, "146.8"],
          [1514765400, "146.8"],
          [1514765460, "146.8"],
          [1514765520, "146.8"],
          [1514765580, "146.8"],
          [1514765640, "146.8"],
          [1514765700, "146.8"],
        ]
      }
    ]
  }
}
```

---

18 A scalar result is converted into an instant vector with a single time series with no labels with the same value, as if the `vector` function was used. Range vector results are not supported.

There are a few aspects of this that you should take note of. The first is that the sample timestamps align with the start time and step, as each result comes from a different instant query evaluation and instant query results always use their evaluation time as the timestamp of results.

The second is that the last sample here is at the end time, which is to say that the range is inclusive and the last point will be the end time if it happens to line up with the step.

The third is that I selected a range of 5 minutes for the rate function, which is larger than the step. Since query_range is doing repeated instant query evaluations, there is no state being passed between the evaluations. If the range was smaller than the step, then I would have been skipping over data. For example, a 1-minute range with a 5-minute step would have ignored 80% of the samples. To prevent this you should use ranges that are at least one or two scrape intervals larger than the step you are using.

When using range vectors with query_range, you should usually use a range that is longer than your step in order to not skip data.

The fourth is that some of the samples are not particularly round, and that any numbers are round at all is due to this being a simple setup of the sample values. When working with metrics your data is rarely perfectly clean; different targets are scraped at different times and scrapes can be delayed. When performing queries that are not perfectly aligned with the underlying data or aggregating across multiple hosts, you will rarely get round results. In addition, the nature of floating-point calculations can lead to numbers that are almost round.

Here there is a sample for each step. If it happened that there was no result for a given time series for a step, then that sample would simply be missing in the end result.

If there would be more than 11,000 steps for a query_range, Prometheus will reject the query with an error. This is to prevent accidentally sending extremely large queries to Prometheus, such as a 1-second step for a week. As monitors with a horizontal resolution of over 11,000 pixels are rare, you are unlikely to run into this when graphing.

If you are writing reporting scripts, you can split up query_range requests that would hit this limit. This limit allows for a minute resolution for a week or an hour of resolution for a year, so most of the time it should not apply.

Aligned data

When using tools like Grafana it's common for the alignment of query_range to be based on the current time, and so your results will not align perfectly with minutes, hours, or days. While this is fine when you are looking at dashboards, it is rarely what you want with reporting scripts.

query_range does not have an option to specify alignment, instead it is up to you to specify a start parameter with the right alignment. For example, if you wanted to have samples every hour on the hour in Python, the expression (time.time() // 3600) * 3600 will return the start of the current hour,[19] which you can adjust in steps of 3,600 and use as the start and end URL parameters and then use a step parameter of 3600.

Now that you know the basics of how to use PromQL and execute queries via the HTTP APIs, I will go into more detail on aggregation.

---

19 // performs integer division in Python.

Aggregation Operators

You already learned about aggregation in "Aggregation Basics" on page 211; how-ever, this is only a small taste of what is possible. Aggregation is important. With applications with thousands or even just tens of instances it's not practical for you to sift through each instance's metrics individually. Aggregation allows you to summa-rise metrics not just within one application, but across applications too.

There are 11 aggregation operators in all, with 2 optional clauses, without and by. In this chapter you'll learn about the different ways you can use aggregation.

Grouping

Before talking about the aggregation operators themselves, you need to know about how time series are grouped. Aggregation operators work only on instant vectors, and they also output instant vectors.

Let's say you have the following time series in Prometheus:

```
node_filesystem_size_bytes{device="/dev/sda1",fstype="vfat",
    instance="localhost:9100",job="node",mountpoint="/boot/efi"} 100663296
node_filesystem_size_bytes{device="/dev/sda5",fstype="ext4",
    instance="localhost:9100",job="node",mountpoint="/"} 90131324928
node_filesystem_size_bytes{device="tmpfs",fstype="tmpfs",
    instance="localhost:9100",job="node",mountpoint="/run"} 826961920
node_filesystem_size_bytes{device="tmpfs",fstype="tmpfs",
    instance="localhost:9100",job="node",mountpoint="/run/lock"} 5242880
node_filesystem_size_bytes{device="tmpfs",fstype="tmpfs",
    instance="localhost:9100",job="node",mountpoint="/run/user/1000"} 826961920
node_filesystem_size_bytes{device="tmpfs",fstype="tmpfs",
    instance="localhost:9100",job="node",mountpoint="/run/user/119"} 826961920
```

There are three instrumentation labels: device, fstype, and mountpoint. There are also two target labels: job and instance. Target and instrumentation labels are a notion that you and I have, but which PromQL knows nothing about. All labels are the same when it comes to PromQL, no matter where they originated from.

without

Generally you will always know the instrumentation labels, as they rarely change. But you do not always know the target labels in play, as an expression you write might be used by someone else on metrics originating from different scrape configs or Prometheus servers that might also have added in other target labels across a job, such as a env or cluster label. You might even add in such target labels yourself at some point, and it'd be nice not to have to update all your expressions.

When aggregating metrics you should usually try to preserve such target labels, and thus you should use the without clause when aggregating to specify the specific labels you want to remove. For example, the query:

```
sum without(fstype, mountpoint)(node_filesystem_size_bytes)
```

will group the time series, ignoring the fstype and mountpoint labels, into three groups:

```
# Group {device="/dev/sda1",instance="localhost:9100",job="node"}
node_filesystem_size_bytes{device="/dev/sda1",fstype="vfat",
    instance="localhost:9100",job="node",mountpoint="/boot/efi"} 100663296

# Group {device="/dev/sda5",instance="localhost:9100",job="node"}
node_filesystem_size_bytes{device="/dev/sda5",fstype="ext4",
    instance="localhost:9100",job="node",mountpoint="/"} 90131324928

# Group {device="tmpfs",instance="localhost:9100",job="node"}
node_filesystem_size_bytes{device="tmpfs",fstype="tmpfs",
    instance="localhost:9100",job="node",mountpoint="/run"} 826961920
node_filesystem_size_bytes{device="tmpfs",fstype="tmpfs",
    instance="localhost:9100",job="node",mountpoint="/run/lock"} 5242880
node_filesystem_size_bytes{device="tmpfs",fstype="tmpfs",
    instance="localhost:9100",job="node",mountpoint="/run/user/1000"} 826961920
node_filesystem_size_bytes{device="tmpfs",fstype="tmpfs",
    instance="localhost:9100",job="node",mountpoint="/run/user/119"} 826961920
```

and the sum aggregator will apply within each of these groups, adding up the values of the time series and return one sample per group:

```
{device="/dev/sda1",instance="localhost:9100",job="node"} 100663296
{device="/dev/sda5",instance="localhost:9100",job="node"} 90131324928
{device="tmpfs",instance="localhost:9100",job="node"} 2486128640
```

Notice that the instance and job labels are preserved, as would be any other labels that had been present. This is useful because any alerts you created that included this expression somehow would have additional target labels like env or cluster

---

preserved. This provides context for your alerts and makes them more useful (also useful when graphing).

The metric name has also been removed, as this is an aggregation of the `node_file system_size_bytes` metric rather than the original metric. When a PromQL operator or function could change the value or meaning of a time series, the metric name is removed.

It is valid to provide no labels to the `without`. For example:

```
sum without()(node_filesystem_size_bytes)
```

will give you the same result as:

```
node_filesystem_size_bytes
```

with the only difference being the metric name being removed.

by

In addition to `without` there is also the by clause. Where `without` specifies the labels to remove, by specifies the labels to keep. Accordingly, some care is required when using by to ensure you don't remove target labels that you would like to propagate in your alerts or use in your dashboards. You cannot use both by and `without` in the same aggregation.

The query:

```
sum by(job, instance, device)(node_filesystem_size_bytes)
```

will produce the same result as the querying in the preceding section using `without`:

```
{device="/dev/sda1",instance="localhost:9100",job="node"} 100663296
{device="/dev/sda5",instance="localhost:9100",job="node"} 90131324928
{device="tmpfs",instance="localhost:9100",job="node"} 2486128640
```

However, if `instance` or `job` had not been specified, then they wouldn't have defined the group and would not be in the output. Generally, you should prefer to use `without` rather than by for this reason.

There are two cases where you might find by more useful. The first is that unlike `without`, by does not automatically drop the __name__ label. This allows you to use expressions like:

```
sort_desc(count by(__name__)({__name__=~".+"}))
```

to investigate how many time series have the same metric names.[1]

---

1 This is potentially an expensive query as it touches every active time series; use it carefully.

The second is cases where you do want to remove any labels you do not know about. For example, info metrics, as discussed in "Info" on page 90, are expected to add more labels over time. To count how many machines were running each kernel version you could use:

```
count by(release)(node_uname_info)
```

which on my single machine test setup returns:

```
{release="4.4.0-101-generic"} 1
```

You can use sum with an empty by, and can even omit the by. That is to say that:

```
sum by()(node_filesystem_size_bytes)
```

and:

```
sum(node_filesystem_size_bytes)
```

are exactly equivalent and will give a result like:

```
{} 92718116864
```

This is a single time series, and that time series has no labels.

If you executed the expression:

```
sum(non_existent_metric)
```

the result would be an instant vector with no time series, which will show up in the expression browser's Console tab as *"no data."*

> If the input to an aggregation operator is an empty instant vector, it will output an empty instant vector. Thus count by(foo) (non_existent_metric) will be empty rather than 0, as count and other aggregators don't have any labels to work with. count(non_existent_metric) is consistent with this, and also returns an empty instant vector.

Operators

All 11 aggregation operators use the same grouping logic. You can control this with one of without or by. What differs between aggregation operators is what they do with the grouped data.

sum

sum is the most common aggregator; it adds up all the values in a group and returns that as the value for the group. For example:

```
sum without(fstype, mountpoint, device)(node_filesystem_size_bytes)
```

would return the total size of the filesystems of each of your machines.

When dealing with counters,[2] it is important that you take a `rate` before aggregating with `sum`:

```
sum without(device)(rate(node_disk_read_bytes_total[5m]))
```

If you were to take a `sum` across counters directly, the result would be meaningless, as different counters could have been initialised at different times depending on when the exporter started, restarted, or any particular children were first used.

count

The `count` aggregator counts the number of time series in a group, and returns it as the value for the group. For example:

```
count without(device)(node_disk_read_bytes_total)
```

would return the number of disk devices a machine has. My machine only has one disk, so I get:

```
{instance="localhost:9100",job="node"} 1
```

Here it is okay not to use `rate` with a counter, as you care about the existence of the time series rather than its value.

Unique label values

You can also use `count` to count how many unique values a label has. For example, to count the number of CPUs in each of your machines you could use:

```
count without(cpu)(count without (mode)(node_cpu_seconds_total))
```

The inner `count`[3] removes the other instrumentation label, `mode`, returning one time series per CPU per instance:

```
{cpu="0",instance="localhost:9100",job="node"} 8
{cpu="1",instance="localhost:9100",job="node"} 8
{cpu="2",instance="localhost:9100",job="node"} 8
{cpu="3",instance="localhost:9100",job="node"} 8
```

The outer `count` then returns the number of CPUs that each instance has:

```
{instance="localhost:9100",job="node"} 4
```

---

2 Including the _sum, _count, and _bucket of histograms and summary metrics.

3 The inner aggregation does not have to be count; anything that returns the same set of time series such as sum would also work. This is because the outer count ignores the values of these time series.

If you didn't want a per-machine breakdown, such as if you were investigating if certain labels had high cardinality, you could use the by modifier to look at only one label:

```
count(count by(cpu)(node_cpu_seconds_total))
```

Which would produce a single sample with no labels, such as:

```
{} 4
```

avg

The avg aggregator returns the average of the values[4] of the time series in the group as the value for the group. For example:

```
avg without(cpu)(rate(node_cpu_seconds_total[5m]))
```

would give you the average usage of each CPU mode for each Node exporter instance with a result such as:

```
{instance="localhost:9100",job="node",mode="idle"} 0.9095948275861836
{instance="localhost:9100",job="node",mode="iowait"} 0.005543103448275879
{instance="localhost:9100",job="node",mode="irq"} 0
{instance="localhost:9100",job="node",mode="nice"} 0.0013620689655172522
{instance="localhost:9100",job="node",mode="softirq"} 0.0001465517241379329
{instance="localhost:9100",job="node",mode="steal"} 0
{instance="localhost:9100",job="node",mode="system"} 0.015836206896552414
{instance="localhost:9100",job="node",mode="user"} 0.06054310344827549
```

This gives you the exact same result as:

```
    sum without(cpu)(rate(node_cpu_seconds_total[5m]))
/
    count without(cpu)(rate(node_cpu_seconds_total[5m]))
```

but it is both more succinct and more efficient to use avg.

When using avg sometimes you may find that a NaN in the input is causing the entire result to become NaN. This is because any floating-point arithmetic that involves NaN will have NaN as a result.

You may wonder how to filter out these NaNs in the input, but that is the wrong question to ask. Usually this is due to attempting to average averages, and one of the denominators of the first averages was 0.[5] Averaging averages is not statistically valid, so what you should do instead is aggregate using sum and then finally divide, as shown in "Summary" on page 214.

---

4 Technically it is called an *arithmetic mean*. In the unlikely event you need a *geometric mean*, the ln and exp functions combined with the avg aggregator can be used to calculate that.

5 This is as 1 / 0 = NaN.

stddev and stdvar

The *standard deviation* is a statistical measure of how spread out a set of numbers is. For example, if you had the numbers [2,4,6] then the standard deviation would be 1.633.[6] The numbers [3,4,5] have the same average of 4, but a standard deviation of 0.816.

The main use of the standard deviation in monitoring is to detect outliers. In normally distributed data you would expect that about 68% of samples would be within one standard deviation of the mean, and 95% within two standard deviations.[7] If one instance in a job has a metric several standard deviations away from the average, that's a good indication that something is wrong with it.

For example, you could find all instances that were at least two standard deviations above the average using an expression such as:

```
  some_gauge
> ignoring (instance) group_left()
  (
      avg without(instance)(some_gauge)
    +
      2 * stddev without(instance)(some_gauge)
  )
```

This uses one-to-many vector matching, which will be discussed in "Many-to-One and group_left" on page 248. If your values are all tightly bunched then this may return some time series that are more than two standard deviations away, but still operating normally and close to the average. You could add an additional filter that the value has to be at least say 20% higher than the average to protect against this. This is also a rare case where it is okay to take an average of an average, such as if you applied this to average latency.

The *standard variance* is the standard deviation squared[8] and has statistical uses.

---

6 Prometheus uses the *population standard deviation* rather than the *sample standard deviation*, as you will usually be looking at all the values you are interested in rather than a random subset.

7 For nonnormally distributed data, *Chebyshev's inequality* provides a weaker bound.

8 If the exponentiation operator had existed at the time I was adding stdvar and stddev, then stdvar would probably not have been added.

min and max

The min and max aggregators return the minimum or maximum value within a group as the value of the group, respectively. The same grouping rules apply as elsewhere, so the output time series will have the labels of the group.[9] For example:

```
max without(device, fstype, mountpoint)(node_filesystem_size_bytes)
```

will return the size of the biggest filesystem on each instance, which for me returns:

```
{instance="localhost:9100",job="node"} 90131324928
```

The max and min aggregators will only return NaN if all values in a group are NaN.[10]

topk and bottomk

topk and bottomk are different from the other aggregators discussed so far in three ways. First, the labels of time series they return for a group are not the labels of the group; second, they can return more than one time series per group; and third, they take an additional parameter.

topk returns the k time series with the biggest values, so for example:

```
topk without(device, fstype, mountpoint)(2, node_filesystem_size_bytes)
```

would return up to two[11] time series per group, such as:

```
node_filesystem_size_bytes{device="/dev/sda5",fstype="ext4",
    instance="localhost:9100",job="node",mountpoint="/"} 90131324928
node_filesystem_size_bytes{device="tmpfs",fstype="tmpfs",
    instance="localhost:9100",job="node",mountpoint="/run"} 826961920
```

As you can see, topk returns input time series with all their labels, including the __name__ label, which holds the metric name. The result is also sorted.

bottomk is the same as topk, except that it returns the k time series with the smallest values rather than the k biggest values. Both aggregators will where possible avoid returning time series with NaN values.

There is a gotcha when using these aggregators with the query_range HTTP API endpoint. As was discussed in "query_range" on page 225, the evaluation of each step is independent. If you use topk, it is possible that the top time series will change from

---

9 If you want the input time series returned, use topk or bottomk.

10 In floating-point math, any comparison with NaN always returns false. Aside from causing oddities such as NaN != NaN returning false, a naive implementation of min and max would (and once did) get stuck on a NaN if it was the first value examined.

11 The k is 2 in this case.

step to step. So a `topk(5, some_gauge)` for a `query_range` with 1,000 steps could in the worst case return 5,000 different time series.

The way to handle this is to first determine which time series you care about across the whole time range by using the `query` API endpoint with an expression such as:

```
topk(5, avg_over_time(some_gauge[1h]))
```

that calculates the biggest time series on average over the past hour (presuming the graph's time range was an hour). You can then use the label values in the returned time series in a matcher for your `query_range` expression such as:

```
some_gauge{instance=~"a|b|c|d|e"}
```

Grafana does not currently support this fully, but you can use Grafana's templating feature with a PromQL query with a fixed range to select the time series you want.

quantile

The `quantile` aggregator returns the specified quantile of the values of the group as the group's return value. As with `topk`, `quantile` takes a parameter.

So, for example, if I wanted to know across the different CPUs in each of my machines what the 90th percentile of the system mode CPU usage is I could use:

```
quantile without(cpu)(0.9, rate(node_cpu_seconds_total{mode="system"}[5m]))
```

which produces a result like:

```
{instance="localhost:9100",job="node",mode="system"} 0.024558620689654007
```

This means that 90% of my CPUs are spending at least 0.02 seconds per second in the system mode. This would be a more useful query if I had tens of CPUs in my machine, rather than the four it actually has.

In addition to the mean, you could use `quantile` to show the median, 25th, and 75th percentiles[12] on your graphs. For example, for process CPU usage the expressions would be:

```
# average, arithmetic mean
avg without(instance)(0.5, rate(process_cpu_seconds_total[5m]))

# 0.25 quantile, 25th percentile, 1st or lower quartile
quantile without(instance)(0.25, rate(process_cpu_seconds_total[5m]))

# 0.5 quantile, 50th percentile, 2nd quartile, median
quantile without(instance)(0.5, rate(process_cpu_seconds_total[5m]))
```

---

12 Also known as the 1st and 3rd *quartiles*.

```
# 0.75 quantile, 75th percentile, 3rd or upper quartile
quantile without(instance)(0.75, rate(process_cpu_seconds_total[5m]))
```

This would give you a sense of how your different instances for a job are behaving, without having to graph each instance individually. This allows you to keep your dashboards readable as the number of underlying instances grows. Personally I find that per-instance graphs break down somewhere around three to five instances.

---

quantile, histogram_quantile, and quantile_over_time

As you may have noticed by now, there is more than one PromQL function or operator with quantile in the name.

The quantile aggregator works across an instant vector in an aggregation group.

The quantile_over_time function works across a single time series at a time in a range vector.

The histogram_quantile function works across the buckets of one histogram metric child at a time in an instant vector.

---

count_values

The final aggregation operator is count_values. Like topk it takes a parameter and can return more than one time series from a group. What it does is build a *frequency histogram* of the values of the time series in the group, with the count of each value as the value of the output time series and the original value as a new label.

That's a bit of a mouthful, so I'll show you an example. Say you had a time series called software_version with the following values:

```
software_version{instance="a",job="j"} 7
software_version{instance="b",job="j"} 4
software_version{instance="c",job="j"} 8
software_version{instance="d",job="j"} 4
software_version{instance="e",job="j"} 7
software_version{instance="f",job="j"} 4
```

If you evaluated the query:

```
count_values without(instance)("version", software_version)
```

on these time series you would get the result:

```
{job="j",version="7"} 2
{job="j",version="8"} 1
{job="j",version="4"} 3
```

There were two time series in the group with a value of 7, so a time series with a version="7" plus the group labels was returned with the value 2. The result is similar for the other time series.

There is no bucketing involved when the frequency histogram is created; the exact values of the time series are used. Thus this is only really useful with integer values and where there will not be too many unique values.

This is most useful with version numbers,[13] or with the number of objects of some type that each instance of your application sees. If you have too many versions deployed at once, or different applications are continuing to see different numbers of objects, something might be stuck somewhere.

count_values can be combined with count to calculate the number of unique values for a given aggregation group. For example, the number of versions of software that are deployed can be calculated with:

```
count without(version)(
  count_values without(instance)("version", software_version)
)
```

which in this case would return:

```
{job="j"} 3
```

You could also combine count_values with count in the other direction; for example, to see how many of your machines had how many disk devices:

```
count_values without(instance)(
  "devices",
  count without(device) (node_disk_io_now)
)
```

In my case I have one machine with five disk devices:

```
{devices="5",job="node"} 1
```

Now that you understand aggregators, we will look at binary operators, like addition and subtraction, and how vector matching works.

---

13 For versions that cannot be represented as floating-point values, you can use an info metric as discussed in "Info" on page 90.

Binary Operators

You will want to do more with your metrics than simply aggregate them, which is where the *binary operators* come in. Binary operators are operators that take two operands,[1] such as the addition and equality operators.

Binary operators in Prometheus allow for more than simple arithmetic on instant vectors; you can also apply a binary operator to two instant vectors with grouping based on labels. This is where the real power of PromQL comes out, allowing classes of analysis that few other metrics systems offer.

PromQL has three sets of binary operators: arithmetic operators, comparison operations, and logical operators. This chapter will show you how to use them.

Working with Scalars

In addition to instant vectors and range vectors, there is another type of value known as a *scalar*.[2] Scalars are single numbers with no dimensionality. For example, 0 is a scalar with the value zero, while {} 0 is an instant vector containing a single sample with no labels and the value zero.[3]

---

1 In contrast to *unary operators*, which only take one operand. PromQL has + and - unary operators.

2 Internally, PromQL also has a *string* type, but this is only used as an argument to count_values, label_replace, and label_join.

3 You may also see the convention {}: 0 to represent a single sample.

Arithmetic Operators

You can use scalars in arithmetic with an instant vector to change the values in the instant vector. For example:

```
process_resident_memory_bytes / 1024
```

would return:

```
{instance="localhost:9090",job="prometheus"} 21376
{instance="localhost:9100",job="node"} 13316
```

which is the process memory usage, in kilobytes.[4] You will note that the division operator was applied to all time series in the instant vector returned by the `process_resident_memory_bytes` selector and that the metric name was removed as it is no longer the metric `process_resident_memory_bytes`.

 Even when you are using arithmetic operators in a way that doesn't change the value, the metric name will still be removed for consistency. For example, the result of `some_gauge + 0` will not have a metric name.

All six arithmetic operations work similarly, with the semantics you'd expect from other programming languages. They are:

- + addition
- - subtraction
- * multiplication
- / division
- % modulo
- ^ exponentiation

The *modulo* operator is a floating-point modulo and can return noninteger results if you provide it with noninteger input. For example:

```
5 % 1.5
```

will return:

```
0.5
```

---

4 If you are using a dashboarding tool like Grafana, it's generally best to let it handle creating human-readable units for metrics that are already in base units such as bytes.

As this example demonstrates, you can also use binary arithmetic operators when both operands are scalars. The result will be a scalar. This is mostly useful for readability, as it is much easier to understand the intent of (1024 * 1024 * 1024) than it is 1073741824.

In addition, you can put the scalar operand on the left side of the operator and an instant vector on the right, so:

```
1e9 - process_resident_memory_bytes
```

for example would subtract the process memory from a billion.

You can also use arithmetic operators with instant vectors on both sides, which is covered in "Vector Matching" on page 245.

Comparison Operators

The *comparison operators* are as follows, with the usual meanings:

- == equals
- != not equals
- > greater than
- < less than
- >= greater than or equal to
- <= less than or equal to

What is a little different is that the comparison operators in PromQL are *filtering*. That is to say that if you had the samples:

```
process_open_fds{instance="localhost:9090",job="prometheus"} 14
process_open_fds{instance="localhost:9100",job="node"} 7
```

and used an instant vector in a comparison with a scalar such as in the expression:

```
process_open_fds > 10
```

then you would get the result:

```
process_open_fds{instance="localhost:9090",job="prometheus"}  14
```

As the value can't change, the metric name has been preserved. When comparing a scalar and an instant vector it doesn't matter which side each is on, it is always elements of the instant vector that are returned.

As PromQL deals with floating-point numbers, some care is required when using == and !=. Floating-point calculations can produce results that are very slightly different depending on exactly what the values are and in what order operations they are performed.

If you want to do equality on noninteger values, it is better to instead check that their difference is less than some small number which is called an *epsilon*. For example, you could do:

```
(some_gauge - 1) < 1e-6 > -1e-6
```

to check if a gauge has a value of one allowing for inaccuracy of one in a million.

You cannot do a filtering comparison between two scalars, as to be consistent with arithmetic operations between two scalars it'd have to return a scalar. This doesn't allow for filtering, as there's no way to have an empty scalar like you can have an empty instant vector.

bool modifier

Filtering comparisons are primarily useful in alerting rules, as discussed in Chapter 18, and generally to be avoided elsewhere.[5] I will show you why.

Continuing on from the preceding example, say you wanted to see how many of your processes for each job had more than ten open file descriptors. The obvious way to do this would be:

```
count without(instance)(process_open_fds > 10)
```

which would return the result:

```
{job="prometheus"}  1
```

This correctly indicates that there is one Prometheus process with more than 10 open file descriptions. It does not report that the Node exporter has zero such processes. This is can be a subtle gotcha because as long as one time series is not filtered away everything seems to be okay.

What you need is some way to do the comparison but not have it filter. This is what the bool modifier does; for each comparison it returns a 0 for false or a 1 for true.

For example:

```
process_open_fds > bool 10
```

---

5 It is possible to use filtering correctly with careful application of the or operator, but it's more complicated and error prone.

will return:

```
{instance="localhost:9090",job="prometheus"} 1
{instance="localhost:9100",job="node"} 0
```

which as expected has one output sample per sample in the input instant vector.

From there you can `sum` up to get the number of processes for each job that have more than 10 open file descriptors:

```
sum without(instance)(process_open_fds > bool 10)
```

which produces the result you originally wanted:

```
{job="prometheus"} 1
{job="node"} 0
```

You could use a similar approach to find the proportion of machines with more than four disk devices:

```
avg without(instance)(
  count without(device)(node_disk_io_now) > bool 4
)
```

This works by first using a `count` aggregation to find the number of disks reported by each Node exporter, then seeing how many have more than four, and finally averaging across machines to get the proportion. The trick here is that the values returned by the `bool` modifier are all 0 and 1, so the count is the total number of machines, and the sum is the number of machines meeting the criteria. The `avg` is the count divided by the sum, giving you a ratio or proportion.

The `bool` modifier is the only way you can compare scalars, as:

```
42 <= bool 13
```

will return:

```
0
```

where the 0 indicates false.

Vector Matching

Using operators between scalars and instant vectors will cover many of your needs, but using operators between two instant vectors is where PromQL's power really starts to shine.

When you have a scalar and an instant vector, it is obvious that the scalar can be applied to each sample in the vector. With two instant vectors, which samples should apply to which other samples? This matching of the instant vectors is known as *vector matching*.

One-to-One

In the simplest cases there will be a one-to-one mapping between your two vectors. Say that you had the following samples:

```
process_open_fds{instance="localhost:9090",job="prometheus"} 14
process_open_fds{instance="localhost:9100",job="node"} 7
process_max_fds{instance="localhost:9090",job="prometheus"} 1024
process_max_fds{instance="localhost:9100",job="node"} 1024
```

Then when you evaluated the expression:

```
  process_open_fds
/
  process_max_fds
```

you would get the result:

```
{instance="localhost:9090",job="prometheus"} 0.013671875
{instance="localhost:9100",job="node"} 0.0068359375
```

What has happened here is that samples with exactly the same labels, except for the metric name in the label __name__, were matched together. That is to say that the two samples with the labels {instance="localhost:9090",job="prometheus"} got matched together, and the two samples with the labels {instance="localhost:9100",job="node"} got matched together.

In this case there was a perfect match, with each sample on both sides of the operator being matched. If a sample on one side had no match on the other side, then it would not be present in the result, as binary operators need two operands.

 If a binary operator returns an empty instant vector when you were expecting a result, it is probably because the labels of the samples in the operands don't match. This is often due to a label that is present on one side of the operator but not the other.

Sometimes you will want to match two instant vectors whose labels do not quite match. Similar to how aggregation allows you to specify which labels matter, as discussed in "Grouping" on page 229, vector matching also has clauses controlling which labels are considered.

You can use the ignoring clause to ignore certain labels when matching, similar to how without works for aggregation. Say you were working with node_cpu_seconds_total, which has cpu and mode as instrumentation labels, and wanted to know what proportion of time was being spent in the idle mode for each instance. You could use the expression:

```
sum without(cpu)(rate(node_cpu_seconds_total{mode="idle"}[5m]))
/ ignoring(mode)
sum without(mode, cpu)(rate(node_cpu_seconds_total[5m]))
```

This will give you a result such as:

```
{instance="localhost:9100",job="node"} 0.8423353718871361
```

Here the first `sum` produces an instant vector with a `mode="idle"` label, whereas the second `sum` produces an instant vector with no `mode` label. Usually vector matching will fail to match the samples, but with `ignoring(mode)` the `mode` label is discarded when the vectors are being grouped, and matching succeeds. As the `mode` label was not in the match group it is not in the output.[6]

You can tell the preceding expression is correct in terms of vector matching by inspection, without having to know anything about the underlying time series. The removal of `cpu` is balanced on both sides, and `ignoring(mode)` handles one side having a `mode` and the other not.

This can be trickier when there are different time series with different labels in play, but looking at expressions in terms of how the labels flow is a handy way for you to spot errors.

The on clause allows you to consider only the labels you provide, similar to how by works for aggregation. The expression:

```
sum by(instance, job)(rate(node_cpu_seconds_total{mode="idle"}[5m]))
/ on(instance, job)
sum by(instance, job)(rate(node_cpu_seconds_total[5m]))
```

will produce the same result as the preceeding expression,[7] but as with by, the on clause has the disadvantage that you need to know all labels that are currently on the time series or that may be present in the future in other contexts.

The value that is returned for the arithmetic operators is the result of the calculation, but you may be wondering what happens for the comparison operators when there are two instant vectors. The answer is that the value from the left-hand side is returned. For example, the expression:

```
process_open_fds
>
(process_max_fds * .5)
```

---

6 The cpu label was aggregated away by both sums, so is not present in the output either.

7 You could exclude the on(instance, job) here as the left- and right-hand side both have only instance and job labels.

will return for you the value of `process_open_fds` for all instances whose open file descriptors are more than halfway to the maximum.[8]

If you had instead used:

```
(process_max_fds * .5)
 <
process_open_fds
```

you would get half the maximum file descriptors as the return value. While the result will have the same labels, this value is less useful when alerting[9] or when used in a dashboard! In general, a current value is more informative than the limit, so you should try to structure your math so that the most interesting number is on the left-hand side of a comparison.

Many-to-One and group_left

If you were to remove the matcher on `mode` from the preceding section and try to evaluate:

```
  sum without(cpu)(rate(node_cpu_seconds_total[5m]))
/ ignoring(mode)
  sum without(mode, cpu)(rate(node_cpu_seconds_total[5m]))
```

you would get the error:

```
multiple matches for labels:
  many-to-one matching must be explicit (group_left/group_right)
```

This is because the samples no longer match one-to-one, as there are multiple samples with different mode labels on the left-hand side for each sample on the right-hand side. This can be a subtle failure mode, as a time series may appear later on that breaks your expression. You can see that this is a potential issue, as looking at the label flow there's nothing restricting the `mode` label to one potential value[10] on the left-hand side.

Errors like this are usually due to incorrectly written expressions, so PromQL does not attempt to do anything smart by default. Instead, you must specifically request that you want to do many-to-one matching using the `group_left` modifier.

---

8 Running out of file descriptors can break applications in fun ways, and you should usually try to ensure that your applications always have enough.

9 Alert templates have ready access to the value of an alert's PromQL expression. This is discussed in "Annotations and Templates" on page 298.

10 A missing `mode` label due to aggregating it away would count as a single label value of the empty string.

`group_left` lets you specify that there can be multiple matching samples in the group of the left-hand operand.[11] For example:

```
sum without(cpu)(rate(node_cpu_seconds_total[5m]))
/ ignoring(mode) group_left
    sum without(mode, cpu)(rate(node_cpu_seconds_total[5m]))
```

will produce one output sample for each different `mode` label within each group on the left-hand side:

```
{instance="localhost:9100",job="node",mode="irq"} 0
{instance="localhost:9100",job="node",mode="nice"} 0
{instance="localhost:9100",job="node",mode="softirq"} 0.00005226389784152013
{instance="localhost:9100",job="node",mode="steal"} 0
{instance="localhost:9100",job="node",mode="system"} 0.01720353303949279
{instance="localhost:9100",job="node",mode="user"} 0.10345203045243238
{instance="localhost:9100",job="node",mode="idle"} 0.8608691486211044
{instance="localhost:9100",job="node",mode="iowait"} 0.01842302398912871
```

`group_left` always takes all of its labels from samples of your operand on the left-hand side. This ensures that the extra labels that are on the left side that require this to be many-to-one vector matching are preserved.[12]

This is much easier than having to run a one-to-one expression with a matcher for each potential `mode` label: `group_left` does it all for you in one expression. You can use this approach to determine the proportion each label value within metric represents of the whole, as shown in the preceding example, or to compare a metric from a leader of a cluster against the replicas.

There is another use for `group_left`—adding labels from info metrics to other metrics from a target. Instrumentation with info metrics was covered in "Info" on page 90. The role of info metrics is to allow you to provide labels that would be useful for a target or metric to have but that would clutter up the metric if you were to use it as a normal label.

The `prometheus_build_info` metric, for example, provides you with build information from Prometheus:

```
prometheus_build_info{branch="HEAD",goversion="go1.10",
    instance="localhost:9090",job="prometheus",
    revision="bc6058c81272a8d938c05e75607371284236aadc",version="2.2.1"}
```

---

11 There can still only be one sample per group on the right-hand side of the operand, as `group_left` only enables many-to-one matching, not many-to-many matching.

12 If the labels from the right-hand side were used you would get the same labels for each sample from the groups on the left, which would clash.

You can join this with metrics such as up:

```
up
* on(instance) group_left(version)
  prometheus_build_info
```

which will produce a result like:

```
{instance="localhost:9090",job="prometheus",version="2.2.1"} 1
```

You can see that the version label has been copied over from the right-hand operand to the left-hand operand as was requested by group_left(version), in addition to returning all the labels from the left-hand operand as group_left usually does. You can specify as many labels as you like to group_left, but usually it's only one or two.[13] This approach works no matter how many instrumentation labels the left-hand side has, as the vector matching is many-to-one.

The preceding expression used on(instance), which relies on each instance label only being used for one target within your Prometheus. While this is often the case, it isn't always, so you may also need to add other labels such as job to the on clause.

prometheus_build_info applies to a whole target. There are also info-style[14] metrics such as node_hwmon_sensor_label mentioned in "Hwmon Collector" on page 120 that apply to children of a different metric:

```
node_hwmon_sensor_label{chip="platform_coretemp_0",instance="localhost:9100",
    job="node",label="core_0",sensor="temp2"} 1
node_hwmon_sensor_label{chip="platform_coretemp_0",instance="localhost:9100",
    job="node",label="core_1",sensor="temp3"} 1

node_hwmon_temp_celsius{chip="platform_coretemp_0",instance="localhost:9100",
    job="node",sensor="temp1"} 42
node_hwmon_temp_celsius{chip="platform_coretemp_0",instance="localhost:9100",
    job="node",sensor="temp2"} 42
node_hwmon_temp_celsius{chip="platform_coretemp_0",instance="localhost:9100",
    job="node",sensor="temp3"} 41
```

The node_hwmon_sensor_label metric has children that match with some (but not all) of the time series in node_hwmon_temp_celsius. In this case you know that there is only one additional label (which is called label), so you can use ignoring with group_left to add this label to the node_hwmon_temp_celsius samples:

---

13 There's no way for you to request all the labels to be copied over, as then you would no longer know what labels the output metric had.

14 The convention for whether a metric that has a single info-style label should have an _info suffix is not fully resolved yet.

```
    node_hwmon_temp_celsius
 * ignoring(label) group_left(label)
    node_hwmon_sensor_label
```

which will produce results such as:

```
{chip="platform_coretemp_0",instance="localhost:9100",
    job="node",label="core_0",sensor="temp2"} 42
{chip="platform_coretemp_0",instance="localhost:9100",
    job="node",label="core_1",sensor="temp3"} 41
```

Notice that there is no sample with `sensor="temp1"` as there was no such sample in `node_hwmon_sensor_label` (how to match sparse instant vectors will be covered in "or operator" on page 251).

There is also a `group_right` modifier that works in the same way as `group_left` except that the one and the many side are switched, with the many side now being your operand on the right-hand side. Any labels you specify in the `group_right` modifier are copied from the left to the right. For the sake of consistency, you should prefer `group_left`.

Many-to-Many and Logical Operators

There are three logical or set operators you can use:

- `or` union
- `and` intersection
- `unless` set subtraction

There is no *not* operator, but the `absent` function discussed in "Missing Series and absent" on page 266 serves a similar role.

All the logical operators work in a many-to-many fashion, and they are the only operators that work many-to-many. They are different from the arithmetic and comparison operators you have already seen in that no math is performed; all that matters is whether a group contains samples.

or operator

In the preceding section, `node_hwmon_sensor_label` did not have a sample to go with every `node_hwmon_temp_celsius`, so results were only returned for samples that were present in both instant vectors. Metrics with inconsistent children, or whose children are not always present, are tricky to work with, but you can deal with them using the or operator.

How the or operator works is that for each group where the group on the left-hand side has samples, then they are returned; otherwise, the samples in the group on the right-hand side are returned. If you are familiar with SQL this operator can be used in a similar way as the SQL COALESCE function, but with labels.

Continuing the example from the preceding section, or can be used to substitute the missing time series from node_hwmon_sensor_label. All you need is some other time series that has the labels you need, which in this case is node_hwmon_temp_celsius. node_hwmon_temp_celsius does not have the label label, but all the other labels match up so you can ignore this using ignoring:

```
    node_hwmon_sensor_label
  or ignoring(label)
    (node_hwmon_temp_celsius * 0 + 1)
```

The vector matching produced three groups. The first two groups had a sample from node_hwmon_sensor_label so that was what was returned, including the metric name as there was nothing to change it. For the third group, however, which included sensor="temp1", there was no sample in the group for the left-hand side, so the values in the group from the right-hand side were used. Because arithmetic operators were used on the value, the metric name was removed.

 x * 0 + 1 will change all[15] the values of the x instant vector to 1. This is also useful when you want to use group_left to copy labels, as 1 is the identity element for multiplication, which is to say it does not change the value you are multiplying.

This expression can now be used in the place of node_hwmon_sensor_label:

```
    node_hwmon_temp_celsius
  * ignoring(label) group_left(label)
    (
        node_hwmon_sensor_label
      or ignoring(label)
        (node_hwmon_temp_celsius * 0 + 1)
    )
```

which will produce:

```
{chip="platform_coretemp_0",instance="localhost:9100",
    job="node",sensor="temp1"} 42
{chip="platform_coretemp_0",instance="localhost:9100",
    job="node",label="core_0",sensor="temp2"} 42
{chip="platform_coretemp_0",instance="localhost:9100",
    job="node",label="core_1",sensor="temp3"} 41
```

---

15 NaN will stay as NaN, but in practice there will be another time series with the same labels and no NaN values you could use instead.

The sample with `sensor="temp1"` is now present in your result. It has no label called `label`, which is the same as saying that that `label` label has the empty string as a value.

In simpler cases you will be working with metrics without any instrumentation labels. For example, you might be using the textfile collector, as covered in "Textfile Collector" on page 122, and expecting it to expose a metric called `node_custom_metric`. In the event that metric doesn't exist you would like to return 0 instead. In cases like this, you can use the up metric that is associated with every target:

```
  node_custom_metric
or
  up * 0
```

This has a small problem in that it will return a value even for a failed scrape, which is not how scraped metrics work.[16] It will also return results for other jobs. You can fix this with a matcher and some filtering:

```
  node_custom_metric
or
  (up{job="node"} == 1) * 0
```

Another way you can use the or operator is to return the larger of two series:

```
  (a >= b) or b
```

If a is larger it will be returned by the comparison, and then the or operator since the group on the left-hand side was not empty. If on the other hand b is larger, then the comparison will return nothing, and or will return b as the group on the left-hand side was empty.

unless operator

The `unless` operator does vector matching in the same way as the or operator, working based on whether groups from the right and left operands are empty or have samples. The `unless` operator returns the left-hand group, unless the right-hand group has members, in which case it returns no samples for that group.

You can use `unless` to restrict what time series are returned based on an expression. For example, if you wanted to know the average CPU usage of processes except those using less than 100 MB of resident memory you could use the expression:

```
  rate(process_cpu_seconds_total[5m])
unless
  process_resident_memory_bytes < 100 * 1024 * 1024
```

---

16 up is not a scraped metric; Prometheus adds it after every scrape whether the scrape succeeds or fails.

`unless` can also be used to spot when a metric is missing from a target. For example:

```
up{job="node"} == 1
unless
  node_custom_metric
```

would return a sample for every instance that was missing the `node_custom_metric` metric, which you could use in alerting.

By default, as with all binary operators, `unless` looks at all labels when grouping. If `node_custom_metric` had instrumentation labels you could use `on` or `ignoring` to check that at least one relevant time series existed without having to know the values of the other labels:

```
up == 1
unless on (job, instance)
  node_custom_metric
```

Even if there are multiple samples from the right operand in a group, this is okay as `unless` uses many-to-many matching.

and operator

The `and` operator is the opposite of the `unless` operator. It returns a group from the left-hand operand only if the matching right-hand group has samples; otherwise, it returns no samples for that match group. You can think of it as an *if* operator.[17]

You will use the `and` operator most commonly in alerting to specify more than one condition. For example, you might want to return when both latency is high and there is more than a trickle of user requests. To do this for Prometheus for handlers that were taking over a second on average and had at least one request per second[18] you could use:

```
(
    rate(http_request_duration_microseconds_sum{job="prometheus"}[5m])
  /
    rate(http_request_duration_microseconds_count{job="prometheus"}[5m])
) > 1000000
and
  rate(http_request_duration_microseconds_count{job="prometheus"}[5m]) > 1
```

---

17 Prior to Prometheus 2.x, PromQL had an `IF` keyword that was used in alerting, so while I had wondered if renaming the `and` operator to `if` would have been a good idea, it was not possible.

18 This was the one remaining latency metric in the Prometheus server that was not using seconds, but from 2.3.0 was replaced by a metric called `prometheus_http_request_duration_seconds`.

This will return a sample for every individual handler on every prometheus job, so it could get a little spammy even with the one request per second restriction. Usually you would want to aggregate across a job when alerting.

You can use on and ignoring with the and operator, as you can with the other binary operators. In particular, on() can be used to have a condition that has no common labels at all between the two operands. You can use this, for example, to limit the time of day an expression will return results for:

```
(
    rate(http_request_duration_microseconds_sum{job="prometheus"}[5m])
  /
    rate(http_request_duration_microseconds_count{job="prometheus"}[5m])
) > 1000000
and
  rate(http_request_duration_microseconds_count{job="prometheus"}[5m]) > 1
and on()
  hour() > 9 < 17
```

The hour function is covered in "minute, hour, day_of_week, day_of_month, days_in_month, month, and year" on page 263; it returns an instant vector with one sample with no labels and the hour of the UTC day of the query evaluation time as the value.

Operator Precedence

When evaluating an expression with multiple binary operators, PromQL does not simply go from left to right. Instead, there is an order of operators that is largely the same as the order used in other languages:

1. ^
2. * / %
3. + -
4. == != > < >= <=
5. unless and
6. or

For example, a or b * c + d is the same as a or ((b * c) + d).

All operators except ^ are left-associative. That means that a / b * c is the same as (a / b) * c, but a ^ b ^ c is a ^ (b ^ c).

You can use parentheses to change the order of evaluation. I also recommend adding parentheses where the evaluation order may not be immediately clear for an expression, as not everyone will have memorised the operator precedence.

Now that you understand both aggregators and operators, let's look at the final part of PromQL: functions.

Functions

PromQL has 46 functions as of 2.2.1, and offers you a wide variety of functionality, from common math to functions specifically for dealing with counter and histogram metrics. In this chapter you will learn about how all the functions work and how they can be used.

Almost all PromQL functions return instant vectors, and the two that don't (time and scalar) return scalars. No functions return range vectors, though multiple functions, including rate and avg_over_time that you have already seen, take a range vector as input.

Put another way, functions generally work either across the samples of a single time series at a time or across the samples of an instant vector. There is no single function or feature of PromQL that you can use to process an entire range vector at once.

PromQL is statically typed, functions do not change their return value based on the input types. In fact, the input types for each function are also fixed. Where a function needs to work with two different types, two different names are used. For example, you use the avg aggregator on instant vectors and the avg_over_time function on range vectors.

There are no official categories for the functions, but I have grouped related functions together.

Changing Type

At times you will have a vector but need a scalar, or vice versa. There are two functions that allow you to do so.

vector

The vector function takes a scalar value, and converts it into an instant vector with one labelless sample and the given value. For example, the expression:

```
vector(1)
```

will produce:

```
{} 1
```

This is useful if you need to ensure an expression returns a result, but can't depend on any particular time series to exist. For example:

```
sum(some_gauge) or vector(0)
```

will always return one sample, even if some_gauge has no samples. Depending on the use case, "bool modifier" on page 244 may be a better choice than the or operator (see "or operator" on page 251).

scalar

The scalar function takes an instant vector with a single sample and converts it to a scalar with the value the input sample had. If there is not exactly one sample, then NaN will be returned to you.

This is mostly useful when working with scalar constants, but you should use math functions that only work on instant vectors. For example, if you wanted the natural logarithm of two as a scalar, rather than typing out 0.6931471805599453 and hoping anyone reading it recognised the significance of number, you could use:

```
scalar(ln(vector(2)))
```

This can also make certain expressions simpler to write. For example, if you wanted to see which servers were started in the current year, you could do:

```
year(process_start_time_seconds)
==
scalar(year())
```

rather than:

```
year(process_start_time_seconds)
== on() group_left
year()
```

as scalar comparisons are a little easier to understand than vector matching with group_left, and this is okay as you know that year here will only ever return one sample.

But use of the scalar function should be limited because using `scalar` loses all of your labels and with it your ability to do vector matching. For example:

```
sum(rate(node_cpu_seconds_total{mode!="idle",instance="localhost:9090"}[5m]))
/
    scalar(count(node_cpu_seconds_total{mode="idle",instance="localhost:9090"))
```

will give you the proportion of time a machine's CPU is not idle, but you would then have to alter and reevaluate this expression for every single instance.

Taking advantage of the full power of PromQL, you can do:

```
sum without (cpu, mode)(
    rate(node_cpu_seconds_total{mode!="idle"}[5m])
)
/
    count without(cpu, mode)(node_cpu_seconds_total{mode="idle"})
```

and calculate the proportion of nonidle CPU for all your machines at once.

Math

The math functions perform standard mathematical operations on instant vectors, such as calculating absolute values or taking a logarithm. Each sample in the instant vector is handled independently, and the metric name is removed in the return value.

abs

abs takes an instant vector and returns the absolute value for each of its values, which is to say any negative numbers are changed to positive numbers.

The expression:

```
abs(process_open_fds - 15)
```

will return how far away each process's open file descriptors count is from 15. Counts of 5 and 25 would both return 10.

ln, log2, and log10

The functions ln, log2, and log10 take an instant vector and return the logarithm of the values and use different bases for the logarithm, Euler's number e, 2, and 10, respectively. ln is also known as the *natural logarithm*.

These functions can be used to get an idea of the different orders of magnitude of numbers. For example, to calculate the number of 9s[1] of successes an API endpoint had over the past hour, you could do:

```
log10(
  1 - (
     sum without(instance)(rate(requests_failed_total[1h]))
    /
     sum without(instance)(rate(requests_total[1h]))
  )
) * -1
```

 If you want a logarithm to a different base, you can use the *change of base* formula. For example, for a logarithm base three on the instant vector x, you would use:

```
ln(x) / ln(3)
```

These can also be useful for graphing in certain circumstances where normal linear graphs can't suitably represent a large variance in values. However, it is usually best to rely on the in-built logarithm graphing options in tools such as Grafana rather than using these functions, as they tend to gracefully handle edge cases such as negative logarithms returning NaN.

exp

The exp function provides the natural exponent, and is the inverse to the ln function. For example:

```
exp(vector(1))
```

returns:

```
{} 2.718281828459045
```

which is Euler's number, *e*.

sqrt

The sqrt function returns a square root of the values in an instant vector. For example:

```
sqrt(vector(9))
```

---

1 A 99% success rate is two 9s.

will return:

```
{} 3
```

sqrt predates the exponent operator ^, so this is equivalent to:

```
vector(9) ^ 0.5
```

If you need other roots you can use the same approach. For example, the cube or third root can be calculated with:

```
vector(9) ^ (1/3)
```

ceil and floor

ceil and floor allow you to round the values in an instant vector. ceil always rounds up to the nearest integer, and floor always rounds down. For example:

```
ceil(vector(0.1))
```

will return:

```
{} 1
```

round

round rounds the values in an instant vector to the nearest integer. If you provide a value that is exactly halfway between two integers, it is rounded up. That is to say that:

```
round(vector(5.5))
```

will return:

```
{} 6
```

round is also one of the functions that you can optionally provide with an additional argument. The additional argument is a scalar, and the values will be rounded to the nearest multiple of this number:

```
round(vector(2446), 1000)
```

will return:

```
{} 2000
```

for example. This is equivalent to:

```
round(vector(2446) / 1000) * 1000
```

but easier for you to use and understand.

clamp_max and clamp_min

Sometimes you will find that a metric returns spurious values well outside the normal range, such as a gauge that you expect to be positive occasionally being massively negative. clamp_max and clamp_min allow you to put upper and lower bounds, respectively, on the values in an instant vector.

For example, if you didn't believe that your processes could have fewer than 10 open file descriptors you could use:

```
clamp_min(process_open_fds, 10)
```

which would produce a result like:

```
{instance="localhost:9090",job="prometheus"} 46
{instance="localhost:9100",job="node"} 10
```

Time and Date

Prometheus offers you several functions dealing with time, most of which are convenience functions around time to save you from having to implement date-related logic yourself. Prometheus works entirely in UTC, and has no notion of time zones.

time

The time function is the most basic time-related function. It returns the evaluation time of the query as seconds since the Unix epoch[2] as a scalar. For example:

```
time()
```

might return:

```
1518618359.529
```

If you were to use time with the query_range endpoint, then every result would be different, as each step has a different evaluation time.

The Prometheus best practice is to expose the the Unix time in seconds at which something of interest happened, and not how long it has been since it happened. This is more reliable, as it's not susceptible to failure to update the metric. The time function then lets you convert these to durations. For example, if you wanted to see how long your processes have been running you would use:

```
time() - process_start_time_seconds
```

---

2 Midnight January 1st, 1970 UTC.

which will return a result such as:

```
{instance="localhost:9090",job="prometheus"} 313.5699999332428
{instance="localhost:9100",job="node"} 322.25999999046326
```

Here both Node exporter and Prometheus have been running for a bit over 5 minutes. If you had a batch job pushing the last time it succeeded to the Pushgateway, as discussed in "Pushgateway" on page 71, you could find jobs that hadn't succeeded in the past hour with:

```
time() - my_job_last_success_seconds > 3600
```

minute, hour, day_of_week, day_of_month, days_in_month, month, and year

time covers most use cases, but sometimes you will want to have logic based on the the clock or calendar. Converting to minutes and hours from time isn't too difficult,[3] but beyond that you have to consider issues like leap days.

All of these functions return the given value for the query evaluation time as an instant vector with one sample and no labels. As I write this it is currently 13:39 on Wednesday, February 14, 2018, in the UTC timezone. The outputs of these functions when evaluated at this time are:

Expression	Result
minute()	{} 39
hour()	{} 13
day_of_week()	{} 3
day_of_month()	{} 14
days_in_month()	{} 28
month()	{} 2
year()	{} 2018

day_of_week starts with 0 for Sunday, so the 3 here is Wednesday. If you wanted to check if today was the last day of the month you could compare the output of day_of_month to days_in_month.

You may be wondering why these functions don't return scalars, as that'd seem more convenient to work with. The answer is that these functions all take an optional argu-

---

3 Minutes are floor(vector(time() / 60 % 60)), for example.

ment[4] so that you can pass in instant vectors. For example, to see what year your processes started in you could use:

```
year(process_start_time_seconds)
```

which would produce a result such as:

```
{instance="localhost:9090",job="prometheus"} 2018
{instance="localhost:9100",job="node"} 2018
```

This could also be used to count how many processes were started this month:

```
sum(
    (year(process_start_time_seconds) == bool scalar(year()))
  *
    (month(process_start_time_seconds) == bool scalar(month()))
)
```

Here I am taking advantage of the fact that the multiplication operator acts like an *and operator* when used on booleans with the value 1 for true and 0 for false.

timestamp

The `timestamp` function is different from the other time functions in that it looks at the timestamp of the samples in an instant vector rather than the values. As was mentioned in "Instant Vector" on page 219 and "query" on page 223, the timestamps for samples returned from all operators, functions, the `query_range` HTTP API, and query HTTP API when it returns an instant vector will be the query evaluation time.

However, the timestamp of samples in an instant vector from an instant vector selector will be the actual timestamps.[5] The `timestamp` function allows you to access these. For example, you can see when the last scrape started for each target with:

```
timestamp(up)
```

This is because the default timestamp for data from a scrape is the time that the scrape started. Similarly the timestamp for samples from recording rules, as covered in Chapter 17, is the rule group execution time.

If you want to see raw data with samples for debugging, using a range vector selector with the query HTTP API is best, but `timestamp` does have some uses. For example:

```
node_time_seconds - timestamp(node_time_seconds)
```

would return the difference between when the scrape of the Node exporter was started by Prometheus and what time the Node exporter thought was the current

---

4 The default value of this argument is `vector(time())`.

5 As will the timestamps of samples if you provide a range vector selector to the query HTTP API.

time. While this isn't 100% accurate (it will vary with machine load), it will allow you to know if time is out of sync by a few seconds without needing a 1-second scrape interval.

Labels

In an ideal world the label names and label values used by different parts of your system would be consistent, so you wouldn't have customer in one place and cust in another. While it is best to resolve such inconsistencies in the source code, or failing that with metric_relabel_configs as discussed in "metric_relabel_configs" on page 148, this is not always possible. Thus the two label functions allow you to change labels.

label_replace

label_replace allows you to do regular expression substitution on label values. For example, if you needed the device label on node_disk_read_bytes_total to be dev instead for vector matching to work as you needed you could do:[6]

```
label_replace(node_disk_read_bytes_total, "dev", "${1}", "device", "(.*)")
```

which would return a result like:

```
node_disk_read_bytes_total{dev="sda",device="sda",instance="localhost:9100",
    job="node"} 4766305792
```

Unlike most functions, label_replace does not remove the metric name, as it is presumed that you are doing something unusual if you have to resort to label_replace, and removing the metric name could make that harder for you.

The arguments to label_replace are the instant vector input, the name of the output label, the replacement, the name of the source label, and the regular expression. label_replace is similar to the replace relabelling action, but you can only use one label as a source label. If the regular expression does not match for a given sample, then that sample is returned unchanged.

label_join

label_join allows you to join label values together, similarly to how source_labels is handled in relabelling. For example, if you wanted to join the job and instance labels together into a new label you could do:

```
label_join(node_disk_read_bytes_total, "combined", "-", "instance", "job")
```

---

6 In reality, as node_disk_read_bytes_total is a counter, you would use rate first and then label_replace.

which would return a result such as:

```
node_disk_read_bytes_total{combined="localhost:9100-node",device="sda",
    instance="localhost:9100",job="node"} 4766359040
```

As with `label_replace`, `label_join` does not remove the metric name. The arguments are the instant vector input, the name of the output label, the separator, and then zero or more label names.

You could combine `label_join` with `label_replace` to provide the full functionality of the `replace` relabel action, but at that point you should seriously consider `metric_relabel_configs` or fixing the source metrics instead.

Missing Series and absent

As mentioned in "Many-to-Many and Logical Operators" on page 251, the `absent` function plays the role of a *not* operator. If you pass a nonempty instant vector, it returns an empty instant vector. If you pass an empty instant vector, it returns an instant vector with one sample and a value of 1.

You might expect that this sample has no labels, since there are no labels to work with. However, `absent` is a little smarter than that, and if the argument is an instant vector selector, it uses the labels from any equality matchers present.

Expression	Result
absent(up)	empty instant vector
absent(up{job="prometheus"})	empty instant vector
absent(up{job="missing"})	{job="missing"} 1
absent(up{job=~"missing"})	{} 1
absent(non_existent)	{} 1
absent(non_existent{job="foo",env="dev"})	{job="foo",env="dev"} 1
absent(non_existent{job="foo",env="dev"} * 0)	{} 1

`absent` is useful for detecting if an entire job has gone missing from service discovery. Alerting on `up == 0` doesn't work too well when you have no targets to produce up metrics! Even when using `static_configs` it can be wise to have such an alert in case generation of your *prometheus.yml* goes awry.

If you want instead to alert on specific metrics that are missing from a target, you can use `unless`, which was covered in "unless operator" on page 253.

Sorting with sort and sort_desc

PromQL generally does not specify the order of elements within an instant vector, so it can change from evaluation to evaluation. But if you use sort or sort_desc as the last thing that is evaluated in a PromQL expression, then the instant vector will be sorted by value. For example:

```
sort(node_filesystem_size_bytes)
```

might return:

```
node_filesystem_free_bytes{device="tmpfs",fstype="tmpfs",
    instance="localhost:9100",job="node",mountpoint="/run/lock"} 5238784
node_filesystem_free_bytes{device="/dev/sda1",fstype="vfat",
    instance="localhost:9100",job="node",mountpoint="/boot/efi"} 70300672
node_filesystem_free_bytes{device="tmpfs",fstype="tmpfs",
    instance="localhost:9100",job="node",mountpoint="/run"} 817094656
node_filesystem_free_bytes{device="tmpfs",fstype="tmpfs",
    instance="localhost:9100",job="node",mountpoint="/run/user/1000"} 826912768
node_filesystem_free_bytes{device="/dev/sda5",fstype="ext4",
    instance="localhost:9100",job="node",mountpoint="/"} 30791843840
```

The effect of these functions is cosmetic, but may save you some effort in reporting scripts. NaNs are always sorted to the end, so sort and sort_desc are not quite the reverse of each other.

> The instant vectors returned from the topk and bottomk aggregators already come with their samples sorted within the aggregation groups.

Histograms with histogram_quantile

The histogram_quantile function was already touched on in "Histogram" on page 215. It is internally a bit like an aggregator, since it groups samples together like a without(le) clause would and then calculates a quantile from their values. For example:

```
histogram_quantile(
    0.90,
    rate(prometheus_tsdb_compaction_duration_seconds_bucket[1d]))
```

would calculate the 0.9 quantile (also known as the 90th percentile) latency of Prometheus's compaction latency over the past day. Values outside of the range from zero to one do not make sense for quantiles, and will result in infinities.

As discussed in "Cumulative Histograms" on page 52, the values in the buckets must be cumulative and there must be a +Inf bucket.

You must always use `rate` first for buckets exposed by Prometheus's histogram metric type, as shown in "The Histogram" on page 50, as `histogram_quantile` needs gauges to work on. But there are a very small number of exporters that expose histogram-like time series where the buckets are gauges rather than counters. If you come across one of these it is okay to use `histogram_quantile` on them directly.

Counters

Counters include not just the counter metric, but also the _sum, _count, and _bucket time series from summary and histogram metrics. Counters can only go up. When an application starts or restarts, counters will initialise to 0, and the counter functions take this into account automatically.

The values of counters are not particularly useful on their own; you will almost always want to convert them to gauges using one of the counter-related functions.

Functions working on counters all take a range vector as an argument and return an instant vector. Each of the time series in the range vector is processed individually, and returns at most one sample. If there is only one sample for one of your time series within the range you provide, you will get no output for it when using these functions.

rate

The `rate` function is the primary function you will use with counters, and indeed likely the main function you will use from PromQL. `rate` returns how fast a counter is increasing per second for each time series in the range vector passed to it. You have already seen many examples of `rate`, such as:

```
rate(process_cpu_seconds_total[1m])
```

which returns a result like:

```
{instance="localhost:9090",job="prometheus"} 0.0018000000000000683
{instance="localhost:9100",job="node"} 0.005
```

`rate` automatically handles counter resets, and any decrease in a counter is considered to be a counter reset. So, for example, if you had a time series that had values [5,10,4,6], it would be treated as though it was [5,10,14,16]. `rate` presumes that the targets it is monitoring are relatively long-lived compared to a scrape interval, as it cannot detect multiple resets in a short period of time. If you have targets that are expected to regularly live for less than a handful of scrape intervals you may wish to consider a log-based monitoring solution instead.

`rate` has to handle scenarios like time series appearing and disappearing, such as if one of your instances started up and then later crashed. For example, if one of your instances had a counter that was incrementing at a rate of around 10 per second, but was only running for half an hour, then a `rate(x_total[1h])` would return a result of around 5 per second.

Values are rarely exact. Since scrapes for different targets happen at different times, there can be jitter over time, the steps of a `query_range` call will rarely align perfectly with scrapes, and scrapes are expected to fail every now and then. In the face of such challenges, `rate` is designed to be robust, and the result of `rate` is intended to be correct when looked at on average over time.

`rate` is not intended to catch every single increment, as it is expected that increments will be lost, such as if an instance dies between scrapes. This may cause artifacts if you have very slow moving counters, such as if they're only incremented a few times an hour. `rate` can also only deal with changes in counters, because if a counter time series appears with a value of 100, `rate` has no idea if those increments were just now or if the target has been running for years and has only just started being returned by service discovery to be scraped.

It is recommended to use a range for your range vector that is at least four times your scrape interval. This will ensure that you always have two samples to work with even if scrapes are slow, ingestion is slow, and there has been a single scrape failure. Such issues are a fact of life in real-world systems, so it is important to be resilient. For example, for a 1-minute scrape interval you might use a 4-minute rate, but usually that is rounded up to a 5-minute rate.[7]

Generally you should aim to have the same range used on all your rate functions within a Prometheus for the sake of sanity, since outputs from rates over different ranges are not comparable and tend to be hard to keep track of.

You may wonder with all these implementation details and caveats if `rate` could be changed to be simpler. There are several ways you can approach this problem, but at the end of the day they all have both advantages and disadvantages. If you fix one apparent problem, you will cause a different problem to pop up. The `rate` function is a good balance across all of these concerns, and provides a robust solution suitable for operational monitoring. If you run into a situation where any rate-like function isn't giving you quite what you need, I would suggest continuing your debugging based on logs data, which does not have these particular concerns and can produce exact answers.

---

7 *Five-minute rate* is a colloquial way to say a `rate` function on a range vector with a 5-minute range, such as `rate(x_total[5m])`.

increase

increase is merely syntactic sugar on top of rate. increase(x_total[5m]) is exactly equivalent to rate(x_total[5m]) * 300, which is to say the result of rate multiplied by the range of the range vector. The logic is otherwise identical.

Seconds are the base unit for Prometheus, so you should use increase only when displaying values to humans. Within your recording rules and alerts it is best to stick to rate for consistency.

One of the outcomes of the robustness of rate and increase is that they can return noninteger results when given integer inputs. Consider that you had the following data points for a time series:

```
21@2
22@7
24@12
```

And you were to calculate increase(x_total[15s]) with a query time of 15 seconds. The increase here is 3 over a period of 10 seconds, so you might expect a result of 3. However, the rate was taken over a 15-second period, so to avoid underestimating the correct answer, the 10 seconds of data you have is extrapolated out to 15 seconds, producing a result of 4.5 for the increase.

rate and increase presume that a time series continues beyond the bound of the range if the first/last samples is within 110% of the average interval of the data. If this is not the case, it is presumed the time series exists for 50% of an interval beyond the samples you have, but not with the value going below zero.

irate

irate is like rate in that it returns the per-second rate at which a counter is increasing. The algorithm it uses is much simpler though; it only looks at the last two samples of the range vector it is passed. This has the advantage that it is much more responsive to changes and you don't have to care so much about the relationship between the vector's range and the scrape interval, but comes with the corresponding disadvantage that as it is only looking at two samples, it can only be safely used in graphs that are fully zoomed in.[8] Figure 16-1 shows a comparison of a 5-minute rate against an irate.

---

8 If the step for a query_range is greater than the scrape interval, you would skip data when using irate.

Due to the lack of averaging that `irate` brings, the graphs can be more volatile[9] and harder to read. It is not advisible to use `irate` in alerts due to it being sensitive to brief spikes and dips; use `rate` instead.

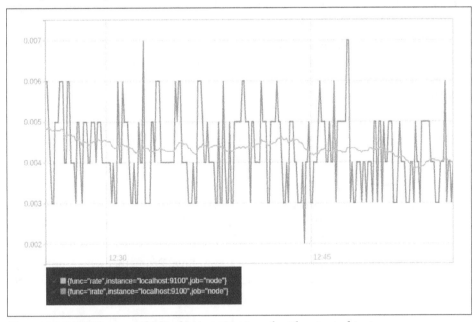

Figure 16-1. CPU usage of a Node exporter viewed with rate and irate

resets

You may sometimes suspect that a counter is resetting more often than it should be. The `resets` function returns how many times each time series in a range vector has reset. For example, the expression:

```
resets(process_cpu_seconds_total[1h])
```

will indicate how many times the CPU time of the process has reset in the past hour. This should be the number of times the process has restarted,[10] but if you had a bug that was causing it to go backwards, the value would be higher.

`resets` is intended as a debugging tool for counters, since counters might reset too often and nonmonotonic counters will cause artifacts in the form of large spikes in your graphs. However, some users have found occasional uses for it when they want to know how many times a gauge has been seen to decrease.

---

9 `irate` is short for *instant rate*, though that the function is called *irate* still brings me minor amusement.

10 `changes(process_start_time_seconds[1h])` is a better way to count restarts.

Changing Gauges

Unlike counters, the values of gauges are useful on their own and you can use binary operators and aggregators directly on them. But sometimes you will want to analyse the history of a gauge, and there are several functions for this purpose.

As with the counter functions, these functions also take a range vector and return an instant vector with at most one sample for each time series in your input.

changes

Some gauges are expected to change very rarely. For example, the start time of a process does not change in the lifetime of a process.[11] The changes function allows you to count how many times a gauge has changed value, so

```
changes(process_start_time_seconds[1h])
```

will tell you how many times your process has restarted in the past hour. If you aggregated this across entire applications it would allow you to spot if your applications were in a slow crash loop.

Due to the fundamental nature of metrics sampling, Prometheus may not scrape often enough to see every possible change. However, if a process is restarting that frequently, you will still detect it either via this method or by up being 0.

You can use changes beyond process_start_time_seconds for other situations where the fact that a gauge has changed is interesting to you.

deriv

Often you will want to know how quickly a gauge is changing; for example, how quickly a backlog is increasing if it is increasing at all. This would allow you to alert on not only the backlog being higher than you'd like but also that it has not already started to go down.

You could do x - x offset 1h, but this only uses two samples, and thus lacks robustness because it is susceptible to individual outlier values. The deriv function uses *least-squares regression*[12] to estimate the slope of each of the time series in a range vector. For example:

```
deriv(process_resident_memory_bytes[1h])
```

---

11 Although there have been cases, such as *https://github.com/prometheus/client_golang/issues/289*, where a cloud provider's kernel was providing bad metrics.

12 Also known as *simple linear regression*.

would calculate how fast resident memory is changing per second based on samples from the past hour.

predict_linear

predict_linear goes a step further than deriv and predicts what the value of a gauge will be in the future based on data in the provided range. For example:

```
predict_linear(node_filesystem_free_bytes{job="node"}[1h], 4 * 3600)
```

would predict how much free space would be left on each filesystem in four hours based on the past hour of samples. This expression is roughly equivalent to:

```
deriv(node_filesystem_free_bytes{job="node"}[1h]) * 4 * 3600
+
  node_filesystem_free_bytes{job="node"}[1h]
```

but predict_linear is slightly more accurate because it uses the intercept from the regression.

predict_linear is useful for resource limit alerts, where static thresholds such as 1 GB free or percentage thresholds such as 10% free tend to have false positives and false negatives depending on whether you are working with relatively large or small filesystems. A 1 GB threshold on a 1 TB filesystem would alert you too late, but would also alert you too early on a 2 GB filesystem. predict_linear works better across all sizes.

It can take some tweaking to choose good values for the range and to determine how far to predict forward. If there was a regular sawtooth pattern in the data you would want to ensure that the range was long enough not to extrapolate the upward part of the cycle out indefinitely.

delta

delta is similar to increase, but without the counter reset handling. This function should be avoided as it can be overly affected by single outlier values. You should use deriv instead, or x - x offset 1h if you really want to compare with the value a given time ago.

idelta

idelta takes the last two samples in a range and returns their difference. idelta is intended for advanced use cases. For example, the way rate and irate work is not to everyone's personal tastes, so using idelta and recording rules allows users to implement what they'd like without polluting PromQL with various subtle variations of the rate function.

holt_winters

The holt_winters function[13] implements *Holt-Winters double exponential smoothing*. Gauges can at times be very spiky and hard to read so some smoothing is often good. At the simplest you could use avg_over_time, but you might want something more sophisticated.

This function works through the samples for a time series and tracks the smoothed value so far and provides an estimate of the trend in the data. Each new sample is taken into account based on the *smoothing factor*, which indicates how much old data is important relative to new data, and the *trend factor*, which controls how important the trend is. For example:

```
holt_winters(process_resident_memory_bytes[1h], 0.1, 0.5)
```

would smooth memory usage with a smoothing factor of 0.1 and a trend factor of 0.5. Both factors must be between 0 and 1.

Aggregation Over Time

Aggregators such as avg work across the samples in an instant vector. There is also a set of functions such as avg_over_time that apply the same logic, but across the values of a time series in a range vector. These functions are:

- sum_over_time
- count_over_time
- avg_over_time
- stddev_over_time
- stdvar_over_time
- min_over_time
- max_over_time
- quantile_over_time

For example, to see the peak memory usage that Prometheus saw for a process you could use:

```
max_over_time(process_resident_memory_bytes[1h])
```

and even go a step further and calculate that across the application:

```
max without(instance)(max_over_time(process_resident_memory_bytes[1h]))
```

---

13 It is possible this function is misnamed; see *https://github.com/prometheus/prometheus/issues/2458*.

These functions only work from the values of the samples; there is no weighting based on the length of time between samples or any other logic relating to time-stamps. This means that if you change the scrape interval, for example, there will be a bias toward the time period with the more frequent scrapes for functions such as avg_over_time and quantile_over_time. Similarly if there are failed scrapes for a period of time, that period will be less represented in your result.

These functions are used with gauges.[14] If you want to take an avg_over_time of a rate this isn't possible as that function returns instant rather than range vectors. However, rate already calculates an average over time, so you can increase the range on the rate. For example, instead of trying to do:

```
avg_over_time(rate(x_total[5m])[1h])
```

which will produce a parse error, you can instead do:

```
rate(x_total[1h])
```

How to use the instant vector output of functions as the input of functions that require range vectors is covered in the next chapter on recording rules.

---

14 Though as count_over_time ignores values, it can be useful for debugging any type of metric.

Recording Rules

The HTTP API is not the only way in which you can access PromQL. You can also use *recording rules* to have Prometheus evaluate PromQL expressions regularly and ingest their results. This is useful to speed up your dashboards, provide aggregated results for use elsewhere, and to compose range vector functions. Other monitoring systems might call their equivalent feature standing queries or continuous queries. Alerting rules (covered in Chapter 18) are also a variant of recording rules. This chapter will show you how and when to use recording rules.

Using Recording Rules

Recording rules go in separate files from your *prometheus.yml*, which are known as *rule files*. As with *prometheus.yml*, rule files also use the YAML format. You can specify where your rule files are located using the `rule_files` top-level field in your *prometheus.yml*. For example, Example 17-1 loads a rule file called *rules.yml*, in addition to scraping two targets.

Example 17-1. prometheus.yml scraping two targets and loading a rule file

```
global:
  scrape_interval: 10s
  evaluation_interval: 10s
rule_files:
 - rules.yml
scrape_configs:
 - job_name: prometheus
   static_configs:
    - targets:
       - localhost:9090
 - job_name: node
   static_configs:
```

```
  - targets:
    - localhost:9100
```

Similar to the `files` field of `file_sd_configs`, as covered in "File" on page 130, `rule_files` takes a list of paths, and you can use globs in the filename. Unlike file service discovery, `rule_files` does not use inotify nor does it automatically pick up changes you make to rule files. Instead, you must either restart Prometheus or reload its configuration.

To ask Prometheus to reload its configuration you can send it the `SIGHUP` signal using a command like:

```
kill -HUP <pid>
```

where *pid* is the process ID of Prometheus. You can also send a HTTP `POST` to the */-/reload* endpoint of Prometheus, but for security reasons this requires that the `--web.enable-lifecycle` flag is specified. If the reload fails, Prometheus will log this, and you will see the `prometheus_config_last_reload_successful` metric change to 0.

To detect bad configuration files or rules in advance, you can use the `promtool check config` command to check your *prometheus.yml*. This will also check all the rule files referenced by the *prometheus.yml*. You might have this as a pre-submit check or unit test that is applied before the configuration file is rolled out. If you want to check the syntax of individual rule files you can use `promtool check rules`.

Rule files themselves consist of zero[1] or more groups of rules. Example 17-2 shows a rule file.

Example 17-2. rules.yml with one group containing two rules

```
groups:
 - name: example
   rules:
    - record: job:process_cpu_seconds:rate5m
      expr: sum without(instance)(rate(process_cpu_seconds_total[5m]))
    - record: job:process_open_fds:max
      expr: max without(instance)(process_open_fds)
```

You will notice that the group has a `name`. This must be unique within a rule file, and is used in the Prometheus UI and metrics. `expr` is the PromQL expression to be evaluated and output into the metric name specified by `record`.

---

1 I'm not sure why you would want an empty rule file.

It is possible to specify an `evaluation_interval` for a group, but as with `scrape_interval` you should aim for only one interval in a Prometheus for sanity. You can also specify a set of labels in the `labels` field to be added to the output, but this is rarely appropriate for recording rules.[2]

Each rule in a group is evaluated in turn, and the output of your first rule is ingested into the time series database before your second rule is run. While rules within a group are executed sequentially, different groups will be run at different times just as different targets are scraped at different times. This is to spread out the load on your Prometheus.

Once your rules are loaded and running you can view them on the Rules status page at *http://localhost:9090/rules*, as shown in Figure 17-1.

Figure 17-1. Rules status page of Prometheus

In addition to listing your rules, how long each group as a whole took to last evaluate and how long each rule took to execute are also displayed. You can use this to find expensive rules that may need adjustment or reconsideration. The `prometheus_rule_group_last_duration_seconds` metric will also tell you how long the last evaluation of each group took, which you can use to determine if there have been recent changes in the cost of your rules. There is no metric with the duration of individual rules as that could cause cardinality issues. In this case, the rules are taking less than a millisecond, which is well under the evaluation interval, so there is nothing to worry about.

---

2 However, `labels` is used in virtually all alerting rules.

There is no API to upload or change rules. As with Prometheus configuration generally, files are intended to be a base upon which you could build such a system on top of if you so wish.

When to Use Recording Rules

There are several cases when you might want to use recording rules. Recording rules are mainly used to reduce cardinality in order to make your queries more efficient. This is common for dashboards, federation, and before storing the metrics in long-term storage. You might also use recording rules to compose range vector functions and on occasion offering APIs of metrics to other teams.

Reducing Cardinality

If you have an expression such as:

```
sum without(instance)(rate(process_cpu_seconds_total{job="node"}[5m]))
```

in a dashboard you will find you get a prompt response from Prometheus if you have a few targets. As the number of targets grows to the hundreds and thousands you will find that the response time for a `query_range` is not as snappy.

Rather than asking PromQL to access and process thousands of time series for the entire range of each graph on your dashboard, you can precompute this value using a rule group using something like:[3]

```
groups:
 - name: node
   rules:
    - record: job:process_cpu_seconds:rate5m
      expr: >
        sum without(instance)(
          rate(process_cpu_seconds_total{job="node"}[5m])
        )
```

which will output to a metric called `job:process_cpu_seconds:rate5m`.

Now you only need to fetch that one time series when your dashboard is being rendered. The same applies even if you have instrumentation labels in play, as you are reducing the number of time series to process by a factor of how many instances you have. Effectively you are trading an ongoing resource cost against much lower latency and resource cost for your queries. Due to this tradeoff it is not generally wise to have

---

3 The > here is one of the ways to have multiline strings in YAML.

rules that use long vector ranges, as such queries tend to be expensive, and running them regularly can cause performance problems.

You should try to put all rules for one job in one group. That way they will have the same timestamp and avoid artifacts when you do further math on them. All recording rules in a group have the same query evaluation time for an execution, and all output samples will also have that timestamp.

You will find aggregation rules like these are useful beyond making your dashboards faster. When using federation, as discussed in "Going Global with Federation" on page 334, you will always want to pull aggregated metrics, as otherwise you would be pulling in large swathes of instance-level metrics. At that point, the Prometheus using federation would be better off scraping the targets directly itself from a performance standpoint.[4]

Similar logic applies if you want to save some metrics on a long-term basis. When doing capacity planning over months or years of data, details of individual instances are not relevant. By keeping primarily aggregated metrics long term you can save a lot of resources with little loss in useful information.

You will often have aggregation rules based off the same metric but with different sets of labels. Rather than calculating each aggregation individually, you can be efficient by having one rule use the output of another. For example:

```
groups:
 - name: node
   rules:
    - record: job_device:node_disk_read_bytes:rate5m
      expr: >
        sum without(instance)(
          rate(node_disk_read_bytes_total{job="node"}[5m])
        )
    - record: job:node_disk_read_bytes:rate5m
      expr: >
        sum without(device)(
          job_device:node_disk_read_bytes:rate5m{job="node"}
        )
```

For this to work properly, the rules in a given hierarchy must be in order within a single rule group.[5] It is generally best to explicitly specify the job that your rules apply to in your selectors, so that your groups don't step on each others' toes.

---

4 Performance-wise, many small scrapes staggered over time is better than the samples from all those scrapes being combined into one massive scrape.

5 Prior to Prometheus 2.0 this approach was not practical. There was no notion of rule groups, so you couldn't guarantee that one rule would only run after another rule had completed.

Composing Range Vector Functions

As mentioned in "Aggregation Over Time" on page 274, you cannot use range vector functions on the output of functions that produce instant vectors. For example, `max_over_time(sum without(instance)(rate(x_total[5m]))[1h])` is not possible, and will produce a parse error. PromQL does not feature any form of subquery support, but you can use recording rules to the same effect:

```
groups:
 - name: j_job_rules
   rules:
    - record: job:x:rate5m
      expr: >
        sum without(instance)(
          rate(x_total{job="j"}[5m])
        )
    - record: job:x:max_over_time1h_rate5m
      expr: max_over_time(job:x:rate5m{job="j"}[1h])
```

This approach can be used with any range vector function, including not only the `_over_time` functions but also `predict_linear`, `deriv`, and `holt_winters`.

However, this technique should not be used with `rate`, `irate`, or `increase`, as an effective expression of `rate(sum(x_total)[5m])` would have massive spikes every time one of its constituent counters reset or disappeared.

 Always `rate` and then `sum`, never `sum` and then `rate`.

You are not required to have the outer function in a recording rule. With the preceding example it might make more sense to have the `max_over_time` performed as you need it. For example, the primary use for this particular example would be capacity planning, as you need to plan for peak rather than average traffic. Since capacity planning is often performed once a month or once a quarter, there is not much point in you evaluating the `max_over_time` at least once a minute rather than running the query just when you need it. Functions over longer time ranges can also get expensive due to the amount of data they have to process. Be careful with ranges over an hour and particularly across many many time series.

Rules for APIs

Usually the Prometheus servers you run are going to be used entirely by you and your team. But you may run into situations where other teams wish to pull metrics from your Prometheus. If their usage is just informational or depends on metrics that are unlikely to change, that's generally okay, because if you break things on them it's not the end of the world. But if the metrics are being used as part of automated systems or processes outside of your control, it may be a good idea to create metrics just for other teams to consume as a form of public API. Then if you need to change the labels or rules inside your Prometheus you can do so, while still ensuring that the metrics the other team depends on keep the same semantics.

The naming of such metrics doesn't tend to follow the normal naming conventions, and you will typically put the name of the consuming team either in the metric name or a label.

Such uses of rules are quite rare. If another team's use of your Prometheus is getting to the stage where it is placing a nontrivial maintenance burden on you, you might want to ask them to run their own Prometheus for the metrics they need.

How Not to Use Rules

I have noticed a few common antipatterns with recording rules that I would like to help you avoid.

The first of these is rules that undo the benefits of labels. For example:

```
- record: job_device:node_disk_read_bytes_sda:rate5m
  expr: >
    sum without(instance)(
      rate(node_disk_read_bytes_total{job="node",device="sda"}[5m])
    )
- record: job_device:node_disk_read_bytes_sdb:rate5m
  expr: >
    sum without(instance)(
      rate(node_disk_read_bytes_total{job="node",device="sdb"}[5m])
    )
```

This would require you to have a rule per potential device label, and you cannot easily aggregate across these metrics. This basically defeats the entire purpose of labels, one of the most powerful features of Prometheus. You should avoid moving label values into metric names, and if you want to limit what time series are returned based on a label value, use a matcher at query time. Similarly do not move the job label into the metric name.

Another antipattern is preaggregating every metric an application exposes. While it is true that aggregation is a good idea to reduce cardinality for performance, it is counterproductive to overdo it. In a metrics-based monitoring system it is not uncommon to never use over 90% of your metrics,[6] so aggregating everything by default is a waste of resources and would require unnecessary maintenance as metrics are added and

---

6 I have heard numbers around this mark from multiple monitoring systems.

removed over time. Instead, you should add aggregation as you need it. Those other 90% of metrics are still accessible for when you end up debugging some weird issue in the bowels of your system, and the only cost of not aggregating them is that your queries on them will take slightly longer.

The primary purpose of recording rules is to reduce cardinality, so there is often not much point in having recording rules that still have an instance label in their output. Querying ten time series at query time isn't notably more expensive than querying one. If you have metrics with high cardinality within a target, recording rules with instance labels can make sense, though you should also consider if those instrumentation labels should be removed on cardinality grounds.

With rules such as:

```
- record: job:x:max_over_time1h_rate5m
  expr: max_over_time(job:x:rate5m{job="j"}[1h])
```

from the preceding section, you might be tempted to change their evaluation_inter val to an hour in order to save resources. This is not a good idea for three reasons. First, as the input metric came from a recording rule that already reduced cardinality, any resource savings will likely be tiny in the grand scheme of things. Second, Prometheus only guarantees that the rule will be executed once an hour, not when in the hour it will be executed. As you likely want results around the start of the hour, this, combined with staleness handling, will not work out. Third, for the sake of your sanity, you should aim for one interval inside your Prometheus servers.

The final pattern I would advise you to avoid is using recording rules to fix poor metric names and labels. This pattern loses the original timestamps of the data, and makes it harder to figure out where a metric came from and what it means. First, you should try improving the metrics at their source, and if that is not possible for technical or political reasons, consider whether using "metric_relabel_configs" on page 148 to improve them is worth the downsides of them differing from what everyone else expects them to be named.

Unfortunately, there will always be cases where systems expose metrics that are too far outside the Prometheus way of doing things, and you have no choice but to fix them up however you can.

Naming of Recording Rules

By using a good convention for naming recording rules, you can not only tell at a glance what a given recording rule metric name means, but it will also be easier to share your rules with others due to a shared vocabulary.

As mentioned in "What Should I Name My Metrics?" on page 58, colons are valid characters to have in metric names but are to be avoided in instrumentation. The reason for this is so you the user can take advantage of them to add your own structure in recording rules. The convention I use here balances precision and succinctness and comes from years of experience.

The way this convention works is to have your metric names contain the labels that are in play, followed by the metric name, followed by the operations that have been performed on the metric. These three sections are separated by colons, so you will always have either zero or two colons in a metric name. For example, given the metric name:

```
job_device:node_disk_read_bytes:rate5m
```

I can tell that it has `job` and `device` labels, the metric it is based off is `node_disk_read_bytes`, and that it is a counter that `rate(node_disk_read_bytes _total[5m])` was applied to. These parts are the *level*, *metric*, and *operations*.

level
>The level indicates the aggregation level of the metric by the labels it has. This will always include the instrumentation labels (if they have not been aggregated away yet), the `job` label that should be present, and any other target labels that are relevant. Which target labels to include depends on context. If you have an `env` label across all your targets that doesn't affect your rules, then there's no need to bloat your metric names with it. But if a job was broken up by a `shard` label you should probably include it.

metric
>The metric is just that—the metric or time series name. It's normal to remove the `_total` on counters to make things more succinct, but otherwise this should be the exact metric name. The benefits of keeping the metric name is that it is then easy to search your code base for that metric name, and vice versa if you are looking at code to find if the metric has been aggregated. For ratios you would use `foo_per_bar`, but there's a special rule for dealing with `_sum` and `_count` ratios.

operations
>The operations are a list of functions and aggregators that have been applied to the metric, the most recent first. If you have two `sum` or `max` operations you only need to list one, as a sum of a sum is still a sum. Since sum is the default aggregation, you generally don't need to list it. But if you have no other operation to use, or haven't applied any operations yet, `sum` is a good default. Depending on what operations you plan on applying at other levels, `min` and `max` can make sense for a base metric name. The operation you should use for division is `ratio`.

To take some examples, if you had a `foo_total` counter with a `bar` instrumentation label, then aggregating away the `instance` label would look like:

```
- record: job_bar:foo:rate5m
  expr: sum without(instance)(rate(foo_total{job="j"}[5m]))
```

Going from there to aggregate away the bar label would look like:

```
- record: job:foo:rate5m
  expr: sum without(bar)(job_bar:foo:rate5m{job="j"})
```

You can start to see some of the advantages of this approach. It is clear from inspection that the label handling is as expected here, as the input time series had job_bar as the level, bar was removed using a without clause, and the output had job as the level. In more complex rules and hierarchies this can be helpful to spot mistakes. For example, the rule:

```
- record: job:foo_per_bar:ratio_rate5m
  expr: >
    (
        job:foo:rate5m{job="j"}
      /
        job:bar:rate10m{job="j"}
    )
```

seems to be following the naming scheme for ratios, but there is a mismatch between the rate5m and the rate10m, which you should notice and realise that this expression and the resulting recording rule don't make sense. A correct ratio might look like:

```
- record: job_mountpoint:node_filesystem_avail_bytes_per_
              node_filesystem_size_bytes:ratio
  expr: >
    (
        job_mountpoint:node_filesystem_avail_bytes:sum{job="node"}
      /
        job_mountpoint:node_filesystem_size_bytes:sum{job="node"}
    )
```

Here you can see that the numerator and denominator have the same level and operations, which are propagated to the output metric name.[7] Here the sum is removed, as it doesn't tell you anything. This would not be the case if there was a rate5m operation in the input metrics.

Using the preceding notation for average event sizes would be a bit wordy, so instead the metric name is preserved and mean5m is used as the output operation as it is based on a rate5m and is thus a mean over 5 minutes:

---

7 Arguably you could remove the _bytes here as it cancels out, but that might make it harder to find the original metrics in the source code.

```
- record: job_instance:go_gc_duration_seconds:mean5m
  expr: >
    (
        job_instance:go_gc_duration_seconds_sum:rate5m{job="prometheus"}
      /
        job_instance:go_gc_duration_seconds_count:rate5m{job="prometheus"}
    )
```

If you later saw the rule:

```
- record: job:go_gc_duration_seconds:mean5m
  expr:
    avg without(instance)(
      job_instance:go_gc_duration_seconds:mean5m{job="prometheus"}
    )
```

it would be immediately obvious that this is attempting to take an average of an average, which doesn't make sense. The correct aggregation would be:

```
- record: job:go_gc_duration_seconds:mean5m
  expr:
    (
        sum without(instance)(
          job_instance:go_gc_duration_seconds_sum:rate5m{job="prometheus"})
        )
      /
        sum without(instance)(
          job_instance:go_gc_duration_seconds_count:rate5m{job="prometheus"})
        )
    )
```

You should sum to aggregate, and only perform division for averaging at the last step of your calculation.

While the preceding cases are straightforward, like metric naming in general, once you get off the beaten track, recording rule naming can be more of an art than a science. You should endeavour to ensure that your recording rule names are clear in what their semantics and labels are, while also attempting to make it easy to tie back recording rule names to the code that produced the original metrics.

Aside from the very rare exception (see "Rules for APIs" on page 282), metric names should indicate the identity of a metric name so that you can know what it is. Metric names should not be used as a way to store annotations for policy.

For example, you should not feel tempted to add :federate or :longterm or similar to metric names to indicate that you want such and such a metric transferred to another system. This bloats metric names, and will cause problems when your policy changes. Instead, define and implement your policy via matchers when extracting the data, such as, say, pulling all metric names matching job:.*, rather than trying to micro-optimise which exact metrics will and won't be fetched. By the time a metric has been through a recording rule, it has likely been aggregated sufficiently that its cardinality is negligible, and thus it is probably not worth your time to worry about the resource costs downstream.

Now that you know how to use recording rules, the next chapter will look at alerting rules. Alerting rules also live in rule groups, and have a similar syntax.

Alerting

If you want to be woken up at 3 a.m. by your monitoring system,[1] these are the chapters for you.

Building on the previous chapter, Chapter 18 covers alerting rules in Prometheus, which offer you the ability to alert on far more than simple thresholds.

Once you have alerts firing in Promethus, the Alertmanager converts those into notifications while attempting to group and throttle notifications to increase the value of each notification, as explained in Chapter 19.

---

1 Hopefully when there's a true emergency.

Alerting

Back in "What Is Monitoring?" on page 4 I stated that alerting was one of the components of monitoring, allowing you to notify a human when there is a problem. Prometheus allows you to define conditions in the form of PromQL expressions that are continuously evaluated, and any resulting time series become alerts. This chapter will show you how to configure *alerts* in Prometheus.

As you saw from the example in "Alerting" on page 30, Prometheus is not responsible for sending out *notifications* such as emails, chat messages, or pages. That role is handled by the *Alertmanager*.

Prometheus is where your logic to determine what is or isn't alerting is defined. Once an alert is *firing* in Prometheus, it is sent to an Alertmanager, which can take in alerts from many Prometheus servers. The Alertmanager then groups alerts together and sends you throttled notifications (Figure 18-1).

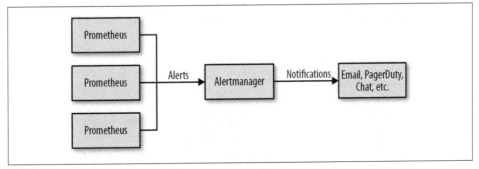

Figure 18-1. Prometheus and Alertmanager architecture

This architecture shown in Figure 18-1 allows you not only flexibility, but also the ability to have a single notification based on alerts from multiple different Prometheus servers. For example, if you had an issue propagating serving data to all of your datacenters, you could configure your alert grouping so that you got only a single notification rather than being spammed by a notification for each datacenter you have.

Alerting Rules

Alerting rules are similar to recording rules, which were covered in Chapter 17. You place alerting rules in the same rule groups as recording rules, and can mix and match as you see fit. For example, it is normal to have all the rules and alerts for a job in one group:[1]

```
groups:
 - name: node_rules
   rules:
    - record: job:up:avg
      expr: avg without(instance)(up{job="node"})
    - alert: ManyInstancesDown
      expr: job:up:avg{job="node"} < 0.5
```

This defines an alert with the name ManyInstancesDown that will fire if more than half of your Node exporters are down. You can tell that it is an alerting rule because it has an alert field rather than a record field.

In this example I am careful to use without rather than by so that any other labels the time series have are preserved and will be passed on to the Alertmanager. Knowing details such as the job, environment, and cluster of your alert is rather useful when you get the eventual notification.

For recording rules, you should avoid filtering in your expressions, as time series appearing and disappearing are challenging to deal with. For alerting rules, filtering is essential. If evaluating your alert expression results in an empty instant vector, then no alerts will fire, but if there are any samples returned, each of them will become an alert.

Due to this, a single alerting rule like:

```
 - alert: InstanceDown
   expr: up{job="node"} == 0
```

automatically applies to every instance in the node job that service discovery returns, and if you had a hundred down instances you would get a hundred firing alerts. If on the next evaluation cycle some of those instances are back up, those alerts are considered *resolved*.

---

1 If a group gets too large to be calculated in one interval, you may have to split it up if trimming it down is not an option.

An alert is identified across evaluation cycles by its labels and does not include the metric name label __name__, but which does include an alertname label with the name of the alert.

In addition to sending alerts to the Alertmanager, your alerting rules will also populate a metric called ALERTS. In addition to all the labels of your alert, an alertstate label is also added. The alertstate label will have a value of firing for firing alerts and pending for pending alerts as discussed in "for" on page 294. Resolved alerts do not have samples added to ALERTS. While you can use ALERTS in your alerting rules as you would any other metric, I would advise caution as it may indicate that you are overcomplicating your setup.

Correct staleness handling for resolved alerts in ALERTS depends on alerts always firing from the same alerting rule. If you have multiple alerts with the same name in a rule group, and a given alert can come from more than one of those alerting rules, then you may see odd behaviour from ALERTS.[2]

If you want notifications for an alert to be sent only at certain times of the day, the Alertmanager does not support routing based on time. But you can use the date functions "minute, hour, day_of_week, day_of_month, days_in_month, month, and year" on page 263. For example:

```
- alert: ManyInstancesDown
  expr: >
    (
        avg without(instance)(up{job="node"}) < 0.5
      and on()
        hour() > 9 < 17
    )
```

This alert will only fire from 9 a.m. to 5 p.m. UTC. It is common to use the "and operator" on page 254 to combine alerting conditions together. Here I used on() as there were no shared labels between the two sides of the and, which is not usually the case.

For batch jobs, you will want to alert on the job not having succeeded recently:

```
- alert: BatchJobNoRecentSuccess
  expr: >
    time() - my_batch_job_last_success_time_seconds{job="batch"} > 86400*2
```

---

2 This also applies to recording rules, but it is quite rare to have multiple recording rules with the same metric name in a group.

As discussed in "Idempotency for Batch Jobs" on page 56, with idempotent batch jobs you can avoid having to care about or be notified by a single failure of a batch job.

for

Metrics-based monitoring involves many race conditions—a scrape may timeout due to a lost network packet, a rule evaluation could be a little delayed due to process scheduling, and the systems you are monitoring could have a brief blip.

You don't want to be woken up in the middle of the night for every artifact or oddity in your systems; you want to save your energy for real problems that affect users. Accordingly, firing alerts based on the result of a single rule evaluation is rarely a good idea. This is where the for field of alerting rules comes in:

```
groups:
- name: node_rules
  rules:
  - record: job:up:avg
    expr: avg without(instance)(up{job="node"})
  - alert: ManyInstancesDown
    expr: avg without(instance)(up{job="node"}) < 0.5
    for: 5m
```

The for field says that a given alert must be returned for at least this long before it starts firing. Until the for condition is met, an alert is considered to be pending. An alert in the pending state but that has not yet fired is not sent to the Alertmanager. You can view the current pending and firing alerts at *http://localhost:9090/alerts*, which will look like Figure 18-2 after you click on an alert name.

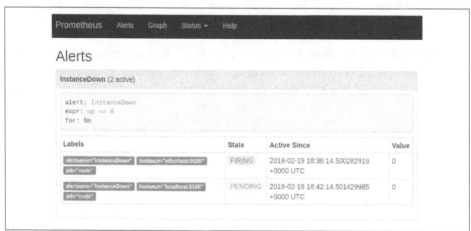

Figure 18-2. The Alert status page displays firing and pending alerts

Prometheus has no notion of hysteresis or flapping detection for alerting. You should choose your alert thresholds so that the problem is sufficiently bad that it is worth calling in a human, even if the problem subsequently subsides.

I generally recommend using a for of at least 5 minutes for all of your alerts. This will eliminate false positives from the majority of artifacts, including from brief flaps. You may worry that this will prevent you from jumping immediately on an issue, but keep in mind that it will likely take you the guts of 5 minutes to wake up, boot up your laptop, login, connect to the corporate network, and start debugging. Even if you are sitting in front of your computer all ready to go, it is my experience that once your system is well developed, the alerts you will handle will be nontrivial and it will take you at least 20–30 minutes just to get an idea of what is going on.

While wanting to immediately jump on every problem is commendable, a high rate of alerts will burn you and your team out and greatly reduce your effectiveness. If you have an alert that requires a human to take an action in less than 5 minutes, then you should work toward automating that action as such a response time comes at a high human cost if you can even reliably react in less than 5 minutes.

You may have some alerts that are less critical or a bit more noisy, with which you would use a longer duration in the for field. As with other durations and intervals, try to keep things simple. For example, across all of your alerts a 5m, 10m, 30m, and 1h for are probably sufficient in practice and there's not much point in micro-optimising by adding a 12m or 20m on top of that.

 The state of for is not currently persisted across restarts of Prometheus (*https://github.com/prometheus/prometheus/issues/422*), so I advise avoiding for durations of over an hour. If you need a longer duration, you must currently handle that via the expression.

Because for requires that your alerting rule return the same time series for a period of time, your for state can be reset if a single rule evaluation does not contain a given time series. For example, if you are using a gauge metric that comes directly from a target, if one of the scrapes fails, then the for state will be reset if you had an alerting rule such as:

```
- alert: FDsNearLimit
  expr: >
    process_open_fds > process_max_fds * .8
  for: 5m
```

To protect against this gotcha you can use the _over_time functions discussed in "Aggregation Over Time" on page 274. Usually you will want to use either avg_over_time or max_over_time:

```
- alert: FDsNearLimit
  expr:
    (
        max_over_time(process_open_fds[5m])
      >
        max_over_time(process_max_fds[5m]) * 0.9
    )
  for: 5m
```

The up metric is special in that it is always present even if a scrape fails, so you do not need to use an _over_time function. So if you were running the Blackbox exporter, as covered in "Blackbox" on page 177, and wanted to catch both failed scrapes or failed probes[3] you could use:

```
- alert: ProbeFailing
  expr: up{job="blackbox"} == 0 or probe_success{job="blackbox"} == 0
  for: 5m
```

Alert Labels

Just like with recording rules, you can specify labels for an alerting rule. Using labels with recording rules is quite rare, but it is standard practice with alerting rules.

When routing alerts in the Alertmanager, as covered in "Routing Tree" on page 307, you do not want to have to mention the name of every single alert you have individually in the Alertmanager's configuration file. Instead, you should take advantage of labels to indicate intent.

It is usual for you to have a severity label indicating whether an alert is intended to page someone, and potentially wake them up, or that it is a ticket that can be handled less urgently.

For example, a single machine being down should not be an emergency, but half your machines going down requires urgent investigation:

```
- alert: InstanceDown
  expr: up{job="node"} == 0
  for: 1h
  labels:
    severity: ticket
- alert: ManyInstancesDown
  expr: job:up:avg{job="node"} < 0.5
  for: 5m
  labels:
    severity: page
```

---

3 While the Blackbox exporter should return a response before it times out, things can always go wrong, such as the network being slow or the Blackbox exporter being down.

The `severity` label here does not have any special semantic meaning; it's merely a label added to the alert that will be available for your use when you configure the Alertmanger. As you add alerts in Prometheus you should set things up so you only need to add a `severity` label to get the alert routed appropriately, and rarely have to adjust your Alertmanager configuration.

In addition to the `severity` label, if a Prometheus can send alerts to different teams it's not unusual to have a `team` or `service` label. If an entire Prometheus was only sending alerts to one team, you would use external labels (as discussed in "External Labels" on page 303). There should be no need to mention labels like `env` or `region` in alerting rules; they should already either be on the alert due to being target labels that end up in the output of the alerting expression, or will be added subsequently by `external_labels`.

Because all the labels of an alert, from both the expression and the `labels`, define the identity of an alert, it is important that they do not vary from evaluation cycle to evaluation cycle. Aside from such alerts never satisfying the `for` field, they will spam the time series database within Prometheus, the Alertmanager, and you.

Prometheus does not permit an alert to have multiple thresholds, but you can define multiple alerts with different thresholds and labels:

```
- alert: FDsNearLimit
  expr: >
    process_open_fds > process_max_fds * .95
  for: 5m
  labels:
    severity: page
- alert: FDsNearLimit
  expr: >
    process_open_fds > process_max_fds * .8
  for: 5m
  labels:
    severity: ticket
```

Note that if you are over 95% of the file descriptor limit then both of these alerts will fire. Attempting to make only one of them fire would be dangerous, as if the value was oscillating around 95% then neither alert would ever fire. In addition, an alert firing should be a situation where you have already decided it is worth demanding a human take a look at an issue. If you feel this may be spammy then you should try and adjust the alerts themselves and consider if they are worth having in the first place, rather than trying to put the genie back in the bottle when the alert is already firing.

> ## Alerts Need Owners
>
> I purposefully did not include a severity of `email` or `chat` in my examples. To explain why, let me tell you a story.
>
> I was once on a team that had to create a team mailing list every few months. There was a mailing list for email alerts, but alerts sent there didn't always get the attention that was desired as there were just too many of them and responsibility was diffuse, which is to say it wasn't actually anyone's job to take care of them. There were some alerts considered important, but not important enough to page the oncall engineer. So these alerts were sent to the main team mailing list, in the hope that someone would take a look. Fast forward a bit and the exact same thing happened to the team mailing list, which now had regular automated alerts coming in. At some point it got bad enough that a new team mailing list was created, and this story repeated itself, at which point this team had three email alert lists.
>
> Based on this experience and that of others, I strongly discourage email alerts and alerts that go to a team.[4] Instead, I advocate having alert notifications going to a ticketing system of some form, where they will be assigned to a specific person whose job it is to handle them. I have also seen it work out to have a daily email to the oncall that lists all currently firing alerts.
>
> After an outage it is everyone's fault for not looking at the email alerts,[5] but still not anyone's responsibility. The key point is that there needs to be ownership and not merely using email as logging.
>
> The same applies to chat messages for alerts, with messaging systems such as IRC, Slack, and Hipchat. Having your pages duplicated to your messaging system is handy, and pages are rare. Having nonpages duplicated has the same issues as email alerts, and is worse as it tends to be more distracting. You can't filter chat messages away to a folder you ignore like you do with emails.

Annotations and Templates

Alert labels define the identity of the alert, so you can't use them to provide additional information about the alert such as its current value as that can vary from evaluation cycle to evaluation cycle. Instead, you can use *alert annotations*, which are similar to labels and can be used in notifications. However, annotations are not part

---

4 I am also strongly against any form of email that was not written by hand by a human going to team mailing lists, including from alerts, pull requests, and bug/issue trackers.

5 Invariably among the thousands of spam alerts that everyone ignored there was one alert that foreshadowed the outage. Hindsight is 20/20, but to spot that email you would have had to also investigate the thousands of irrelevant notifications.

of an alert's identity, so they cannot be used for grouping and routing in the Alertmanager.

The `annotations` field allows you to provide additional information about an alert, such as a brief description of what is going wrong. In addition, the values of the `annotations` field are templated using Go's templating system (*https://golang.org/pkg/text/template/*). This allows you to format the value of the query to be more readable, or even perform additional PromQL queries to add additional context to alerts.

Prometheus does not send the value of your alerts to the Alertmanager. Because Prometheus allows you to use the full power of PromQL in alerting rules, there is no guarantee that the value of an alert is in any way useful or even meaningful. Labels define an alert rather than a value, and alerts can be more than a simple threshold on a single time series.

For example, you may wish to present the number of instances that are up as a percentage in an annotation. It's not easy to do math in Go's templating system, but you can prepare the value in the alert expression:[6]

```
groups:
 - name: node_rules
   rules:
    - alert: ManyInstancesDown
      for: 5m
      expr: avg without(instance)(up{job="node"}) * 100 < 50
      labels:
        severity: page
      annotations:
        summary: 'Only {{printf "%.2f" $value}}% of instances are up.'
```

Here `$value` is the value of your alert. It is being passed to the `printf` function,[7] which formats it nicely. Curly braces indicate template expressions.

In addition to `$value`, there is `$labels` with the labels of the alert. For example, `$labels.job` would return the value of the `job` label.

You can evaluate queries in annotation templates by using the `query` function. Usually you will want to then `range` over the result of the query, which is a for loop:

```
    - alert: ManyInstancesDown
      for: 5m
      expr: avg without(instance)(up{job="node"}) < 0.5
      labels:
```

---

6 For more advanced cases than this, you can consider using the and operator with the value for templating usage on the left-hand side and the alerting expression on the right-hand side.

7 Despite the name, this is actually a sprintf as it returns the output rather than writing it out. This allows you to build up a query that is passed to the query function using printf.

```
      severity: page
    annotations:
      summary: 'More than half of instances are down.'
      description: >
        Down instances: {{ range query "up{job=\"node\"} == 0" }}
          {{ .Labels.instance }}
        {{ end }}
```

The value of the element will be in `.`, which is a single period or full stop character. So `.Labels` is the labels of the current sample from the instant vector, and `.Labels.instance` is the instance label of that sample. `.Value` contains the value of the sample within the `range` loop.

 Every alert that results from an alerting rule has its templates evaluated independently on every evaluation cycle. If you had an expensive template for a rule producing hundreds of alerts, it could cause you performance issues.

You can also use annotations with static values, such as links to useful dashboards or documentation:

```
- alert: InstanceDown
  for: 5m
  expr: up{job="prometheus"} == 0
  labels:
    severity: page
  annotations:
    summary: 'Instance {{$labels.instance}} of {{$labels.job}} is down.'
    dashboard: http://some.grafana:3000/dashboard/db/prometheus
```

In a mature system, attempting to provide all possible debug information in an alert would not only be slow and confuse the oncall, but would likely also be of minimal use for anything but the simplest of issues. You should consider alert annotations and notifications primarily as a signpost to point you in the right direction for initial debugging. You can gain far more detailed and up-to-date information in a dashboard than you can in a few lines of an alert notification.

Notification templating (covered in "Notification templates" on page 317) is another layer of templating performed in the Alertmanager. In terms of what to put where, think of notification templating as being an email with several blanks that need to be filled in. Alert templates in Prometheus provide values for those blanks.

For example, you may wish to have a playbook for each of your alerts linked from the notification, and you will probably name the wiki pages after the alerts. You could add a `wiki` annotation to every alert, but any time you find yourself adding the same annotation to every alerting rule, you should probably be using notification templating in the Alertmanager instead. The Alertmanager already knows the alert's name so it can default to `wiki.mycompany/Alertname`, saving you from having to repeat your-self in alerting rules. As with many things in configuration management and moni-toring, having consistent conventions across your team and company make life easier.

 Alerting rule `labels` are also templated in the same fashion as `anno tations`, but this is only useful in advanced use cases, and you will almost always have simple static values for `labels`. If you do use templating on `labels`, it is important that the label values do not vary from evaluation cycle to evaluation cycle.

What Are Good Alerts?

In Nagios-style monitoring, it would be typical to alert on potential issues such as high load average, high CPU usage, or a process not running. These are all potential *causes* of problems, but they do not necessarily indicate a problem that requires the urgent intervention by a human that paging the oncall implies.

As systems grow ever more complex and dynamic, having alerts on every possible thing that can go wrong is not tractable. Even if you could manage to do so, the vol-ume of false positives would be so high that you and your team would get burnt out and end up missing real problems buried among the noise.

A better approach is to instead alert on *symptoms*. Your users do not care whether your load average is high; they care if their cat videos aren't loading quickly enough. By having alerts on metrics such as latency and failures experienced by users,[8] you will spot problems that really matter, rather than things that maybe might possibly indicate an issue.

For example, nightly cronjobs may cause CPU usage to spike, but with few users at that time of day you probably will have no problems serving them. Conversely, inter-mittent packet loss can be tricky to alert on directly, but will be fairly clearly exposed by latency metrics. If you have Service-Level Agreements (SLAs) with your users, then those provide good metrics to alert on and good starting points for your thresh-olds. You should also have alerts to catch resource utilisation issues, such as running out of quota or disk space, and alerts to ensure that your monitoring is working.

The ideal to aim for is that every page to the oncall, and every alert ticket filed, requires intelligent human action. If an alert doesn't require intelligence to resolve, then it is a prime candidate for you to automate. As a nontrivial oncall incident can take a few hours to resolve, you should aim for less than two incidents per day. For

---

8 Users don't have to be customers of your company, such as if you are running an internal service within a company.

nonurgent alerts going to your ticketing system you don't have to be as strict, but you wouldn't want too many more than you have pages.

If you find yourself responding to pages with "it went away," that is an indication that the alert should not have fired in the first place. You should consider bumping the threshold of the alert to make it less sensitive, or potentially deleting the alert.

For further discussion of how to approach alerting on and managing systems I would recommend reading "My Philsophy on Alerting" (*http://bit.ly/2MCIS1W*) by Rob Ewaschuk. Rob also wrote Chapter 6 of *Site Reliability Engineering* (O'Reilly), which also has more general advice on how to manage systems.

Configuring Alertmanagers

You configure Prometheus with a list of Alertmanagers to talk to using the same service discovery configuration covered in Chapter 8. For example, to configure a single local Alertmanager you might have a *prometheus.yml* that looks like:

```
global:
  scrape_interval: 10s
  evaluation_interval: 10s
alerting:
  alertmanagers:
    - static_configs:
        - targets: ['localhost:9093']
rule_files:
 - rules.yml
scrape_configs:
 - job_name: node
   static_configs:
     - targets:
       - localhost:9100
 - job_name: prometheus
   static_configs:
     - targets:
       - localhost:9090
```

Here the `alertmanagers` field works similarly to a scrape config, but there is no `job_name` and labels output from relabelling have no impact since there is no notion of target labels when discovering the Alertmanagers to send alerts to. Accordingly, any relabelling will typically only involve `drop` and `keep` actions.

You can have more than one Alertmanager, which will be further covered in "Alertmanager Clustering" on page 346. Prometheus will send all alerts to all the configured alertmanagers.

The `alerting` field also has `alert_relabel_configs`, which is relabelling as covered in "Relabelling" on page 135 but applied to alert labels. You can adjust alert labels, or even drop alerts. For example, you may wish to have informational alerts that never make it outside your Prometheus:

```
alerting:
  alertmanagers:
   - static_configs:
      - targets: ['localhost:9093']
  alert_relabel_configs:
   - source_labels: [severity]
     regex: info
     action: drop
```

You could use this to add `env` and `region` labels to all your alerts, saving you hassle elsewhere, but there is a better way to do this using `external_labels`.

External Labels

External labels are labels applied as defaults when your Prometheus talks to other systems, such as the Alertmanager, federation, remote read, and remote write,[9] but not the HTTP query APIs. External labels are the identity of Prometheus, and every single Prometheus in your organisation should have unique external labels. `external_labels` is part of the `global` section of *prometheus.yml*:

```
global:
  scrape_interval: 10s
  evaluation_interval: 10s
  external_labels:
    region: eu-west-1
    env: prod
    team: frontend
alerting:
  alertmanagers:
   - static_configs:
      - targets: ['localhost:9093']
```

It is easiest to have labels such as `region` in your `external_labels` as you don't have to apply them to every single target that is scraped, keep them in mind when writing PromQL, or add them to every single alerting rule within a Prometheus. This saves you time and effort, and also makes it easier to share recording and alerting rules across different Prometheus servers as they aren't tied to one environment or even to one organisation. If a potential external label varies within a Prometheus, then it should probably be a target label instead.

---

9 Covered in "Going Global with Federation" on page 334 and "Long-Term Storage" on page 337.

Since external labels are applied after alerting rules are evaluated,[10] they are not available in alert templating. Alerts should not care which of your Prometheus servers they are being evaluated in, so this is okay. The Alertmanager will have access to the external labels just like any other label in its notification templates, and that is the appropriate place to work with them.

External labels are only defaults; if one of your time series already has a label with the same name then that external label will not apply. Accordingly, I advise not having targets whose label names overlap with your external labels.

Now that you know how to have Prometheus evaluate and fire useful alerts, the next step is to configure the Alertmanager to convert them into notifications, the topic of the next chapter.

---

10 `alert_relabel_configs` happens after `external_labels`.

CHAPTER 19

Alertmanager

In Chapter 18 you saw how to define alerting rules in Prometheus, which result in alerts being sent to the Alertmanager. It is the responsibility of your Alertmanager to take in all the alerts from all of your Prometheus servers and convert them to notifications such as emails, chat messages, and pages. Chapter 2 gave you a brief introduction to using the Alertmanager, but in this chapter you will learn how to configure and use the full power of it.

Notification Pipeline

The Alertmanager does more for you than blindly convert alerts into notifications on a one-to-one basis. In an ideal world you would receive exactly one notification for each production incident. While this is a stretch, the Alertmanager tries to get you there by providing you with a controllable pipeline for how your alerts are processed as they become notifications. Just as labels are at the core of Prometheus itself, labels are also key to the Alertmanager:

Inhibition

> On occasion, even when using symptom-based alerting, you will want to prevent notifications for some alerts if another more severe alert is firing, such as preventing alerts for your service if a datacenter it is in is failing but is also receiving no traffic. This is the role of *inhibition*.

Silencing

> If you already know about a problem or are taking a service down for maintenance, there's no point in paging the oncall about it. *Silences* allow you to ignore certain alerts for a while, and are added via the Alertmanager's web interface.

Routing

It is intended that you would run one Alertmanager per organisation, but it wouldn't do for all of your notifications to go to one place. Different teams will want their notifications delivered to different places; and even within a team you might want alerts for production and development environments handled differently. The Alertmanager allows you to configure this with a *routing tree*.

Grouping

You now have the production alerts for your team going to a route. Getting an individual notification for each of the machines in a rack[1] that failed would be spammy, so you could have the Alertmanager group alerts and only get one notification per rack, one notification per datacenter, or even one notification globally about the uncontactable machines.

Throttling and repetition

You have your group of alerts that are firing due to the rack of machines being down, and the alert for one of the machines on the rack comes in after you have already sent out the notification. If you sent a new notification every time a new alert comes in from a group, that would defect the purpose of grouping. Instead, the Alertmanager will throttle notifications for a given group so you don't get spammed.

In an ideal world all notifications would be handled promptly, but in reality the oncall or other system might let an issue slip through the cracks. The Alertmanager will repeat notifications so that they don't get lost for too long.

Notification

Now that your alerts have been inhibited, silenced, routed, grouped, and throttled, they finally get to the stage of being sent out as notifications through a *receiver*. Notifications are templated, allowing you to customise their content and emphasise the details that matter to you.

Configuration File

As with all the other configurations you have seen, the Alertmanager is configured via a YAML file often called *alertmanager.yml*. As with Prometheus, the configuration file can be reloaded at runtime by sending a SIGHUP or sending a HTTP POST to

---

1 In datacenters, machines are typically organised in vertical racks, with each rack usually having its own power setup and a network switch. It is thus not uncommon for an entire rack to disappear at once due to a power or switch issue.

the */-/reload* endpoint. To detect bad configuration files in advance, you can use the `amtool check-config` command to check your *alertmanager.yml*.[2]

For example, a minimal configuration that sends everything to an email address using a local SMTP server would look like:

```
global:
  smtp_smarthost: 'localhost:25'
  smtp_from: 'youraddress@example.org'

route:
  receiver: example-email

receivers:
 - name: example-email
   email_configs:
    - to: 'youraddress@example.org'
```

You must always have at least one route and one receiver. There are various global settings, which are almost all defaults for the various types of receivers. I'll now cover the various other parts of the configuration file. You can find a full *alertmanager.yml* combining the examples in this chapter on GitHub (*http://bit.ly/2t9kD26*).

Routing Tree

The `route` field specifies the top-level, *fallback*, or *default* route. Routes form a tree, so you can and usually will have multiple routes below that. For example, you could have:

```
route:
  receiver: fallback-pager
  routes:
   - match:
       severity: page
     receiver: team-pager
   - match:
       severity: ticket
     receiver: team-ticket
```

When an alert arrives it starts at the default route and tries to match against its first *child route*, which is defined in the (possibly empty) `routes` field. If your alert has a label that is exactly `severity="page"`, it matches this route and matching halts, as this route has no children to consider.

If your alert does not have a `severity="page"` label, then the next child route of the default route is checked; in this case, for a `severity="ticket"` label. If this matches

---

2 amtool can also be used to query alerts, and work with silences.

your alert, then matching will also halt. Otherwise, since all the child routes have failed to match, matching goes back up the tree and matches the default route. This is known as a *post-order tree transversal*, which is to say that children are checked before their parent, and the first match wins.

There is also a `match_re` field that requires that the given label match the given regular expression. As with almost[3] all other places, regular expressions are fully anchored. For a refresher on regular expressions, see "Regular Expressions" on page 138.

You could use `match_re` if there were variants in what label values were used for a given purpose, such as if some teams used `ticket`, others used `issue`, and others had yet to be convinced that `email` was possibly not the best place to send notifications:

```
route:
  receiver: fallback-pager
  routes:
  - match:
      severity: page
    receiver: team-pager
  - match_re:
      severity: (ticket|issue|email)
    receiver: team-ticket
```

Both `match` and `match_re` can be used in the same route, and alerts must satisfy all of the match conditions.

 All alerts must match some route, and the top-level route is the last route checked, so it acts as a fallback that all alerts must match. Thus it is an error for you to use `match` or `match_re` on the default route.

Rarely will it just be one team using an Alertmanager, and different teams will want alerts routed differently. You should have a standard label such as `team` or `service` across your organisation that distinguishes who owns what alerts. This label will usually but not always come from `external_labels`, as discussed in "External Labels" on page 303. Using this `team`-like label you would have a route per team, and then the teams would have their own routing configuration below that:

---

3 The `reReplaceAll` function in alert and notification templates is not anchored, as that would defeat its purpose.

```
route:
  receiver: fallback-pager
  routes:
  # Frontend team.
  - match:
      team: frontend
    receiver: frontend-pager
    routes:
    - match:
        severity: page
      receiver: frontend-pager
    - match:
        severity: ticket
      receiver: frontend-ticket
  # Backend team.
  - match:
      team: backend
    receiver: backend-pager
    routes:
    - match:
        severity: page
        env: dev
      receiver: backend-ticket
    - match:
        severity: page
      receiver: backend-pager
    - match:
        severity: ticket
      receiver: backend-ticket
```

The frontend team has a simple setup, with pages going to the pager, tickets going to the ticketing system, and any pages with unexpected `severity` labels going to the pager.

The backend team has customised things a little. Any pages from the development environment will be sent to the `backend-ticket` receiver, which is to say that they will be downgraded to just tickets rather than pages.[4] In this way you can have alerts from different environments routed differently in the Alertmanager, saving you from having to customise alerting rules per environment. This approach allows you to only have to vary the `external_labels` in most cases.

---

4 Receiver naming is just a convention, but if your configuration does not result in the `backend-ticket` receiver creating a ticket, it would be quite misleading.

It can be a little challenging to come to grips with an existing routing tree, particularly if it doesn't follow a standard structure. There is a visual routing tree editor (*https://prometheus.io/webtools/alerting/routing-tree-editor/*) on the Prometheus website that can show you the tree and what routes alerts will follow on it.

As such a configuration grows as you gain more teams, you may want to write a utility to combine routing tree fragments together from smaller files. YAML is a standard format with readily available unmarshallers and marshallers, so this is not a difficult task.

There is one other setting I should mention in the context of routing—continue. Usually the first matching route wins, but if continue: true is specified then a match will not halt the process of finding a matching route. Instead, a matching continue route will be matched *and* the process of finding a matching route will continue. In this way an alert can be part of multiple routes. continue is primarily used to log all alerts to another system:

```
route:
  receiver: fallback-pager
  routes:
  # Log all alerts.
  - receiver: log-alerts
    continue: true
  # Frontend team.
  - match:
      team: frontend
    receiver: frontend-pager
```

Once your alert has a route, the grouping, throttling, repetition, and receiver for that route will apply to that alert and all the other alerts that match that route. All settings for child routes are inherited as defaults from their parent route, with the exception of continue.

Grouping

Your alerts have now arrived at their route. By default, the Alertmanager will put all alerts for a route into a single group, meaning you will get one big notification. While this may be okay in some cases, usually you will want your notifications a bit more bite-sized than that.

The group_by field allows you to specify a list of labels to group alerts by; this works in the same way as the by clause that you can use with aggregation operators (discussed in "by" on page 231). Typically you will want to split out your alerts by one or more of alertname, environment, and/or location.

An issue in production is unlikely to be related to an issue in development, and similarly with issues in different datacenters depending on the exact alert. When alerting on symptoms rather than causes, as encouraged by "What Are Good Alerts?" on page 301, it is likely that different alerts indicate different incidents.[5]

To use this in practice you might end up with a configuration such as:

```
route:
  receiver: fallback-pager
  group_by: [team]
  routes:
   # Frontend team.
   - match:
       team: frontend
     group_by: [region, env]
     receiver: frontend-pager
     routes:
      - match:
          severity: page
        receiver: frontend-pager
      - match:
          severity: ticket
        group_by: [region, env, alertname]
        receiver: frontend-ticket
```

Here the default route has its alerts grouped by the team label, so that any team missing a route can be dealt with individually. The frontend team has chosen to group alerts based on the region and env labels. This group_by will be inherited by their child routes, so all their tickets and pages will also be grouped by region and env.

Generally it is not a good idea to group by the instance label, since that can get very spammy when there is an issue affecting an entire application. However, if you were alerting on machines being down in order to create tickets to have a human physically inspect them, grouping by instance may make sense depending on the inspection workflow.

---

5 On the other hand, if you are following the RED method, a high failure ratio and high latency can occur together. In practice, one usually happens a good bit before the other, leaving you plenty of time to mitigate the issue or put in a silence.

There is no way to disable grouping in the Alertmanager, other than listing every possible label in group_by. Grouping is a good thing, because it reduces notification spam and allows you to perform more focused incident response. It is far harder to miss a notification about a new incident among a few pages than a hundred pages.[6]

If you want to disable grouping due to your organisation already having something that fills the Alertmanager's role, you may be better off not using the Alertmanager and working from the alerts sent by Prometheus instead.

Throttling and repetition

When sending notifications for a group, you don't want to get a new notification every time the set of firing alerts changes as that would be too spammy. On the other hand, neither do you only want to learn about additional alerts that started firing many hours after the fact.

There are two settings you can adjust to control how the Alertmanager throttles notifications for a group: group_wait and group_interval.

If you have a group with no alerts and then a new set of alerts starts firing, it is likely that all these new alerts will not all start firing at exactly the same time. For example, as scrapes are spread across the scrape interval, if a rack of machines fails you will usually spot some machines as down one interval before the others. It'd be good if you could delay the initial notification for the group a little to see if more alerts are going to come in. This is exactly what group_wait does. By default, the Alertmanager will wait 30 seconds before sending the first notification. You may worry this will delay reponse to incidents, but keep in mind that if 30 seconds matter, you should be aiming for an automated rather than a human response.

Now that the first notification has been sent for the group, some additional alerts might start firing for your group. When should the Alertmanager send you another notification for the group, now including these new alerts? This is controlled by group_interval, which defaults to 5 minutes. Every group interval after the first notification, a new notification will be sent if there are new firing alerts. If there are no new alerts for a group then you will not receive an additional notification.

Once all alerts stop firing for your group and an interval has passed, the state is reset and group_wait will apply once again. The throttling for each group is independent, so if you were grouping by region, then alerts firing for one region wouldn't make new alerts in another region wait for a group_interval, just a group_wait.

---

6 A hundred pages would be a good-sized pagerstorm.

Let's take an example, where there are four alerts firing at different times:

```
t=  0   Alert firing {x="foo"}
t= 25   Alert firing {x="bar"}
t= 30   Notification for {x="foo"} and {x="bar"}
t=120   Alert firing {x="baz"}
t=330   Notification for {x="foo"}, {x="bar"} and {x="baz"}
t=400   Alert resolved {x="foo"}
t=700   Alert firing {x="quu"}
t=930   Notification for {x="bar"}, {x="baz"}, {x="quu"}
```

After the first alert the group_wait countdown starts, and a second alert comes in while you are waiting. Both these foo and bar alerts will be in a notification sent 30 seconds in. Now the group_interval timer kicks in. In the first interval there is a new baz alert, so 300 seconds (one group interval) after the first notification there is a second notification containing all three alerts that are currently firing. At the next interval one alert has been resolved, but there are no new alerts so there is no notification at t=630. A fourth alert for quu fires, and at the next interval there is a third notification containing all three alerts currently firing.

If an alert fires, resolves, and fires again within a group interval, then it is treated in the same way as if the alert never stopped firing. Similarly if an alert resolves, fires, and resolves again within a group interval, it is the same as if the alert never fired in that interval. This is not something to worry about in practice.

Neither humans nor machines are fully reliable; even if a page got through to the oncall and they acknowledged it, they might forget about the alert if more pressing incidents occur. For ticketing systems, you may have closed off an issue as resolved, but you will want it reopened if the alert is still firing.

For this you can take advantage of the repeat_interval, which defaults to 4 hours. If it has been a repeat interval since a notification was sent for a group with firing alerts, a new notification will be sent. That is to say that a notification sent due to the group interval will reset the timer for the repeat interval. A repeat_interval shorter than the group_interval does not make sense.

If you are getting notifications too often, you probably want to tweak group_interval rather than repeat_interval because the issue is more likely alerts flapping rather than hitting the (usually rather long) repeat interval.

The defaults for these settings are all generally sane, although you may wish to tweak them a little. For example, even a complex outage tends to be under control within 4 hours, so if an alert is still firing after that long it is a good bet that either the oncall forgot to put in a silence or forgot about the issue and the repeated notification is unlikely to be spammy. For a ticketing system, once a day is generally frequent enough to create and poke tickets, so you could set `group_interval` and `repeat_interval` to a day. The Alertmanager will retry failed attempts at notification a few times so there's no need to reduce `repeat_interval` for that reason alone. Depending on your setup you might increase `group_wait` and `group_interval` to reduce the number of pages you receive.

All these settings can be provided on a per-route basis, and are inherited as defaults by child routes. An example configuration using these might look like:

```
route:
  receiver: fallback-pager
  group_by: [team]
  routes:
   # Frontend team.
   - match:
       team: frontend
     group_by: [region, env]
     group_interval: 10m
     receiver: frontend-pager
     routes:
      - match:
          severity: page
        receiver: frontend-pager
        group_wait: 1m
      - match:
          severity: ticket
        receiver: frontend-ticket
        group_by: [region, env, alertname]
        group_interval: 1d
        repeat_interval: 1d
```

Receivers

Receivers are what take your grouped alerts and produce notifications. A receiver contains *notifiers*, which do the actual notifications. As of Alertmanager 0.15.0, the supported notifiers are email, HipChat, PagerDuty, Pushover, Slack, OpsGenie, VictorOps, WeChat, and the webhook. Just as file SD is a generic mechanism for service discovery, the webhook is the generic notifier that allows you to hook in systems that are not supported out of the box.

The layout of receivers is similar to service discovery within a scrape config. All receivers must have a unique name, and then may contain any number of notifiers. In the simplest cases you will have a single notifier in a receiver:

```
receivers:
 - name: fallback-pager
   pagerduty_configs:
    - service_key: XXXXXXXX
```

PagerDuty is one of the simpler notifiers to get going with, since it only requires a service key to work. All notifiers need to be told where to send the notification, whether that's the name of a chat channel, an email address, or whatever other identifiers a system may use. Most notifiers are for commercial Software as a Service (SaaS) offerings, and you will need to use their UI and documentation to obtain the various keys, identifiers, URLs, and tokens that are specific to you and where exactly you want the notification sent to. I'm not going to attempt to give full instructions here, because the notifiers and SaaS UIs are constantly changing.

You might also have one receiver going to multiple notifiers, such as having the frontend-pager receiver sending notifications both to your PagerDuty service and your Slack channel:[7]

```
receivers:
 - name: frontend-pager
   pagerduty_configs:
    - service_key: XXXXXXXX
   slack_configs:
    - api_url: https://hooks.slack.com/services/XXXXXXXX
      channel: '#pages'
```

Some of the notifiers have settings that you will want to be the same across all your uses of that notifier, such as the VictorOps API key. You could specify that in each receiver, but the Alertmanager also has a globals section for these so you only need to specify in the case of VictorOps a routing key in the notifier itself:

```
global:
  victorops_api_key: XXXX-XXXX-XXXX-XXXX-XXXXXXXXXXXX

receivers:
 - name: backend-pager
   victorops_configs:
    - routing_key: a_route_name
```

Since each field like victorops_configs is a list, you can send notifications to multiple different notifiers of one type at once, such as sending to multiple HipChat rooms:[8]

---

7 PagerDuty also has a Slack integration, which permits acknowledging alerts directly from Slack. This sort of integration is quite handy, and can also cover pages coming from sources other than the Alertmanager that are going to PagerDuty.

8 This is preferable to using continue as it is less fragile, and you don't have to keep multiple routes in sync.

```
global:
  opsgenie_api_key: XXXXXXXX
  hipchat_auth_token: XXXXXXXX

receivers:
 - name: backend-pager
   opsgenie_configs:
    - teams: backendTeam   # This is a comma separated list.
   hipchat_configs:
    - room_id: XXX
    - room_id: YYY
```

It is also possible for you to specify no receivers at all, which will not result in any notifications:

```
receivers:
 - name: null
```

It'd be better where possible for you not to send alerts to the Alertmanager in the first place, rather than spending Alertmanager resources on processing alerts just to throw them away.

The webhook notifier is unique in that it doesn't directly notify an existing paging or messaging system that you might already have in place. Instead, it sends all the information the Alertmanager has about a group of alerts as a JSON HTTP message and allows you to do what you like with it. You could use this to log your alerts, to perform an automated action of some form, or to send a notification via some system that the Alertmanager doesn't support directly. A HTTP endpoint that accepts a HTTP POST from a webhook notification is known as a *webhook receiver*.

 While it may be tempting to use webhooks liberally to execute code, it would be wise to keep your control loops as small as possible. For example, rather than going from an exporter to Prometheus to the Alertmanager to a webhook receiver to restart a stuck process, keeping it all on one machine with a supervisor such as Supervisord or Monit is a better idea. This will provide a faster response time, and generally be more robust due to fewer moving parts.

The webhook notifier is similar to the others; it takes a URL to which notifications are sent. If you were logging all alerts you would use continue on the first route, which would go to a webhook:

```
route:
  receiver: fallback-pager
  routes:
   - receiver: log-alerts
     continue: true
   # Rest of routing config goes here.
```

```
receivers:
 - name: log-alerts
   webhook_configs:
    - url: http://localhost:1234/log
```

You could use a Python 3 script such as Example 19-1 to take in these notifications and process the alerts within.

Example 19-1. A simple webhook receiver written in Python 3

```
import json
from http.server import BaseHTTPRequestHandler
from http.server import HTTPServer

class LogHandler(BaseHTTPRequestHandler):
    def do_POST(self):
        self.send_response(200)
        self.end_headers()
        length = int(self.headers['Content-Length'])
        data = json.loads(self.rfile.read(length).decode('utf-8'))
        for alert in data["alerts"]:
            print(alert)

if __name__ == '__main__':
    httpd = HTTPServer(('', 1234), LogHandler)
    httpd.serve_forever()
```

All HTTP-based receivers have a field called `http_config` which, similar to the settings in a scrape config as discussed in "How to Scrape" on page 146, allows setting a `proxy_url`, HTTP Basic Authentication, TLS settings, and other HTTP-related configuration.

Notification templates

The layout of messages from the various notifiers are fine to use when starting out, but you will probably want to customise them as your setup matures. All notifiers except the webhook[9] permit templating using the same Go templating system (*https://golang.org/pkg/text/template/*) as you used for alerting rules in "Annotations and Templates" on page 298. However, the data and functions you have access to are slightly different, as you are dealing with a group of alerts rather than a single alert.

---

9 For the webhook it is expected that the webhook receiver was specifically designed to work with the JSON message that is sent, so no templating of the webhook message sent is required. In fact, the JSON message is the exact same data structure that notification templates use under the covers.

As an example, you might always want the `region` and `env` labels in your Slack notification:

```
receivers:
 - name: frontend-pager
   slack_configs:
    - api_url: https://hooks.slack.com/services/XXXXXXXX
      channel: '#pages'
      title: 'Alerts in {{ .GroupLabels.region }} {{ .GroupLabels.env }}!'
```

This will produce a notification like the one you see in Figure 19-1.

Figure 19-1. A message in Slack with the region and environment

`GroupLabels` is one of the top-level fields you can access in templating, but there are several others:

GroupLabels

> `GroupLabels` contains the group labels of the notification, so will be all the labels listed in the `group_by` for the route that this group came from.

CommonLabels

> `CommonLabels` is all the labels that are common across all the alerts in your notification. This will always include all the labels in `GroupLabels`, and also any other labels that happen to be common. This is useful for opportunistically listing similarities in alerts. For example, if you were grouping by region and a rack of machines failed, the alerts for all the down instances might all have a common `rack` label that you could access in `CommonLabels`. However, if a single other machine in another rack failed, the `rack` label would no longer be in your `Common Labels`.

CommonAnnotations

> `CommonAnnotations` is like `CommonLabels`, but for annotations. This is of very limted use. As your annotations tend to be templated, it is unlikely that there will be any common values. However, if you had a simple string as an annotation, it might show up here.

ExternalURL

> `ExternalURL` will contain the *external URL* of this Alertmanager, which can make it easier to get to the Alertmanger to create a silence. You can also use it to figure out which of your Alertmangers sent a notification in a clustered setup.

There is more discussion of external URLs in "Networks and Authentication" on page 342.

Status

Status will be firing if at least one alert in the notification is firing; if all alerts are resolved, it will be resolved. Resolved notifications are covered in "Resolved notifications" on page 323.

Receiver

The name of the receiver, which is frontend-pager in the preceding example.

GroupKey

An opaque string with a unique identifier for the group. This is of no use to humans, but it helps ticketing and paging systems tie notifications from a group to previous notifications. This could be useful to prevent opening a new ticket in your ticketing system if there was already one open from the same group.

Alerts

Alerts is the actual meat of the notification, a list of all the alerts in your notification.

Within each alert in the Alerts list there are also several fields:

Labels

As you would expect, this contains the labels of your alert.

Annotations

No prizes for guessing that this contains the annotations of your alert.

Status

firing if the alert is firing; otherwise, it'll be resolved.

StartsAt

This is the time the alert started firing as a Go time.Time object. Due to how Prometheus and the alerting protocol work, this is not necessarily when the alert condition was first satisfied. This is of little use in practice.

EndsAt

This is when the alert will stop or has stopped firing. This is of no use for firing alerts, but will tell you when a resolved alert resolved.

GeneratorURL

For alerts from Prometheus,[10] this is a link to the alerting rule on Prometheus's web interface, which can be handy for debugging. To me the real reason this field

---

10 For other systems it should be a link to whatever is generating the alert.

exists is for a future Alertmanager feature that will allow you to drop alerts coming from a particular source, such as if there's a broken Prometheus that you can't shut down sending bad alerts to the Alertmanager.

You can use these fields as you see fit in your templates. For example, you may wish to include all the labels, a link to your wiki, and a link to a dashboard in all of your notifications:

```
receivers:
 - name: frontend-pager
   slack_configs:
    - api_url: https://hooks.slack.com/services/XXXXXXXX
      channel: '#pages'
      title: 'Alerts in {{ .GroupLabels.region }} {{ .GroupLabels.env }}!'
      text: >
        {{ .Alerts | len }} alerts:
        {{ range .Alerts }}
        {{ range .Labels.SortedPairs }}{{ .Name }}={{ .Value }} {{ end }}
        {{ if eq .Annotations.wiki "" -}}
        Wiki: http://wiki.mycompany/{{ .Labels.alertname }}
        {{- else -}}
        Wiki: http://wiki.mycompany/{{ .Annotations.wiki }}
        {{- end }}
        {{ if ne .Annotations.dashboard "" -}}
        Dashboard: {{ .Annotations.dashboard }}&region={{ .Labels.region }}
        {{- end }}

        {{ end }}
```

I'll break this down:

```
{{ .Alerts | len }} alerts:
```

.Alerts is a list, and the in-built len function of Go templates counts how many alerts you have in the list. This is about the most math you can do in Go templates as there are no math operators, so you should use alerting templates in Prometheus as discussed in "Annotations and Templates" on page 298 to calculate any numbers and render them nicely:

```
{{ range .Alerts }}
{{ range .Labels.SortedPairs }}{{ .Name }}={{ .Value }} {{ end }}
```

This iterates over the alerts and then the sorted labels of each alert.

range in Go templates reuses . as the iterator, so the original . is shadowed or hidden while you are inside the iteration.[11] While you could iterate over the label key value pairs in the usual Go fashion, they will not be in a consistent order. The SortedPairs

---

11 To work around this you can set a variable such as {{ $dot := . }} and then access $dot.

method of the various label and annotation fields sorts the label names and provides a list that you can iterate over.

```
{{ if eq .Annotations.wiki "" -}}
Wiki: http://wiki.mycompany/{{ .Labels.alertname }}
{{- else -}}
Wiki: http://wiki.mycompany/{{ .Annotations.wiki }}
{{- end }}
```

Empty labels are the same as no labels, so this checks if the `wiki` annotation exists. If it does it is used as the name of the wiki page to link; otherwise, the name of the alert is used. In this way you can have a sensible default that avoids you having to add a `wiki` annotation to every single alerting rule, while still allowing customisation if you want to override it for one or two alerts. The `{{-` and `-}}` tell Go templates to ignore whitespace before or after the curly braces, allowing you to spread templates across multiple lines for readability without introducing extraneous whitespace in the output.

```
{{ if ne .Annotations.dashboard "" -}}
Dashboard: {{ .Annotations.dashboard }}&region={{ .Labels.region }}
{{- end }}
```

If a `dashboard` annotation is present, it will be added to your notification, and in addition, the region added as a URL parameter. If you have a Grafana template variable with this name, you will have it set to point to the right value. As discussed in "External Labels" on page 303, alerting rules do not have access to the external labels that usually contain things such as `region`, so this is how you can add architectural details to your notifications without your alerting rules having to be aware of how your applications are deployed.

The end result of this is a notification like the one shown in Figure 19-2. When using chat-like notifiers and paging systems, it is wise for you to keep notifications brief. This reduces the chances of your computer or mobile phone screen being overcome with lengthy alert details, making it hard to get a basic idea of what is going on. Notifications such as these should get you going on debugging by pointing to a potentially useful dashboard and playbook that have further information, not try to info dump everything that might be useful in the notification itself.

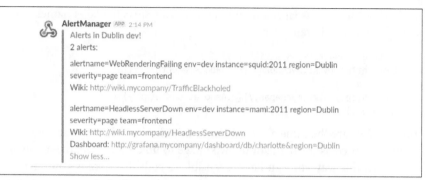

Figure 19-2. A customised Slack message

In addition to templating text fields, the destination of notifications can also be templated. Usually each of your teams has their own part of the routing tree and associated receivers. If another team wanted to send your team alerts they would set labels accordingly to use your team's routing tree. For cases where you are offering a service, particularly to external customers, having to define a receiver for every potential destination could be a little tedious.[12]

Combining the power of PromQL, labels, and notification templating for alert destinations, you can go so far as to define a per-customer threshold and notification destination in a metric and have the Alertmanager deliver to that destination. The first step is to have alerts that include their destination as a label:

```
groups:
 - name: example
   rules:
    - record: latency_too_high_threshold
      expr: 0.5
      labels:
        email_to: foo@example.com
        owner: foo
    - record: latency_too_high_threshold
      expr: 0.7
      labels:
        email_to: bar@example.com
        owner: bar
    - alert: LatencyTooHigh
      expr: |
        # Alert based on per-owner thresholds.
          owner:latency:mean5m
        > on (owner) group_left(email_to)
          latency_too_high_threshold
```

---

12 Alertmanager configuration is expected to change relatively rarely, as your label structure shouldn't change that often. Alerting rules, on the other hand, tend to have ongoing churn and tweaks.

Here the different owners have different thresholds coming from a metric, which also provides an email_to label. This is fine for internal customers who can add their own latency_too_high_threshold to your rule file; for external customers you may have an exporter exposing these thresholds and destinations from a database.

Then in the Alertmanager you can set the destination of the notifications based on this email_to label:

```
global:
  smtp_smarthost: 'localhost:25'
  smtp_from: 'youraddress@example.org'

route:
  group_by: [email_to, alertname]
  receiver: customer_email

receivers:
- name: customer_email
  email_configs:
   - to: '{{ .GroupLabels.email_to }}'
     headers:
       subject: 'Alert: {{ .GroupLabels.alertname }}'
```

The group_by must include the email_to label that you are using to specify the destination, because each destination needs its own alert group. The same approach can be used with other notifiers. Note that anyone with access to Prometheus or the Alertmanager will be able to see the destinations since labels are visible to everyone. This may be a concern if some destination fields are potentially sensitive.

Resolved notifications

All notifiers have a send_resolved field, with varying defaults. If it is set to true then in addition to receiving notifications about when alerts fire, your notifications will also include alerts that are no longer firing and are now resolved. The practical effect of this is that when Prometheus informs the Alertmanager that an alert is now resolved,[13] that a notifier with send_resolved enabled will include this alert in the next notification and will even send a notification with only resolved alerts if no other alerts are firing.

While it may seem handy to know that an alert is now resolved, I advise quite a bit of caution with this feature as an alert no longer firing does not mean that the original issue is handled. In "What Are Good Alerts?" on page 301 I mentioned that responding to alerts with "it went away" was a sign that the alert should probably not have fired in the first place. Getting a resolved notification may be an indication that a sit-

---

13 Resolved alerts will have the annotations from the last firing evaluation of that alert.

uation is improving, but you as the oncall still need to dig into the issue and verify that it is fixed, and not likely to come back. Halting your handling of an incident because the alert stopped firing is essentially the same as saying "it went away." Because the Alertmanager works with alerts rather than incidents, it is inappropriate to consider an incident resolved just because the alerts stopped firing.

For example, machine down alerts being resolved might only mean that the machine running Prometheus has now also gone down. So while your outage is getting worse, you are no longer getting alerts about it.[14]

Another issue with resolved notifications is that they can be a bit spammy. If they were enabled for a notifier such as email or Slack, you could be looking at doubling the message volume, thus halving your signal to noise ratio. As discussed in "Alerts Need Owners" on page 298, using email for notifications is often problematic and more noise will not help with that.

If you have a notifier with `send_resolved` enabled, then in notification templating, `.Alerts` can contain a mix of firing and resolved alerts. While you could filter the alerts yourself using the `Status` field of an alert, `.Alert.Firing` will give you a list of just the firing alerts, and `.Alert.Resolved` the resolved alerts.

Inhibitions

Inhibitions are a feature that allows you to treat some alerts as not firing if other alerts are firing. For example, if an entire datacenter was having issues but user traffic had been diverted elsewhere, there's not much point in sending alerts for that datacenter.

Inhibitions currently[15] live at the top level of *alertmanager.yml*. You must specify what alerts to look for, what alerts they will suppress, and which labels must match between the two:

```
inhibit_rules:
 - source_match:
     severity: 'page-regionfail'
   target_match:
     severity: 'page'
   equal: ['region']
```

---

14 Alerting approaches to detect this are covered in "Meta- and Cross-Monitoring" on page 347, but the salient point here is that you should be in a place where once an alert starts firing, it will get investigated.

15 They may move to per-route at some point (having them as a global setting increases the chances for an inhibition to accidentally supress more than was intended).

Here, if an alert with a `severity` label of `page-regionfail` is firing, it will supress all your alerts with the same `region` label that have a `severity` label of `page`.[16]

Overlap between the `source_match` and `target_match` should be avoided since it can be tricky to understand and maintain otherwise. Having different `severity` labels is one way to avoid a overlap. If there is overlap, any alerts matching the `source_match` will not be suppressed.

I recommend using this feature sparingly. With symptom-based alerting (as discussed in "What Are Good Alerts?" on page 301) there should be little need for dependency chains between your alerts. Reserve inhibition rules for large-scale issues such as datacenter outages.

Alertmanager Web Interface

As you saw in "Alerting" on page 30, the Alertmanager allows you to view what alerts are currently firing and to group and filter them. Figure 19-3 shows several alerts in an Alertmanager grouped by `alertname`; you can also see all of the alerts' other labels.

Figure 19-3. Several alerts showing on the Alertmanager status page

---

16 Using `match_re` in your routes makes it easier to have more specific `severity` labels like these, while still handling all pages in one route. If the source alerts are not meant to result in notifications, that would be a good use of a null receiver, as shown in "Receivers" on page 314.

From the status page you can click on New Silence to create a silence from scratch, or click on the Silence link to prepopulate the silence form with the labels of that alert. From there you can tweak the labels you want your silence to have. When working with an existing alert you will usually want to remove some labels to cover more than just that one alert. To help track silences you must also enter your name and a comment for the silence. Finally, you should preview the silence to ensure it is not too broad, as you can see in Figure 19-4, before creating the silence.

Figure 19-4. Previewing a silence before creating it

If you visit the Silences page you can see all silences that are currently active, the ones that have yet to apply, and the silences that have expired and no longer apply (as shown in Figure 19-5). From here you can also expire silences that no longer apply and recreate silences that have expired.

Figure 19-5. The Alertmanager Silences page showing the active silences

Silences stop alerts with the given labels from being considered as alerting for the purposes of notification. Silences can be created in advance, if you know that maintenance is going to happen and don't want to pointlessly page the oncall, for example. As the oncall you will also use silences to suppress alerts that you've already known about for a while, so you are not disturbed while investigating. You can think of a silence like the snooze button on an alarm clock.

If you want to stop alerts at a set time every day you should not do so with silences, rather add a condition to your alerts that the hour function returns the desired value, as shown in "Alerting Rules" on page 292.

Now that you have seen all the key components of Prometheus, it is time to consider how they all fit together at a higher level. In the next chapter you will learn how to plan a deployment of Prometheus.

Deployment

Playing around with Prometheus on your own machine is one thing, deploying it on a real production system is a different kettle of fish. Chapter 20 looks at the practicalities of running Prometheus in production and how to approach rolling it out.

Putting It All Together

In the preceding chapters you learned about all the components in a Prometheus setup: instrumentation, dashboards, service discovery, exporters, PromQL, alerts, and the Alertmanager. In this final chapter you will learn how to bring all of these together and plan a Prometheus deployment and maintain it in the future.

Planning a Rollout

When you are considering a new technology it's best to start the rollout with something small that doesn't take too much effort, nor prematurely commit you to doing a complete rollout. When starting with Prometheus in an existing system, I recommend starting by running the Node exporter[1] and Prometheus. You already ran both of these in Chapter 2.

The Node exporter covers all the machine-level metrics that might be used from other monitoring systems, and then quite a few more as was covered in Chapter 7. At this stage you will have a wide variety of metrics for little effort, and you should get comfortable with Prometheus, set up some dashboards, and maybe even do some alerting.

Next, I'd suggest looking at what third-party systems you are using and which exporters exist for them and start deploying those. For example, if you have network devices you can run the SNMP exporter, if you have JVM-based applications such as Kafka or Cassandra you would use the JMX exporter, and if you want blackbox monitoring you might use the Blackbox exporter, as covered in Chapter 10. The goal at

---

1 If you are on Windows, use the WMI exporter instead of the Node exporter.

this stage is to gain metrics about as many different parts of your system as you can with as little effort as possible.

By now you will be comfortable with Prometheus, and will have figured out your approach to aspects such as service discovery, as discussed in Chapter 8. You could have done all the previous steps of the rollout alone. The next step is to start instrumenting your organisation's own applications, as covered in Chapter 3, which will likely involve asking other people to also get involved and commit time to monitoring. Being able to demonstrate all of the monitoring and dashboards[2] you have set up so far (which are backed by exporters) will make it quite a bit easier to sell others on using Prometheus, extensively instrumenting all your code as step one would be unlikely to get buy-in.

As before, when adding instrumentation you want to start with metrics that give you the biggest gains. Look for chokepoints in your applications that significant proportions of traffic go through. For example, if you have common HTTP libraries that all of your applications use to communicate with each other and you instrument them with the basic RED metrics, as covered in "Service instrumentation" on page 55, you will get the key performance metrics for large swathes of your online serving systems from just one instrumentation change.

If you have existing instrumentation from another monitoring system you can deploy integrations such as the StatsD and Graphite exporters discussed in Chapter 11 to take advantage of what you already have. Over time you should look to not only transition entirely to Prometheus instrumentation, as covered in Chapter 3, but also to further instrument your applications.

As your usage of Prometheus grows to cover more and more of your monitoring and metrics-monitoring needs, you should start turning down other monitoring systems that are no longer needed. It's not unusual for a company to end up with 10+ different monitoring systems over time, so consolidating where practical is always beneficial.

This plan is a general guideline, which you can and should adapt to your circumstances. For example, if you are a developer you might jump straight to instrumenting your applications. You might even add a client library to your application with no instrumentation yet, in order to take advantage of the out-of-the-box metrics such as CPU usage and garbage collection.

---

2 I continue to be amazed by the seductive power of a pretty dashboard, especially over other factors such as if the metrics in the dashboard are in any way useful. Do not underestimate this when trying to convince others to use Prometheus.

Growing Prometheus

Usually you start out with one Prometheus server per datacenter. Prometheus is intended to be run on the same network as what it is monitoring, because this reduces the ways in which things can fail, aligns failure domains, and provides low latency, high bandwidth network access to the targets that Prometheus is scraping.[3]

A single Prometheus is quite efficient, so you can likely get away with one Prometheus for an entire datacenter's monitoring needs for longer than you'd think. At some point though, operational overhead, performance, or just social considerations will lead you to start splitting out parts of the Prometheus to separate Prometheus servers. For example, it is common to have separate Prometheus servers for network, infrastructure, and application monitoring. This is known as *vertical sharding* and it is the best way to scale Prometheus.

Longer term you may have every team run their own Prometheus servers, empowering them to choose what target labels and scrape intervals make sense for them (as discussed in Chapter 8). You could also run the servers for teams as a shared service, but you must be prepared for teams getting overenthusiastic with labels.

A pattern I have seen play out many times is that starting out it is a struggle to convince teams that they should instrument their own code or deploy exporters. At some point though, it'll click, and they will understand the power of labels. Within a short period of time you will likely find that your Prometheus server has performance issues due to metrics with a cardinality that is far beyond what it is reasonable to use in a metrics-based monitoring system (as discussed in "Cardinality" on page 93). If you are running Prometheus as a shared service and the team consuming these metrics is not the one getting paged, it can be difficult to convince them that they need to cut back on cardinality. But if they run their own Prometheus and are the ones getting woken up at 3 a.m., they are likely going to be more realistic about what belongs in a metrics-based monitoring system and what belongs in a logs-based system.

If your team has particularly large systems they may end up with multiple Prometheus servers per datacenter. An infrastructure team may end up with one Prometheus for Node exporters, one for reverse proxies, and one for everything else. For ease of management, it is normal to run Prometheus servers inside each of your Kubernetes clusters rather than trying to monitor them from outside.

---

3 Monitoring across failure domain boundaries, such as across datacenters, is possible but messy as you introduce a whole slew of network-related failure modes. If you have hundreds of tiny datacenters with only a handful of machines each, one Prometheus per region/continent can be an acceptable tradeoff.

Where you start and end up on this spectrum of setups will depend on your scale and the culture within your organisation. It is my experience that social factors[4] usually result in Prometheus servers being split out before any performance concerns arise.

Going Global with Federation

With a Prometheus per datacenter, how do you perform global aggregations?

Reliability is a key property of a good monitoring system, and a core value of Prometheus. When it comes to graphing and alerting, you want as few moving parts as possible because a simple system is a reliable system. When you want a graph of application latency in a datacenter you have Grafana talk to the Prometheus in that datacenter that is scraping that application, and similarly for alerting on per-datacenter application latency.

This doesn't quite work for global latency, since each of your datacenter Prometheus servers only has a part of the data. This is where *federation* comes in. Federation allows you to have a global Prometheus that pulls aggregated metrics from your datacenter Prometheus servers, as shown in Figure 20-1.

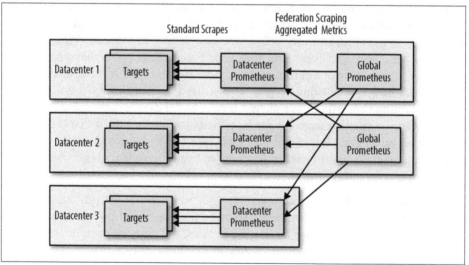

Figure 20-1. Global federation architecture

For example, to pull in all metrics aggregated to the job level you could have a *prometheus.yml* like:

---

4 For example, it is sane only to have one target label hierarchy within a Prometheus. If a team has a different idea of what a region is than everyone else, they should run their own Prometheus.

```
scrape_configs:
  - job_name: 'federate'
    honor_labels: true
    metrics_path: '/federate'
    params:
      'match[]':
        - '{__name__=~"job:.*"}'
    static_configs:
      - targets:
        - 'prometheus-dublin:9090'
        - 'prometheus-berlin:9090'
        - 'prometheus-new-york:9090'
```

The *federate* HTTP endpoint on Prometheus takes a list of selectors (covered in "Selectors" on page 217) in match[] URL parameters. It will return all matching time series following instant vector selector semantics, including staleness, as discussed in "Instant Vector" on page 219. If you supply multiple match[] parameters, a sample will be returned if it matches any of them. To avoid the aggregated metrics having the instance label of the Prometheus target, honor_labels (which was discussed in "Label Clashes and honor_labels" on page 151) is used here.[5] The external labels of the Prometheus (as discussed in "External Labels" on page 303) are also added to the federated metrics, so you can tell where each time series came from.

Unfortunately some users use federation for purposes other than pulling in aggregated metrics. To avoid falling into this trap, you should understand the following:

Federation is not for copying the content of entire Prometheus servers.

Federation is not a way to have one Prometheus proxy another Prometheus.

You should not use federation to pull metrics with an instance label.

Let me explain why you should not use federation beyond its intended use case. First, for reliability you want to have as few moving parts as is practical, pulling all your metrics over the internet to a global Prometheus from where you can then graph and alert on them means that internet connectivity to another datacenter is now a hard dependency on your per-datacenter monitoring working. In general, you want to align your failure domains, so that graphing and alerting for a datacenter does not depend on another datacenter being operational. That is, as far as is practical you

---

5 The *federate* endpoint automatically includes an empty instance label in its output for any metrics lacking an instance label, in the same way the Pushgateway does as mentioned in "Pushgateway" on page 71.

want the Prometheus that is scraping a set of targets to also be the one sending alerts for that target. This is particularly important if there is a network outage or partition.

The second issue is scaling. For reliability, each Prometheus is standalone and running on one machine and thus limited by machine size in terms of how much it can handle. Prometheus is quite efficient, so even limited to a single machine, it is quite plausible for you to have a single Prometheus server monitor an entire datacenter. As you add datacenters you just need to turn up a Prometheus in each of them. A global Prometheus pulling in only aggregated metrics will have greatly reduced cardinality data to deal with compared with the datacenter Prometheus servers,[6] and thus will prevent bottlenecks. Conversely, if the global Prometheus was pulling in all metrics from each datacenter Prometheus, the global Prometheus would become the bottleneck and greatly limit your ability to scale. Put another way, for federation to scale you need to use the same approach discussed in "Reducing Cardinality" on page 280 for dashboards.

Thirdly, Prometheus is designed to scrape many thousands of small to medium size targets.[7] By spreading the scrapes over the scrape interval, Prometheus can keep up with the data volumes with even load. If you instead have it scrape a handful of targets with massive numbers of time series, such as massive federation endpoints, this can cause load spikes and it may not even be possible for Prometheus to complete processing of one massive scrape worth of data in time to start the next scrape.

The fourth issue is semantics. By passing all the data through an extra Prometheus, additional race conditions will be introduced. You would see increased artifacts in your graphs, and you would not get the benefit of the staleness handling the semantics.

One objection to this architecture is if all your metrics don't end up in one Prometheus, how will you know which Prometheus contains a given metric? This turns out not to be an issue in practice. As your Prometheus servers will tend to follow your general architecture, it is usually quite obvious which Prometheus monitors which targets and thus which has a specific metric. For example, Node exporter metrics for Dublin are going to be in the Dublin infrastructure Prometheus. Grafana supports both data source templating and having graphs with metrics from different data sources on them, so this is not an issue for dashboards either.

---

6 Let's say that you were aggregating up every metric from an application with 100 instances and a global Prometheus was pulling these aggregated metrics. For the same resources that a datacenter Prometheus uses, the global Prometheus could federate metrics from 100 datacenters. In reality the global Prometheus can handle far more, as not all metrics would be aggregated.

7 There are no exact numbers, but I would consider 10,000 time series as starting to get large.

Usually you will only have a two-level federation hierarchy with datacenter Prometheus servers and globals. The global Prometheus will perform calculations with PromQL that you cannot do in a lower-level Prometheus, such as how much traffic you are receiving globally.

It is also possible that you will end up with an additional level. For example, it's normal to run a Prometheus inside each Kubernetes cluster you have. If you had multiple Kubernetes clusters in a datacenter you might federate their aggregated metrics to a per-datacenter Prometheus before then federating them from there to your global Prometheus.

Another use for federation is to pull limited aggregated metrics from another team's Prometheus. It is polite to ask first, and if this becomes a common or more formal thing, the considerations in "Rules for APIs" on page 282 may apply. There is no need to do this just for dashboards though, as Grafana supports using multiple data sources in a dashboard and in a panel.

Long-Term Storage

In "What Is Monitoring?" on page 4 I mentioned that monitoring was alerting, debugging, trending, and plumbing. For most alerting, debugging, and plumbing, days to weeks of data is usually more than enough.[8] But when it comes to trending such as capacity planning it's usual for you to want years of data.

One approach to long-term storage is to treat Prometheus like a traditional database and take regular backups that you can restore from in the event of failure. A Prometheus ingesting 10,000 samples per second with a conservative 2 bytes per sample would use a bit under 600 GB of disk space per year, which would fit on a modern machine.

Backups can be taken by sending a HTTP POST to the */api/v1/admin/tsdb/snapshot* endpoint, which will return the name of the snapshot created under Prometheus's storage directory. This uses hard links, so doesn't consume much additional disk space as the data is stored only once between the snapshot and Prometheus's own database. After you are done with a snapshot it is best to delete it to avoid using more disk space than is needed. To restore from a snapshot, replace the Prometheus storage directory with the snapshot.

Only a tiny proportion of your metrics will be interesting to you for long-term trending, usually the aggregated metrics. It's usually not worth keeping everything forever, so you can save a lot of storage space by only keeping metrics from a global

---

8 Indeed, I have heard various different monitoring systems report that around 90% of metrics data is not used after the first 24 hours. The problem, of course, is knowing in advance which 90% you'll never need again.

Prometheus long term[9] or deleting nonaggregated metrics before a certain time. The */api/v1/admin/tsdb/delete* HTTP endpoint takes selectors in its `match[]` URL parameter[10] and has `start` and `end` parameters to restrict the time range. Data will be deleted from disk at the next compaction. It would be reasonable to delete old data, say, once a month.

For security reasons both the snapshot and delete APIs require the `--web.enable-admin-api` flag to be passed to Prometheus for them to be enabled.

Another approach is to send your samples from Prometheus to some form of clustered storage system that can use the resources of many machines. *Remote write* sends samples as they are ingested to another system. *Remote read* allows PromQL to transparently use samples from another system, as if it were stored locally within the Prometheus. These are both configured at the top level of *prometheus.yml*:

```
remote_write:
  - url: http://localhost:1234/write
remote_read:
  - url: http://localhost:1234/read
```

Remote write supports relabelling through `write_relabel_configs`, which works similarly to what you saw in "metric_relabel_configs" on page 148. Your main use of this would be to restrict what metrics are sent to the *remote write endpoint*, as you may find yourself limited by cost. From a bandwidth and memory standpoint, you should take care when pulling in large numbers of time series from long time periods via remote read. When using remote write it is important that each Prometheus has unique external labels so that metrics from different Prometheus servers don't clash.

One way to use remote read and write would be to consider Prometheus as a largely ephemeral cache, and the remote storage as the main storage.[11] If Prometheus is restarted with an empty data store you would rely on remote read for historical graphs. You would also design your alerts to be resilient under such a restart, which is a good idea in any case.

Long-term storage (LTS) for Prometheus is a relatively new and rapidly evolving space. There are several companies and projects that can integrate with Prometheus's remote read and remote write support, but there is not yet enough operational experience to make specific recommendations here.

---

9 As discussed in "Going Global with Federation" on page 334, the global Prometheus will only have aggregated metrics.

10 This works in the same way as the `match[]` URL parameter for federation.

11 Usually a multiweek cache.

When evaluating your options, keep in mind that a load that would be considered light for a single Prometheus server may exceed what another system running across many machines can handle. It is always wise to load test systems based on your own use case rather than relying on headline numbers, as different systems are designed with different data models and access patterns in mind. Simpler solutions can turn out to be both more performant and easier to operate. Clustered does not automatically mean better.

You should expect clustered storage systems to cost at least five times what the equivalent Prometheus would cost for the same load. This is because most systems will replicate the data three times, plus have to take it in and process all the data. Thus you should be judicious about what metrics you keep only locally and which ones are sent to clustered storage.

Running Prometheus

When it comes to actually running the Prometheus server, you will have to consider hardware, configuration management, and how your network is set up.

Hardware

The first question you will probably ask when it comes to running Prometheus is what hardware Prometheus needs. Prometheus is best run on SSDs, though they are not strictly necessary on smaller setups. Storage space is one of the main resources you need to care about. To estimate how much you'll need you have to know how much data you will be ingesting. For an existing Prometheus[12] you can run a PromQL query to report the samples ingested per second:

```
rate(prometheus_tsdb_head_samples_appended_total[5m])
```

While Prometheus can achieve compression of 1.3 bytes per sample in production, when estimating I tend to use 2 bytes per sample to be conservative. The default retention for Prometheus is 15 days, so 100,000 samples per second would be around 240 GB over 15 days. You can increase the retention with the `--storage.tsdb.retention` flag, and control where Prometheus stores data with the `--storage.tsdb.path` flag. There is no particular filesystem recommended or required for Prometheus, and many users have had success using network block devices such as Amazon's EBS. However NFS, including Amazon's EFS, is explicitly not supported by Prometheus because Prometheus expects a POSIX filesystem and NFS implementations have never really had a reputation for offering exact POSIX

---

12 For Prometheus 1.x, use the `prometheus_local_storage_ingested_samples_total` metric instead.

semantics. Each Prometheus needs its own storage directory; you cannot share one storage directory across the network.

The next question is how much RAM you will need. The storage in Prometheus 2.x works in blocks that are written out every two hours and subsequently compacted into larger time ranges. The storage engine does no internal caching, rather it uses your kernel's page cache. So you will need enough RAM to hold a block, plus overheads, plus the RAM used during queries. 12 hours worth of sample ingestion is a good starting point, so for 100,000 samples per second that would be around 8 GB.

Prometheus is relatively light on CPU. A quick benchmark on my machine (which has an i7-3770k CPU) shows only 0.25 CPUs being used to ingest 100,000 samples per second. But that is just ingestion—you will want additional CPU power to cover querying and recording rules. Due to CPU spikes from Go's garbage collection, you should always have at least one core more than you think you need.

Network bandwidth is another consideration. Prometheus 2.x can handle ingesting millions of samples per second, which is similar to the one-machine limit of many other similar systems. Prometheus usually uses compression when scraping, so it uses somewhere around 20 bytes of network traffic to transfer a sample. With a million samples per second, that's 160 Mbps of network traffic. That is a good chunk of a gigabit network card, which may be all you have for an entire rack of machines.

Another resource to keep in mind is file descriptors. I could give you the equation and factors, but these days file descriptors are not a scarce resource so I'd say set your file ulimit to a million and not worry about it.

 Ulimit changes for file descriptors have an annoying habit of not applying, depending on how exactly you start a service. Prometheus logs the file ulimit at startup, and you can also check the value of process_max_fds on /metrics.

These numbers are just starting points. You should benchmark and verify these against your setup. I would generally recommended leaving room for your Prometheus to double in terms of resource usage to give you time to get new hardware as you grow, and it also gives you a buffer to deal with sudden cardinality increases.

Configuration Management

Prometheus does one thing and does it well—that being metrics-based monitoring. Prometheus does not try to fulfull the role of configuration management, secret management, or service database. To that extent Prometheus aims to get out of your way and allow you to use standard configuration management approaches, rather than forcing you to learn and work around some Prometheus specific configuration management contrivance.

If you do not yet have a configuration management tool, I would recommend Ansible for more traditional environments. For Kubernetes, ksonnet (*https://ksonnet.io/*) looks promising, but there are literally tens of tools in this space.

Just because Prometheus allows for standard approaches does not mean it will automatically work perfectly in your environment. Being generic means avoiding the temptation to cater to platform-specific nuances. It means that if you have a mature setup, Prometheus should be quite easy to deploy. You could view Prometheus as a maturity test for your configuration management, because Prometheus is a standard Unix binary that works in the ways you'd expect. It accepts SIGTERM, SIGHUP, logs to standard error, and uses simple text files for configuration.[13]

For example, Prometheus rule files (discussed in Chapter 17) can only come from files on disk. If you want to have an API where you can submit rules, there is nothing stopping you from building such a system, and having it output the rule files in standard YAML format. Prometheus does not offer such an API itself, as how, for example, would you ensure Prometheus had rules immediately after a reboot? By only offering files on disk you will find debugging is simpler since you know exactly what input Prometheus is working from. Those with simpler setups don't have to worry about more intricate configuration management concepts, and those who wish to do something fancier have an interface that permits them to do whatever they like. Put another way, the cost of more complex and nonstandard setups is borne by those with such setups, not by everyone else.

In simpler setups you can get away with having a static *prometheus.yml*. But as you expand you will need to template it using your configuration management system, at a minimum to specify a different external_labels per Prometheus, as Prometheus itself has no templating abilities for configuration files. If you haven't fully progressed to having a configuration management system yet,[14] some runtime environments can provide environment variables to the applications running under them. You could use tools like sed or envsubst[15] to do rudimentary templating. On the far end of sophistication you have tools like the Prometheus Operator from CoreOS (briefly mentioned in Chapter 9), which will completely manage not only your configuration file but also your Prometheus server running on Kubernetes.

---

13 Windows users can use HTTP instead of SIGTERM and SIGHUP, which requires the --web.enable-lifecycle flag to be specified.

14 To avoid confusion, systems like Docker, Docker Compose, and Kubernetes are not configuration management systems; they are potential outputs for a configuration management system.

15 Part of the gettext library.

In Chapter 10 I mentioned that exporters should live right beside the application they are exporting metrics from. You should take the same approach with any daemons that provide configuration data for Prometheus, such as if you are using File service discovery (discussed in "File" on page 130). By having such daemons run beside each Prometheus you will only be affected by the machine running Prometheus having issues, and not other machines that you are relying on to provide key functionality.

If you want to test changes to your Prometheus configuration you can easily spin up a test Prometheus with the new configuration. Since Prometheus is pull based, your targets don't have to know or care about what is monitoring them. When doing this it would be wise to remove any Alertmanagers or remote write endpoints from the configuration file.

Networks and Authentication

Prometheus is designed with the idea that it is on the same network as the targets it is monitoring, and can contact them directly over HTTP and request their metrics. This is known as pull-based monitoring, and comes with advantages such as up indicating if a scrape worked, being able to run a test Prometheus without having to configure all your targets to push to it, and more tactical options for handling sudden load increases, as covered in "Managing Performance" on page 348.

If you have a network setup where there is NAT or a firewall in the way, you should try to run a Prometheus server behind it so that it can directly access the targets. There are also options like PushProx (*https://github.com/RobustPerception/Push Prox*), SSH tunnels, or having Prometheus use a proxy via the `proxy_url` configuration field.

> Do not try to use the Pushgateway to work around network architecture, or more generally to try to convert Prometheus to a push-based system.

As was already covered in "Pushgateway" on page 71, the Pushgateway is for service-level batch jobs to push metrics to once just before they exit. It is not designed for application instances to regularly push metrics to, and you should never be pushing metrics that end up with an `instance` label to the Pushgateway. Trying to use the Pushgateway in this fashion will create a bottleneck,[16] the timestamps of the samples will not be correct (which will lead to graph artifacts), and you lose the up metric so

---

16 For the same reasons that you want to run an StatsD exporter per application instance, rather than one per datacenter.

it's harder to distinguish whether a process has died on purpose or due to a failure. The Pushgateway also has no logic to expire old data, because for service-level batch jobs that the last run of a cronjob was a month ago doesn't change the validity of the last success time metric that cronjob pushed.

Pull is at the very core of Prometheus; work with it rather than against it.

Prometheus components do not currently offer any service-side security support, which is to say that all serving is performed under plain HTTP with no authentication, authorisation, or TLS encryption. This is because, as with configuration management, there are so many ways to do things that Prometheus chooses to offer you a basic way of doing things and lets you build on top of it. In the case of server-side security, that would usually be using a reverse proxy such as nginx or Apache, which both offer a wide range of security-related features. You may also want the reverse proxy to block access to the admin and lifecycle endpoints to protect against Cross-Site Request Forgery (XSRF), and use HTTP headers to protect against Cross-Site Scripting (XSS).

When running Prometheus behind a reverse proxy you should pass Prometheus the URL under which it is available via the `--web.external-url` flag, so that the Prometheus UI and the generator URL in alerts work correctly. If your reverse proxy changes the HTTP path before sending it on to Prometheus, set the `--web.route-prefix` flag to the prefix of the new paths.

 Like Prometheus, the Alertmanager also has `--web.external-url` and `--web.route-prefix` flags.

While Prometheus and the Alertmanager don't support authentication for serving, they do support it for talking to other systems, including alerting, notification, most service discovery mechanisms, remote read, remote write, and scraping, as was covered in "How to Scrape" on page 146.

Planning for Failure

In distributed systems, failure is a fact of life. Prometheus does not take the path of attempting a clustered design to handle machine failures, since such designs are very tricky to get right and turn out to be less reliable than nonclustered solutions more often than you'd expect. Nor does Prometheus attempt to backfill data if a scrape failed. If the scrape failure was due to overload, backfilling when load went back down a bit could only cause the overload to happen again. It's better when monitoring systems have predictable load and don't exacerbate outages.

Due to the design above, if a scrape fails, up will be 0 for that scrape, and you will have a gap in your time series. But this is not something you should worry about. You will not care about the vast majority of your samples, gaps included, a week after they are collected (if not sooner). For monitoring, Prometheus takes the stance that it's more important that your monitoring is generally reliable and available, rather than 100% accurate. For metrics-based monitoring, 99.9% accuracy is fine for most purposes. It is more useful for you to know that latency increased by a millisecond than whether that increase was to 101.2 or 101.3 ms. rate is resilient to the occasional failed scrape, as long as your range is at least four times the scrape interval, as discussed in "rate" on page 268.

When discussing reliability, the first question you should ask is how reliable do you need your monitoring to be? If you are monitoring a system that has a 99.9% SLA then there's no point spending your time and effort designing and maintaining a monitoring system that will be 99.9999% available. Even if you could build such a system, neither the internet connections that your users use nor the response of the humans who are oncall are that reliable.

Taking an example, here in Ireland it is common to use SMS for paging as it is generally fast, cheap, and reliable. However, for a few hours every year it grinds to a halt when the entire country wishes each other Happy New Year, which makes it at most 99.95% reliable over a year. You can have contingencies in place to handle things like this, but as you try backup paging devices and escalating to the secondary oncall, the minutes are ticking away. As mentioned in "for" on page 294, if you have an issue that requires a resolution in under 5 minutes, you should automate it rather than hope your oncall engineers will be able to handle it in time.

In this context I'd like to talk about reliable alerting. If a Prometheus dies for some reason, you should have it automatically restart, and disruption should be minimal beyond for state resetting (as discussed in "for" on page 294).[17] But if the machine Prometheus is on dies and Prometheus cannot restart, you won't have alerts until you replace it. If you are using a cluster scheduler such as Kubernetes you can expect this to happen promptly, which may well suffice.[18] If replacement is a more manual process, this probably won't be acceptable.

The good news is that you can easily make alerting more reliable by eliminating the single point of failure (SPOF). If you run two identical Prometheus servers then as

---

17 For this reason I recommend you design your critical alerts to be up and running in a fresh Prometheus within an hour, if not sooner.

18 If using network storage such as Amazon's EBS, the Prometheus may even continue on with the data of the previous run.

long as one of them is running you will have alerts, and the Alertmanager will automatically deduplicate the alerts because they will have identical labels.

As mentioned in "External Labels" on page 303, every Prometheus should have unique external labels, so to maintain that constraint you can use alert_rela bel_configs (as discussed in "Configuring Alertmanagers" on page 302):

```
global:
  external_labels:
    region: dublin1
alerting:
  alertmanagers:
   - static_configs:
      - targets: ['localhost:9093']
  alert_relabel_configs:
    - source_labels: [region]
      regex: (.+)\d+
      target_label: region
```

This will remove the 1 from dublin1 before sending the alert to the Alertmanager. The second Prometheus would have a region label of dublin2 as an external label.

I've mentioned now a few times that external labels should be unique across all your Prometheus servers. This is so that if you have multiple Prometheus servers in a setup like the preceding one and you are either using remote write or federation from them, the metrics from the different Prometheus servers won't clash. Even in perfect conditions, different Prometheus servers will see slightly different data, which could be misinterpreted as a counter reset, for example. In less optimal conditions, such as a network partition, each of your redundant Prometheus servers could see wildly different information.

This brings me to the question of reliability for dashboards, federation, and remote write. There is no general way you can automatically synthesise the "correct" data from the different Prometheus servers, and going via load balancer for Grafana or federation would lead to artifacts. I suggest taking the easy way out and only dashboarding/federating/writing from one of the Prometheus servers, and if it is down, live with the gap. In the rare event that the gap covers a period you care about, you can always look at the data in the other Prometheus by hand.

For global Prometheus servers, as discussed in "Going Global with Federation" on page 334, the tradeoffs are a bit different. As global Prometheus servers are monitoring across failure zones, it is plausible that the global server could be down for hours or days if there was, for example, a major power outage in the datacenter. This is fine for the datacenter Prometheus servers since they aren't running, but neither is anything they were going to be monitoring. I recommend that you always run at least two global Prometheus servers in different datacenters and in dashboards making graphs available from all of the global servers. Similarly for remote write.[19] It is the responsibility of the person using the dashboards to interpret the data from the differing sources.

Alertmanager Clustering

You will want to run one centralised Alertmanager setup for your entire organisation, so that everyone has one place to look at alerts and silences and you get the maximum benefits from alert grouping. Unless you have a small setup, you will take advantage of the Alertmanager's clustering feature, whose architecture is shown in Figure 20-2.

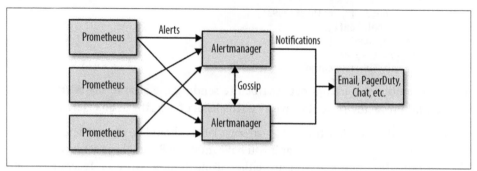

Figure 20-2. Clustering architecture for the Alertmanager

The Alertmanager uses Hashicorp's memberlist (*https://github.com/hashicorp/memberlist*)[20] to gossip information about notifications and silences.[21] This is not a consensus-based design, so there is no need to have an odd number of Alertmanagers. This is what is known as an AP, or Availability and Partition-tolerant, design, so as long as your Prometheus can talk to at least one Alertmanager that can successfully send notifications, your notifications will get through. When there are rare issues such as network partitions you may get duplicate notifications, but that's better than not getting notifications at all.

For the clustering to work, every Prometheus must send its alerts to every Alertmanager. How it works is that the Alertmanagers order themselves. The first Alertmanager sends notifications normally, and if successful, gossips that the notification was sent. The second Alertmanager has a small delay before sending notifications. If it

---

19 Global Prometheus servers are at the top of the federation hierarchy, so nothing generally federates from them.

20 Prior to 0.15.0, the Alertmanager used the Weaveworks Mesh library.

21 Aside from gossiping, the Alertmanager also stores data on local disk, so even in a nonclustered setup you won't lose state by restarting the Alertmanager.

doesn't get the gossip that the first Alertmanager sent the notification, then it will send the notification. The third Alertmanager will have a slightly longer delay and so on. The Alertmanagers should all have identical *alertmanager.yml* files, but the worst that should happen if they don't is that duplicate notifications will be sent.

To get it running with Alertmanager version 0.15.0 on two machines called foo and bar you would start the Alertmanager as follows:

```
# On the machine foo
alertmanager --cluster.peer bar:9094

# On the machine bar
alertmanager --cluster.peer foo:9094
```

The easiest way for you to test if clustering is working is to create a silence on one Alertmanager and see if it appears on the other Alertmanager. There will also be a list of all members of the cluster on the Alertmanager's Status page.

Meta- and Cross-Monitoring

Thus far I have covered monitoring many different types of systems, but among those I have not covered monitoring your monitoring system. It is fairly standard to have each of your Prometheus servers scrape itself, but that doesn't help you when that Prometheus is having issues. How you monitor your monitoring is known as *meta-monitoring*.

The general approach to metamonitoring for you to take is to have one Prometheus per datacenter which monitors all of the other Prometheus servers in that datacenter. This doesn't have to be a Prometheus server dedicated to this purpose as Prometheus is pretty cheap to monitor, and even if you have a setup where each team is entirely responsible for running their own Prometheus servers, it is still wise to offer metamonitoring as a central shared service.

A global Prometheus can then scrape all of your per-datacenter metamonitoring Prometheus servers, likely both for /metrics and federating aggregated metrics about all of the Prometheus servers in your organisation.

This still leaves the question of how you should monitor the global Prometheus servers. *Cross-monitoring* is metamonitoring where Prometheus servers monitor each other, rather than the usual metamonitoring hierarchy where Prometheus servers at the same "level" monitor each other. For example, you will usually have two global Prometheus servers scrape each other's /metrics and alert if the other Prometheus is down. You could also have the datacenter Prometheus servers alerting on the global Prometheus servers.[22]

Even with all this meta- and cross-monitoring, you are still depending on Prometheus to monitor Prometheus. In the absolute worst case, a bug could take out all of your Prometheus servers at the same time, so it would be wise to have alerting that can catch that. One approach would be an end-to-end alerting test. An always firing alert would continuously fire a notification via your paging provider, which feeds into a dead man's switch. The dead man's switch would then page you[23] if it doesn't receive a notification for too long a period. This would test your Prometheus, Alertmanager, and paging provider.

When designing your metamonitoring don't forget to scrape other monitoring-related components, such as the Alertmanager and the /metrics of Blackbox/SNMP-style exporters.

Managing Performance

Unless you have a particularly small and unchanging setup, running into performance issues is more of a when than an if. As discussed in "Cardinality" on page 93 and elsewhere, high cardinality metrics are likely to be the primary cause of the performance problems you encounter.

You may also encounter recording rules and dashboards using overly expensive queries, such as those with ranges vectors over long durations, as mentioned in "Histogram" on page 215. You can use the Rules status page, as you saw in Figure 17-1, to find expensive recording rules.

Detecting a Problem

Prometheus exposes a variety of metrics about its own performance, so you don't just have to rely on noticing that your dashboards have gotten sluggish. While metrics can and do change names and meanings from version to version, it is unusual for a metric to go away completely.

`prometheus_rule_group_iterations_missed_total` can indicate that some rule groups are taking too long to evaluate. Comparing `prometheus_rule_group_`

---

22 With all these alerts ready to fire when a global Prometheus goes down, you should to ensure that they all have the same labels and get automatically deduplicated at the Alertmanager. An explicit alert label of `data center: global` (or whatever you use as a datacenter label) to prevent the datacenter Prometheus's `datacenter` external label applying is one approach you could take.

23 Preferably not solely via your usual paging provider, since that could be what has failed.

last_duration_second against prometheus_rule_group_interval_seconds can tell you which group is at fault and if it is a recent change in behaviour.

prometheus_notifications_dropped_total indicates issues talking to the Alertmanager, and if prometheus_notifications_queue_length is approaching prome theus_notifications_queue_capacity, you may start losing alerts.

Each service discovery mechanism tends to have a metric such as prometheus_ sd_file_read_errors_total and prometheus_sd_ec2_refresh_failures_ total indicating problems. You should keep an eye on the counters for the SD mechanisms you use.

prometheus_rule_evaluation_failures_total, prometheus_tsdb_compactions_ failed_total, and prometheus_tsdb_wal_corruptions_total indicate that something has gone wrong in the storage layer. In the worst case you can always stop Prometheus, delete[24] the storage directory, and start it back up again.

Finding Expensive Metrics and Targets

As was mentioned in "by" on page 231 you can use queries such as:

```
topk(10, count by(__name__)({__name__=~".+"}))
```

to find metrics with high cardinality. You could also aggregate by job to find which applications are responsible for the most time series. But these are potentially very expensive queries as they touch every time series and accordingly should be used with caution.

In addition to up, Prometheus adds three other samples for every target scrape. scrape_samples_scraped is the number of samples that were on the /metrics. As this is a single time series per target, it is much cheaper to work with than the previous PromQL expression. scrape_samples_post_metric_relabeling is similar, but it excludes samples that were dropped by metric_relabel_configs.

The final special sample added is scrape_duration_seconds, which is how long that scrape took. This can be useful to check if timeouts are occurring if it is reaching the timeout value, or as an indication that a target is getting overloaded.

Hashmod

If your Prometheus is so overloaded by data from scrapes that you cannot run queries, there is a way to scrape a subset of your targets. There is another relabel action called hashmod that calculates the hash of a label and takes its modulus. Combined

---

24 Or rename.

with the `drop` relabel action you could use this to scrape an arbitrary 10% of your
targets:

```
scrape_configs:
 - job_name: my_job
   # Service discovery etc. goes here.
   relabel_configs:
    - source_labels: [__address__]
      modulus:       10
      target_label:  __tmp_hash
      action:        hashmod
    - source_labels: [__tmp_hash]
      regex:         0
      action:        keep
```

With only 10% of the targets to scrape, if you can spin up a test Prometheus you
should now be able to find out which metric is to blame. If it is only some targets that
are causing the problem, you can change which 10% of targets to scrape by changing
the `regex` to 1, 2, and so on up to 9.

Reducing Load

Once you have identified expensive metrics you have a few options. The first thing to
do is try to fix the metric in the source code to reduce its cardinality.

While you're waiting for that to happen, you have several tactical options. The first is
to drop the metric at ingestion time using `metric_relabel_configs`:

```
scrape_configs:
 - job_name: some_application
   static_configs:
    - targets:
     - localhost:1234
   metric_relabel_configs:
    - source_labels: [__name__]
      regex: expensive_metric_name
      action: drop
```

This still transfers the metric over the network and parses it, but it's still cheaper than
ingesting it into the storage layer.[25]

If particular applications are being problematic you can also drop those targets with
relabelling.

---

25 The Java and Python clients support fetching specific time series using URL parameters such as /metrics?met-
ric[]=process_cpu_seconds_total. This may not always work for custom collectors, but it can save a lot of
resources on both sides of the scrape if there are only a small number of specific metrics you want.

The final option is to increase the `scrape_interval` and `evaluation_interval` for the Prometheus. This can buy you some breathing room, but keep in mind that it's not practical to increase these beyond 2 minutes. Changing the scrape interval may also break some PromQL expressions that depend on it having a specific value.

There is one other option in the scrape config that can be of use to you called `sample_limit`. If the number of samples after `metric_relabel_configs`[26] is higher than `sample_limit`, then the scrape will fail and the samples will not be ingested. This is disabled by default but can act as an emergency relief valve in the event that one of your targets blows up in cardinality, such as by adding a metric with a customer identifier as a label, for example. This is not a setting to micromanage or to attempt to build some form of quota system on top of; if you are going to use it, choose a single generous value that will rarely need bumping.

I advise having enough buffer room in your Prometheus to be able to handle a moderate spurt in cardinality and targets.

Horizontal Sharding

If you are running into scaling challenges due to `instance` cardinality rather than instrumentation label cardinality, there is a way to horizontally shard Prometheus using the `hashmod` relabel action you saw in "Hashmod" on page 349. This is an approach that is only typically needed if you have many thousands of targets of a single type of application, as vertical sharding is a far simpler way to scale Prometheus (as discussed in "Growing Prometheus" on page 333).

The approach to horizontal shading is to have a master Prometheus and several scraping Prometheus servers. Your scraping Prometheus servers each scrape a subset of the targets:

```
global:
  external_labels:
    env: prod
    scraper: 2
scrape_configs:
 - job_name: my_job
   # Service discovery etc. goes here.
   relabel_configs:
    - source_labels: [__address__]
      modulus:       4
      target_label:  __tmp_hash
      action:        hashmod
    - source_labels: [__tmp_hash]
```

---

26 Which is to say the value of `scrape_samples_post_metric_relabeling`.

```
    regex:         2 # This is the 3rd scraper.
    action:        keep
```

Here you can see there are four scrapers from the `modulus` setting. Each scraper should have a unique external label, plus the external labels of the master Prometheus. The master Prometheus can then use the remote read endpoint of Prometheus itself to transparently pull in data from the scrapers:

```
global:
  external_labels:
    env: prod
remote_read:
  - url: http://scraper0:9090/api/v1/read
    read_recent: true
  - url: http://scraper1:9090/api/v1/read
    read_recent: true
  - url: http://scraper2:9090/api/v1/read
    read_recent: true
  - url: http://scraper3:9090/api/v1/read
    read_recent: true
```

Remote read has an optimisation where it will try not to read in data it should already have locally, which makes sense if it is being used with remote write to work with a long-term storage system. `read_recent: true` disables this. Due to the external labels, the metrics from each scraper will have a `scraper` label matching where they came from.

All the same caveats as with federation, covered in "Going Global with Federation" on page 334, apply here. This is not a way to have one Prometheus that can let you transparently access all of your Prometheus servers. In fact, it would actually be a great way to take out all of your monitoring simultaneously through a single expensive query. When using this it is best to aggregate what you can inside the scrapers (following "Reducing Cardinality" on page 280), to reduce the amount of data that the master needs to pull in from the scrapers.

You should be generous with the number of scrapers and aim to only have to increase every few years. When you do increase it, you should at least double the number of scrapers to avoid having to increase the number again soon.

Managing Change

Over time you will find that you need to change the structure of your target labels due to changes in the architecture of your systems. Which applications will host the metrics used for capacity planning will change over time as your applications split and merge as a natural part of development. Metrics will appear and disappear from release to release.

You have the option of using `metric_relabel_configs` to rename metrics and cram the new hierarchy into your existing target labels. But over time you would find that these tweaks and hacks accumulate and ultimately cause more confusion than you may have been trying to prevent by trying to keep things the same.

I would advise accepting that changes like this are a natural part of the evolution of your system, and as with gaps due to failed scrapes, you usually find that you don't care much about the old names after the fact.

Long-term processes such as capacity planning, on the other hand, do care about history. At the least you should note the names of the metrics over time and possibly consider using the approach in "Rules for APIs" on page 282 in your global Prometheus if the changes are a bit too frequent to manage by hand.

In this chapter you learned how to approach a Prometheus deployment, and in what order to add Prometheus monitoring to your system, how to architect and run Prometheus, and how to handle performance problems when they arise.

Getting Help

Even after reading everything up to this point, you may have questions that are not covered here. There are a number of places you can ask questions. IRC is the primary communication method of the Prometheus project, and the `#prometheus` channel on *irc.freenode.net* is a good place to ask usage questions. The prometheus-users (*https:// groups.google.com/forum/#!forum/prometheus-users*) mailing list is also available for user questions. There are also unofficial venues for questions, including the Prometheus tag on StackOverflow (*https://stackoverflow.com/questions/tagged/prometheus*) and the PrometheusMonitoring subreddit (*https://www.reddit.com/r/PrometheusMo nitoring/*). Finally, there are several companies and individuals offering commercial support listed on the Prometheus Community (*https://prometheus.io/community/*) page, including my company, Robust Perception (*https://www.robustperception.io/*).

I hope you have found this and all of the preceding chapters useful and that Prometheus will help to make your life easier through metrics-based monitoring.

Index

Symbols

!= (negative equality matcher), 218
!~ (negative regular expression matcher), 218
% (modulo) operator, 242
() (parentheses), using to change or clarify
    order of evaluation, 255
/metrics, 20, 40, 63
    (see also metrics)
/probe, 179
9's, 260, 344
= (equality matcher), 217
=~ (regular expression matcher), 218
_ (underscore), beginning metric names, 58
__address__, 143
__metrics_path__, 147, 187
__name__, 84, 218
__param_, 147, 187
__scheme__, 147

A

abs function, 259
absent function, 251, 266
aggregation, 87, 229
    basics of, in PromQL, 211-217
        counters, 213
        gauges, 211-212
        histograms, 215-217
        summarys, 214
    over time, functions for, 274
aggregation operators, 229-239
    avg, 234
    count, 233
    count_values, 238-239
    empty instant vector as input, 232

grouping, 229-232
min and max, 236
quantile, 237
stddev and stdvar, 235
sum, 232
topk and bottomk, 236
alerting, 5, 30-35, 291
    making more reliable, 344
alerting rules, 15, 31, 292-302
    annotations and templates, 298-301
    for field, 294-296
    good alerts, 301
    labels for, 296-297
Alertmanager, 15, 305-327
    clustering, 346-347
    configuration file, 306-325
        grouping, 310
        inhibitions, 324
        notification templates, 317
        receivers, 314
        resolved notifications, 323
        routing tree, 307
        throttling and repetition, 312
    configuring, 33, 302-304
        external labels, 303
    downloading and installing, 33
    notification pipeline, 305
    starting, 34
    web interface, 325
alertname, 293
alerts, 4
    Alerts field, 319
    configuring (see alerting rules)
    inhibiting, 324

Y

YAML, 19

Yammer metrics, 193
year function, 263

About the Author

Brian Brazil is the founder of Robust Perception and a Prometheus developer. He works on monitoring issues with companies ranging from early-stage startups to Fortune 500 corporations. He is well known in the Prometheus community, has given countless presentations at conferences, and covers many aspects of Prometheus and monitoring on his blog on the Robust Perception website.

Colophon

The animal on the cover of *Prometheus: Up & Running* is the tawny eagle (*Aquila rapax*), a bird of prey native to Africa, the Middle East, and India. Measuring 60–75 inches in length with a wingspan of 63–75 inches, the tawny eagle is slightly smaller than other members of the *Aquila* genus. They are brown in color, with their eponymous tawny coloration most prevalent in the upper body, giving way to darker feathers on the tail.

Tawny eagles tend to make their nests atop tall trees, where monogamous breeding pairs lay one to three eggs annually. They favor dry habitats such as deserts, steppes, and savannas in which they feed on carrion, reptiles, and small mammals.

Due to their widespread habitat range, tawny eagles are not believed to be threatened. However, the tawny eagle population is thought to be declining in West Africa due to the encroachment of cultivated land into their habitat.

Many of the animals on O'Reilly covers are endangered; all of them are important to the world. To learn more about how you can help, go to *animals.oreilly.com*.

The cover image is from *British Birds*. The cover fonts are URW Typewriter and Guardian Sans. The text font is Adobe Minion Pro; the heading font is Adobe Myriad Condensed; and the code font is Dalton Maag's Ubuntu Mono.

Learn from experts.
Find the answers you need.

Sign up for a **10-day free trial** to get **unlimited access** to all of the content on Safari, including Learning Paths, interactive tutorials, and curated playlists that draw from thousands of ebooks and training videos on a wide range of topics, including data, design, DevOps, management, business—and much more.

Start your free trial at:

oreilly.com/safari

(No credit card required.)